# XML and Perl

20¢

W9-CHS-733

## Contents at a Glance

* 20*

# XML and Perl

Mark Riehl and Ilya Sterin

**www.newriders.com**
201 West 103rd Street, Indianapolis, Indiana 46290
An Imprint of Pearson Education
Boston • Indianapolis • London • Munich • New York • San Francisco

# XML and Perl

**Copyright © 2003 by New Riders Publishing**

All rights reserved. No part of this book shall be reproduced, stored in a retrieval system, or transmitted by any means—electronic, mechanical, photocopying, recording, or otherwise—without written permission from the publisher, except for the inclusion of brief quotations in a review.

International Standard Book Number: 0-7357-1289-1

Library of Congress Catalog Card Number: 2002100786

Printed in the United States of America

First edition: October 2002

06 05 04 03 02 7 6 5 4 3 2 1

Interpretation of the printing code: The rightmost double-digit number is the year of the book's printing; the rightmost single-digit number is the number of the book's printing. For example, the printing code 02-1 shows that the first printing of the book occurred in 2002.

## Trademarks

All terms mentioned in this book that are known to be trademarks or service marks have been appropriately capitalized. New Riders Publishing cannot attest to the accuracy of this information. Use of a term in this book should not be regarded as affecting the validity of any trademark or service mark.

## Warning and Disclaimer

Every effort has been made to make this book as complete and as accurate as possible, but no warranty of fitness is implied. The information is provided on an as-is basis. The authors and New Riders Publishing shall have neither liability nor responsibility to any person or entity with respect to any loss or damages arising from the information contained in this book or from the use of the CD or programs that may accompany it.

**Publisher**
David Dwyer

**Associate Publisher**
Stephanie Wall

**Editor in Chief**
Chris Nelson

**Production Manager**
Gina Kanouse

**Managing Editor**
Sarah Kearns

**Acquisitions Editor**
Elise Walter

**Senior Product Marketing Manager**
Tammy Detrich

**Publicity Manager**
Susan Nixon

**Senior Development Editor**
Jennifer Eberhardt

**Project Editor**
Michael Thurston

**Copy Editor**
Sarah Cisco

**Senior Indexer**
Cheryl Lenser

**Proofreader**
Linda Seifert

**Composition**
Wil Cruz

**Manufacturing Coordinator**
Jim Conway

**Book Designer**
Brainstorm Design, Inc.

**Cover Production**
Aren Howell

**Media Developer**
Jay Payne

# Table of Contents

# About the Authors

**Mark Riehl** has over 10 years of experience in software development in a number of operating systems using Perl, XML, and C/C++. Most of his software experience is network related, having recently led teams developing a web-based network planning tool and a client/server modeling and simulation effort that combined both live and virtual components. Mark is a Lead Software Engineer with Agile Communications, Inc. (`http://www.agilecommunications.com`), a company dedicated to finding innovative solutions to challenging technical problems. He is also a user and faithful supporter of open source software and contributes to the community whenever time permits. Mark has both BS and MS degrees in Electrical Engineering. In his spare time, Mark enjoys spending time with his wife Alyse, working on house projects, going to the beach, and riding a bicycle up and down the New Jersey coastline.

**Ilya Sterin** has over seven years of experience in systems programming as well as software development. His interests include low-level programming, including parsers, compilers, and so on. Ilya has extensive knowledge in Perl, C/C++, Java, and XML. He's made a lot of contributions to the Perl community, by writing modules that are available on CPAN and by administering the content of the official Perl XML web site (`www.perlxml.net`). Ilya is a senior software developer at Ford Motor Company where he leads the development of Asset Management software. He also teaches programming classes at a local community college. Ilya spends numerous sleepless nights hacking on interesting code and thinking of ideas that will benefit the open source software world. When not in front of the computer, Ilya actually has a life. He loves spending time with his family, especially his 3-year-old son, Elijah.

## About the Technical Reviewers

These reviewers contributed their considerable hands-on expertise to the entire development process for *XML and Perl*. As the book was being written, these dedicated professionals reviewed all the material for technical content, organization, and flow. Their feedback was critical to ensuring that *XML and Perl* fits our reader's need for the highest-quality technical information.

**Greg Feirer** has been playing with computers since the Apple II, and he's built software with just about every computer system since. Greg has been a consultant for the last 10 years and is currently working as a software architect.

**Steve Heckler** is president of Accelebrate (`www.accelebrate.com`), an IT training and technical writing firm based in Atlanta. Prior to founding Accelebrate, he served more than six years as a senior manager and instructor at a leading IT training firm.

Steve has been an avid Perl developer for nearly seven years and an XML developer for three years. He holds Bachelors and Masters degrees from Stanford University.

## Acknowledgments

We'd first like to thank Paul DuBois, who initially gave us the confidence to believe we could actually write this book and then convinced New Riders of the same. We'd also like to acknowledge and thank the people at New Riders for making this project a reality, especially Jennifer Eberhardt, Elise Walter, Michael Thurston, and Stephanie Wall. Stephanie for our initial foundation, guidance, and introduction to the publishing business; Jennifer for being an extraordinary editor and answering our day-to-day questions; Elise, for overseeing the project, keeping a big picture view, and providing a gentle nudge when we were approaching a chapter deadline. It has been our pleasure working with all of you. The entire New Riders team made the daunting project of writing this book as painless as possible. Their comments and suggestions always seemed to guide us in the right direction, almost as if they had a finished manuscript all along. Their professionalism and thoroughness during the project has demonstrated to us first hand why the New Riders team produces the best technical books available.

We'd also like to thank the technical editors Steven Heckler and Greg Feirer. Their valuable comments always seemed to fill in the missing text that tied everything together. We want them to know that their work was greatly appreciated and made this book a much better product.

**Mark Riehl**

I would like to thank my employer Agile Communications, Inc., especially the president Dave Hall and vice-president Edward J. McCarthy for providing the type of environment and flexible schedule that makes a project like this possible. When you're surrounded by basically the sharpest people you've come across throughout your career, you look forward to work every day. I'd like to also thank Ed for his comments throughout the book, especially those in the first few chapters.

I would also like to thank members of my family who have supported me during this busy project. First, I'd like to thank my grandfather, James Fitzgerald Kennedy, who always taught me while growing up to "Work with your head, not with your back"—that was his way of saying work smarter, not harder (no, my grandfather doesn't use Perl, but he probably could).

Second, my parents Richard and Patricia, who always demonstrated an exemplary work ethic and attention to detail that to this day pushes me to strive for perfection in everything that I do. Hopefully a little piece of them is reflected throughout the book. Finally, I need to thank my wife and best friend Alyse. She was the first person that thought writing a book was a great idea and never doubted me (or my dream of someday writing a book). Alyse has been very understanding during the past six months while I worked in my office on so many nights and weekends. Her unwavering support (which included chocolate chip cookies) has contributed to this book (and me) more than she'll ever know.

**Ilya Sterin**

I'd like to first of all thank God, without whom nothing would be possible. Second I'd like to thank my family, without them everything would be meaningless. My son Elijah, your life brought new life and meaning to mine. You are the reason I strive to succeed. I'd write a book just on what you mean to me, but first I need a vacation after this one's done. David, my brother, I love you more than life itself. My mother Sofya, who's dedication and hard work in raising me, and believe me I mean hard work, gave me the toolset I needed to take this life on. There are three people, my late Grandfather Lazar, Grandmother Malia, and late Great-grandmother Tuba, whom I love enormously and who's hard work and sweat in raising and educating me in the early stages on my life laid the foundation for the rest of my life. My best friend Dr. Eugene Zolotarevsky and his wife Michelle with whom I can share anything with and receive any advice or help needed. You guys have been great. All of the people I just listed hold a special part in my heart and the heart can't beat if any piece is missing. I'd also like to thank the rest of my huge family; I can't think of anyone who hasn't contributed to my life in some way.

## Tell Us What You Think

As the reader of this book, you are the most important critic and commentator. We value your opinion and want to know what we're doing right, what we could do better, what areas you'd like to see us publish in, and any other words of wisdom you're willing to pass our way.

As the Associate Publisher for New Riders Publishing, I welcome your comments. You can fax, email, or write me directly to let me know what you did or didn't like about this book—as well as what we can do to make our books stronger. When you write, please be sure to include this book's title, ISBN, and author, as well as your name and phone or fax number. I will carefully review your comments and share them with the author and editors who worked on the book.

*Please note that I cannot help you with technical problems related to the topic of this book, and that due to the high volume of email I receive, I might not be able to reply to every message.*

Fax: 317-581-4663
Email: `stephanie.wall@newriders.com`
Mail: Stephanie Wall
Associate Publisher
New Riders Publishing
201 West 103rd Street
Indianapolis, IN 46290 USA

# Introduction

The purpose of this book is to introduce you to XML programming with Perl. It is not intended as an introduction to either XML or Perl; rather, this book is intended to be used as a both a tutorial as well as a reference. It teaches good program design by following a problem/solution style. We have a number of examples that can be easily used as starting points for larger and more complicated applications. I guess you can call it a cookbook, where you'll start out as a short order cook and end up as a cordon bleu.

## What Does This Book Cover?

This book is about staying on the leading edge of a quickly moving set of technologies. As we all know, technology moves at the speed of light, or at least our brain perceives it that way.

XML is new, and although it has been in existence for a few years, it's now beginning to make its way to the mainstream programming community. Everyone is looking to jump on the XML bandwagon. This book shows you how to use XML with Perl and attempts to convince you that Perl should be the tool of choice for XML application development.

A number of technologies and standards are related to XML. Because both XML and Perl are open source technologies, some of the best developers from around the world are contributing to their development. This is what makes it so exciting; anyone can contribute. Bugs are fixed immediately (not on next release) and software is customized toward a programmer's needs (not the other way around). Everyday users have a voice (through mailing lists and newsgroups) in the development of new capabilities and are welcome to contribute to the effort. We hope that this book acts as a traveler's guide as you set off on your journey, as well as a navigation system if you happen to get lost.

Here are some of the topics covered in this book:

- XML standards
- XML parsing with Perl
    - SAX 1 and 2 modules
    - DOM 1 and 2 modules
    - Other event-driven and in-memory parsers

- Validating XML with Perl
- Generating XML documents with Perl
    - XML writing modules
    - Generating XML from other data formats
- XML transformations with Perl
    - XSLT modules
    - XPath module
    - Other transformations and conversions
- Advanced topics
    - AxKit
    - XML and databases
    - SVG and Perl
- XML web services with Perl
    - SOAP implementation
    - XML-RPC implementation

## Conventions Used

Source code examples and commands are displayed using a proportionally spaced font, like this:

```
<?xml version="1.0" encoding="UTF-8"?>
```

## Who Should Read This Book and Why?

Whether you are a Perl programmer looking to explore Perl's XML facilities or an XML developer in another language with a basic understanding of Perl, we will provide examples of all the tools required for XML processing using Perl. This book is not intended to be your first book on programming, and it is not going to teach you Perl or XML. We assume that the reader has a basic programming knowledge of Perl and an understanding of XML. Our task is to show you how to use these two technologies together. If you're new to both XML and Perl, we've included a couple appendixes to help you get familiar with the topics. Appendixes A, "What is XML?" and B, "Perl Essentials" provide a primer on XML and Perl, respectively.

## Prerequisites for This Book

To get the most out of this book, you'll need a basic understanding of XML, some Perl background, a PC or Unix workstation, and a Perl-supported OS (for example, Unix, Linux, Win32, Mac).

You'll also need the following:

- **Perl version 5.6 or above**

  Binary Distributions are available at:
  `http://www.perl.com/CPAN/ports/index.html`

  Win32 ActivePerl port is available at: `http://www.activestate.com`

  Source distributions are available at: `http://www.perl.com/pub/a/language/info/software.html#sourcecode`

  If you are using Microsoft Windows (NT, 98, 2000, or XP), we strongly recommend that you use ActivePerl (`http://www.activestate.com`).

- **Text or programming editor**

  Any ASCII text editor can be used with examples in this book. On Microsoft Windows, a simple notepad program can be used. Linux/Unix come with VI, and in many cases, PICO. Both will do just fine.

- **XEmacs**—`http://www.xemacs.org/`

All the examples and programs in this book were typed using XEmacs. XEmacs is a very powerful programming editor and so much more. Binary versions are available for most major platforms. The authors have their preferences and usually work with one or all of the following tools during the course of a normal day:

- **UltraEdit**—`http://www.ultraedit.com/`

  Highly customizable Microsoft Windows programming editor. A trial version is available for download.

- **XML Spy**—`http://www.xmlspy.com/`

  Development environment for XML that runs under Microsoft Windows. A trial version is available for download.

- **XML-related Perl modules**

  Throughout the book, you will need to install Perl modules to run the examples. Appendix B contains the standard installation instructions for most platforms.

You must have access to the internet to download and install Perl modules. CPAN (Comprehensive Perl Archive Network) contains all the modules described in this book. You will need a C/C++ compiler and the `make` utility (`nmake` with Microsoft Windows Visual C++) to install them.

The Microsoft Windows Perl distribution from ActivePerl is distributed with the `ppm` utility, which can be used to install precompiled module binaries from repositories using simple commands (see Appendix B). If you are using ActivePerl and `ppm`, you will not need a C/C++ compiler on your machine to install Perl modules. The main ActiveState Perl module repository is hosted by ActiveState (`http://www.activestate.com`).

A number of other repositories are available. For example, the authors host their own repository at `http://www.xmlproj.com`. Microsoft Windows binaries for all the Perl modules used in this book can be installed from `http://www.xmlproj.com`. We will update the modules as new versions become available.

## Support and Errata

Support for this book is available through the authors by email. Please send email correspondence to `xml_and_perl@xmlproj.com`.

Errata is available at `http://www.xmlproj.com/xmlperl/errata.html`.

# I

# The Foundation

# 1

# Basics of XML Processing in Perl

## Chapter Roadmap

Over the last few years, eXtensible Markup Language (XML) and related technologies have grown enormously large and complex. The number of tools available to work with XML is also growing. Luckily, Application Programming Interfaces (APIs) are available that hide some of the complexities of the technology and provide a clean and simple interface for the developer. I'm going to discuss the Practical Extraction and Reporting Language (Perl) module APIs that support XML processing, and as you'll soon see, an API exists to perform just about any XML-related task. You'll also learn how to customize your XML processing facilities to accomplish unique tasks.

This first chapter lays the foundation for the book's approach to XML and Perl processing. I'm going to discuss how XML and Perl create portable, powerful, and easily extensible applications when they're used together. You will be convinced that Perl is a wonderful tool for XML because this book demonstrates how these two technologies are perfectly suited for each other.

## XML—What Is It and Why Should I Use It?

*XML* is a set of language rules that have been defined to describe and structure data. It was originally developed by the World Wide Web Consortium (W3C) as part of an effort that started in 1996 and produced the first XML specification (version 1.0) in 1998. Their goal at the time was to expand web functionality by providing a flexible architecture for exchanging data. The architecture supports more than the typical web client-server relationship between a browser and a web server. That is, XML isn't just for web pages.

XML can store any type of structured information. One benefit of storing standard data (that is, not web related) is that XML can be used to facilitate data communications between two computer platforms that would otherwise be incompatible as well as store configuration or application data for easy access by the applications. A number of features are what make XML so successful—let's take a quick look at them.

### XML Is Extensible

XML is called extensible because it isn't based on a rigid set of rules like HyperText Markup Language (HTML). HTML and XML are both subsets of Standard Generalized Markup Language (SGML) and have their similarities and differences. HTML defines a standard set of tags, and because each tag has a predefined meaning, the language is not extensible. Because HTML tags are already defined as a standard, the HTML interpreter (the browser, for example) does not have to interpret any tags that are not a part of the HTML standard. The interpreter is free to choose whether or not it wants to ignore the tags, throw an exception, display it as plain text, and so on. XML, on the other hand, is a meta-language that can be used to structure your data and define other meta-languages. In essence, when you generate an XML document, you are actually defining a new data format or a new meta-language because you define the start tags, end tags, and so forth. You then create an interpreter for your language using an XML Parser, which will understand the user-defined syntax. You can also create a Document Type Definition (DTD) to further validate and restrict your language's syntax.

> **Note**
> Even though XML is a meta-language, it still has to follow a set of syntax rules to render a valid XML document. These rules are defined in Appendix A, "What is XML?"

## XML Separates Data from the Presentation of the Data

The data contained in an XML document is separated from the presentation of the document. This feature enables you to decide how to display the data contained in an XML document based on the client viewing the XML document (that is, different clients can view the same data in different ways). Technologies such as eXtensible Stylesheet Language Transformation (XSLT), XML Path Language (XPath), Cascading Style Sheets (CSS), and so forth can be used to transform XML documents for varying presentations to the viewer.

## XML Documents Are Stored As Text

An XML document is stored as text. You can view and edit an XML document easily using any text editor because its legibility makes development and debugging much easier than in binary or other illegible formats. Because an XML document is a text file, it is not platform specific. By that, I mean an XML document generated on one platform—for example, a PC running Microsoft Windows—can be used (viewed, read, or processed) on another platform, such as a Unix workstation. Cross platform portability can sometimes be an issue when applications store their data in a proprietary binary format (such as a word processor document or a spreadsheet). Think of an XML document as a clear glass container that holds data—everyone can see inside of it and nothing is hidden, which is how information or data should be treated.

## XML Provides a Solid Foundation for a Family of Technologies

XML itself is the specification that describes the rules designed to store and represent data. It specifies how start and end tags are defined, which characters are allowed for element names, how comments are written, and so on. In addition to XML, a large number of related specifications are designed from the beginning to closely integrate with XML. Here is a short list of some of the more popular specifications.

- **XLink**—Defines the syntax for adding hyperlinks to XML documents. In XML, any element can be designated as a link. XLink is more flexible than a standard hyperlink because it can support several types of links. For example, XLink can be used to create a standard HTML link, a bi-directional link that will return the user to the main document, or a multi-directional link that can provide multiple paths to the same document. Currently, most browsers support simple XLink functionality; however, custom applications can tap into the full functionality of XLink.

- **XPointer**—Enables you to specify a particular point or range in an XML document. XPointer is similar in concept to a URL. However, rather than pointing off to a document somewhere on a web server, the link points to data inside an XML document.
- **Cascading Style Sheet (CSS)**—Enables you to specify how to display an XML document in a browser. CSS is a non-XML syntax that doesn't change the content of the XML data, it only applies display rules to the existing XML data.
- **eXtensible Stylesheet Language (XSLT)**—Supports transformation of an XML document into another format, whether it's another XML document, an HTML page, or any data format (such as a small summary report generated from a large XML document). XSLT stylesheets contain rules (or templates) regarding format and content of an XML document. XSLT applies the templates found in an XSLT stylesheet and applies them to an input XML document, generating a new document. The contents of the new document are XSLT stylesheet dependent, and the stylesheet can describe a new XML document, an HTML document, or any number of different output formats.
- **XPath**—A language specification used to query XML data to locate and identify parts of XML documents that are specified using XPath expressions.
- **Document Object Model (DOM)**—Defines a language independent (such as Perl, C++, or Java) method of storing structured documents in memory. Once stored in memory, an application can walk up and down the branches of the tree containing elements and attributes and easily retrieve or modify elements and attributes.
- **Simple API for XML (SAX)**—Defines an interface for event-based XML parsing. The event-based parsing concept is a stream-based, sequential parsing model that enables you to parse XML data without storing the entire document in memory. Because it doesn't store the entire XML document in memory, SAX is usually used to parse large XML documents.

### XML Is Not a Transport Protocol

One of the few misconceptions about XML is that it is a transport protocol—it isn't. You cannot use or open an XML-based socket between two processes (for example, a browser client and a web server) to exchange data. You can, however, open up a TCP socket (for example, a browser client and a web server) and exchange a file that contains data stored in XML.

### XML Is Not a Programming Language

Another popular misconception about XML is that it is considered a programming language. XML is not a programming language. XML cannot calculate the average of the first column of a table of data; however, an XML document can store the data from the table. Tools have been written using a number of programming languages (such as Perl, C/C++, and Java) that can generate, build, or parse XML documents, but an XML document is not a script or a source code file.

There are several XML-based languages, and XSLT is a good example. XSLT programs are written using XML constructs, which are then interpreted and executed as defined in the specification. XSLT interpreters can be written in languages such as C, C++, Perl, or Java.

XML-based languages are a hot topic in the compiler and interpreter communities right now because many developers are beginning to see the benefits of using XML-based syntax, which easily defines things such as validations using DTDs or schemas, and namespaces.

## What Can I Do with XML?

Now that you have an understanding of what XML is, let's take a look at how XML might be used in a business application. Let's say you were just hired by a company that manufactures computer parts, and you have several high-profile customers. One of your first responsibilities will be to produce and distribute an electronic version of your company's catalog to your clients every month. The current situation is that each client has a specific requirement for the format of the information in the catalog. Luckily, you're very forward-thinking and see this as a great opportunity to start using XML because you can easily separate the data from the presentation. That's a great idea, but how do you get started? A few steps are involved in trying to start using XML for your catalog distribution, so let's take a look at the process.

### Step 1: Gather Requirements and Data

First, meet with each of the clients and compile a list of all the information required for the catalog and then the subset of the catalog (if applicable) for each client. It may be possible to build a master catalog, and then each client's catalog could be a customized report based in the catalog.

After meeting with the clients, you realize that they'll all need the following information for each manufactured item: part name, part number, description, technical specifications, and pricing information.

### Step 2: Describe the Format of the Data To Be Stored

Now that you have the list of the required data, you will need to work with the clients and describe the format of the data. The format includes ordering of the data, identifying required versus optional data, and valid values (such as enumerated lists or data types). This will assist you in verifying that the required data is present and in the proper format.

### Step 3: Design a DTD or an XML Schema

Formalize the structure and contents of the XML document by developing a DTD or an XML schema. Both DTDs and XML schemas specify the structure and content of an XML document. However, there are differences between DTDs and XML schemas.

Typically, DTDs are easier to develop because their syntax is simpler. However, that ease of use doesn't come without a price. For example, DTDs don't differentiate between data types. A validating XML parser can look at an XML document and the corresponding DTD and verify that a particular element is present, but it cannot verify that the element has the correct data type (such as text versus an integer). Also, DTDs are not valid XML documents, so they cannot be parsed by standard XML parsers.

XML schemas are more difficult to develop. One reason is that you must define a data type for each element. However, this extra work is rewarded with several important benefits. First, XML schemas are XML documents and can be processed by a standard XML parser. Second, XML schemas are much stricter regarding format and data type. For example, in addition to verifying that data is present in a particular element, an XML schema can also verify that the data is the proper type (such as Boolean, float, or string), how many times a particular element can appear, and whether the element value is within the expected range (for example, between 1 and 10). As you can see, a well-defined XML schema can perform nearly all your required input data validation.

> **Note**
> Think of a DTD or a XML schema as a contract—after both sides agree, it cannot be changed without additional negotiation.

At the start of a new project, be sure to spend enough time, and don't rush designing the DTD or XML schema. Try to anticipate any future growth by adding placeholders for data that may be required. Depending on the complexity of the DTD or XML schema, it may be time consuming to modify applications that are dependent on the DTD or XML schema. After you build an application or series of applications based on a particular DTD or XML schema, changes in the DTD or XML schema can sometimes trickle down to additional components in the architecture. For example, let's say that you have an application that parses XML data and stores the data in a database. When either the DTD or XML schema changes, both the parser and the database schema must be modified. If this is a large project, these changes probably won't be trivial. This isn't really an XML issue, it is a basic configuration management issue, but try to localize changes whenever possible.

### Step 4: Exchange and Process XML Documents

Develop and start exchanging XML documents between the manufacturer and the clients. Sounds easy, right? Well, there are a few remaining tasks that must be completed before this can occur.

If you are distributing the documents, you will need to develop an application that generates well-formed and valid XML documents. A well-formed XML document is one that conforms to the XML syntax rules developed by the W3C—this way, it is a legitimate XML file. A valid XML document is one that conforms to your relevant DTD or XML schema. XML documents may contain a lot of data, and trying to generate a large XML document by hand would be tedious and error-prone. Also, XML documents can be generated from a variety of sources—web-based forms, database tables, Comma Separated Values (CSV) files, spreadsheets, and so forth.

If you are on the receiving side of an XML document, you will need to have an application to parse the XML document. Then, after the document is parsed, what do you do with the data? The answer is, just about anything you want—generate another XML document, store the results in a database, or even dynamically generate HTML code to display the XML document (or a subset of the XML document) on a web page. Luckily for us, Perl has a suite of XML-based modules that will perform these tasks (and many others).

> **Learning More About XML**
>
> XML has many mailing lists, newsgroups, and support web sites. I recommend searching and joining some of them because there is no better way to learn about a technology than to listen to the everyday questions and discussions that are raised on these lists, groups, and web sites.
>
> You can find an index of XML mailing lists at `http://www.oasis-open.org/cover/lists.html`.
>
> Because XML is a W3C standard, I strongly suggest that you take a look at `http://www.w3.org` for XML and related standards documentation and resources.

Before I talk about processing XML documents with Perl, let's take a quick look at Perl.

## What Is Perl?

Perl is a high-level, powerful programming language originally developed by Larry Wall. It is an ideal language for quick prototyping of applications and production systems. Perl has file- and text-related functions that make it the ideal language for manipulating text files. In addition, Perl also supports graphical programming, applications requiring database access, network programming (that is, sockets), and web-based programming. As you can see, Perl has support for just about every possible component of an application.

Perl also has several strengths that make it the perfect language for processing XML documents, as you'll see in the following sections.

### Text Manipulation and Processing

One of Perl's major strengths is the suite of built-in tools and functions for text manipulation and processing. Because Perl was designed for data processing, you can do just about anything you want to data with a small Perl script. For example, it's very easy to search, replace, or match any pattern in a string or document using the built-in regular expression engine. A *regular expression* is used by Perl to search for patterns in a text string or file. Because XML data is plain text, it would seem natural to use Perl to process (that is, build, parse, or search) XML data. When Perl operates on XML data, it is just doing what its strength is—manipulating text.

## Extending Perl's Core Functionality Through Modules

Perl's core functionality can be easily extended by the use of modules. A *module* is a self-contained block of Perl code that performs a specific task. It is similar to a library in that it provides an application with additional functionality.

One of the more powerful modules available for Perl is the Database Interface (DBI) module. The Perl DBI module provides you with an API to a large number of supported databases. This module provides you with a standard API, which is independent of any underlying database dependent issues. The end result is a very powerful tool that can be the basis for a number of applications.

Another perfect example of a module is XML::Parser, which I'll be using for several examples throughout the book. *XML::Parser* provides an API to an XML parser library (written in C by James Clark) called *Expat*. Most of the low level parsing work is hidden from the user, and as a result, you interact with the parser through a clean, thought out, and well-defined interface, which makes the task of parsing an XML document much simpler.

Literally hundreds of Perl modules (more than 450 at the time of this writing) have been developed to support XML processing. This means you will find support for just about every XML-related task (such as writing, parsing, searching, and publishing). If not, then chances are someone is working on a module that does exactly what you need. And if not, you can always develop your own modules to support application or project-specific requirements.

As you make your way through this book, you'll see the power of modules, especially when they are utilized in an application. For example, the ability to query multiple database servers, combined with the ability to generate XML files, enables you to generate XML documents from any of the supported database servers. Modules also provide the reverse capability; by combining the XML::Parser module and the DBI module, you can parse XML documents and store their contents in a database. You'll be able to perform a lot of complicated tasks when you take advantage of the power of Perl modules.

## Perl Portability

One of the greatest benefits of using Perl is the fact that it is available for just about every operating system in use today. It is usually included as part of the standard distribution with Unix operating systems; but if not, both source code and binary downloads are readily available. Binary distributions of Perl are available for more than 50 platforms, see `http://www.perl.com/CPAN/ports/index.html` for the list.

You can visit a number of web sites to download a binary distribution of Perl if it wasn't included with your operating system. You can download either source code or binary distributions at `http://www.cpan.org`, `http://www.perl.com`, or from any number of mirror sites. Usually, if you're running a Unix-based system, it's best to download the source code and recompile Perl—this assures you that you are getting the latest (and greatest) version. If you are using a Microsoft Windows-based system, then I recommend using the Perl distribution from ActiveState (`http://www.activestate.com`).

## Web Programming

As dynamic web content came into mainstream web programming, Perl has quickly and surely taken over the market of Common Gateway Interface (CGI) programming, designed to interface between the server side and the client side of the web. Although many technologies now exist (such as Java Servlets, Java Server Pages (JSPs), Active Server Pages (ASPs), Personal Home Pages (PHPs), and so on), Perl continues to dominate the web server-side programming market due to its data processing facilities and ease of use. Because the web is all about processing and displaying data, Perl just naturally fills that position. Even though other technologies (such as Java Servlets) have some benefits over CGI, there are several strong reasons to use Perl. Mod_perl was developed as an answer to the newer technologies, such as JSP, ASP, Java Servlets, and PHP. Mod_perl is an Apache web server plugin module, which provides a built-in Perl interpreter. By using the mod_perl interpreter, scripts can benefit from the power of directly accessing the server API while running much faster and more efficiently. A few Perl technologies also exist to enable the embedding of Perl into HTML to complement technologies like ASP, JSP, and PHP.

## Open Distribution

Perl is available at no cost to users. The original developer of Perl, Larry Wall, believed in an open distribution policy. As a result, Perl is developed and supported by a worldwide network of volunteers. They are (as they say on the Perl web page) "committed to producing better software for free than you could hope to purchase for money." Perl is distributed as part of the GNU software project, but Perl usually falls under a more open license.

## Excellent Support from the Perl Community

Perl is developed and maintained by a community of open-source developers. The Comprehensive Perl Archive Network (CPAN) at `http://www.cpan.org` houses thousands of Perl modules and scripts, developed by many authors, that deal with just about any task at hand. If you need a Perl module to perform a particular task, chances are it already exists on CPAN.

Quite a few companies offer Perl distributions along with support. Some have even developed Perl development environments that they either sell or freely distribute. A variety of tools are available. For example, look at `http://www.perl.com`; this is the main source for Perl information, including an extensive list of Frequently Asked Questions (FAQs) and Perl-related articles and tutorials.

What makes Perl stronger than any other language is the community of dedicated developers and available support. CPAN, as I mentioned, is the central point to look when you are trying to solve a problem and require a module to help you do it.

Numerous mailing lists, newsgroups, and websites related to Perl exist. Some of the most popular ones include

**Newsgroups**

`comp.lang.perl.announce`

`comp.lang.perl.misc`

`comp.lang.perl.modules`

`comp.lang.perl.tk`

**Mailing lists** can be found by going to the following link, which lists most of the Perl-related mailing lists:

`http://www.perl.com/cs/user/query/q/6?id_topic=50`

## And That's Not All

As I demonstrated, the unmatchable power of Perl in the data processing world makes it the ideal candidate for XML processing, which just happens to be text data itself. Perl is great, more than great. As Larry Wall sayings go, "It makes difficult things easy and impossible things possible," and, "There is more than one way to do it with Perl." Both are very true, and you can only begin to realize that with practical experience.

In the following chapters, I will show you how Perl and XML are basically intertwined. As this book focuses on actually providing example solutions to problems, you'll be able to quickly apply these skills in your real world Perl XML application.

## Summary

In this chapter, I showed you why Perl and XML are two powerful, great technologies separately, as well as gave a few reasons why Perl and XML provide a powerful solution to today's information processing challenges. I believe there is nothing like experience and actual examples, so I'll use the rest of the book to convince you why Perl and XML, although not originally intended to work together, are made for each other.

# 2

# Now Let's Start Digging

## Chapter Roadmap

Now that we have presented a high-level concept of XML and Perl, it's time to see some of the tasks that we can accomplish when we combine these two tools. As we mentioned earlier, we will show you how XML and Perl complement each other and make tasks that initially seem to be difficult almost simple (well, at least a lot easier). We're going to discuss XML and Perl, and how they are used together to create portable, powerful, and easily extensible applications.

This chapter covers the concepts and basics of the most popular XML technologies. Each of these technologies is utilized in Perl applications throughout the book, and we provide a working example that clearly illustrates the proper way to use the respective Perl module. Here are the topics that we'll discuss in this chapter:

- What is XML Processing?
- XML Parser Paradigms
- Parsing an XML Document and Extracting Statistics
- Generating XML Documents
- Searching XML Documents

- Transforming XML Documents
- Our First Perl XML Programs
- The Problem: Generating and Parsing an XML Document
- What is XML Processing?

## What Is XML Processing?

What is XML processing? That is an often-asked question today given the popularity of XML. In the context of this book, I'll define XML processing as any task that involves XML data (for example, reading, writing, generating, and transforming).

### Examples of XML Processing

XML processing can mean different things to different people, depending on what is important to them. What are some XML-related tasks? A few of the more important XML-related topics that will be covered throughout the book are XML generation, XML validation, XML parsing, and XML transformation. Each of these topics will be introduced in the next few sections and then discussed in detail a little later in the book.

XML documents must be generated before they can be processed, so generating XML documents is an important topic. There are several Perl modules that are specifically designed to facilitate generating XML from a variety of input sources. The input data source will usually determine the best XML generating module for each situation. For example, if you are converting an input CSV file to XML, you could use either the XML::Writer or XML::SAXDriver::CSV Perl modules. If your input data is store in a Microsoft Excel file, you could use the XML::SAXDriver::Excel Perl module to help with the generation. Finally, if you need to convert the results of a database query to XML, you could use the XML::Writer or the XML::Generator::DBI modules.

As you can see, you have a number of options when it comes to support for generating XML. I'll discuss all of these modules in greater detail and present examples a little later in the book.

### Validating XML

Once we've generated an XML document (or received one from another source), there are Perl modules that will help you validate the XML document. An XML document is considered valid if it complies with a Document Type Definition (DTD) or XML schema. There are several Perl modules that support XML validation (for example, Apache Xerces), and they will be discussed later in the book.

### Parsing XML

Parsing is a concept that goes back a long time (in programmer's time, not historical time). *Parsing* data, in simple terms, is to break the data down into the fundamental components that mean something to the application or the end user. An XML parser is a program that does exactly that—it parses an XML document based on the XML rules and syntax defined in the XML standard, and it provides that information to the requesting application. Information usually comes in a data structure for each construct. If the construct is queried by the application, it will give you information about the construct. For example, for the open element construct (which is recognized whenever the parser encounters a combination of characters similar to <element_name>), the parser provides the element's name and other relevant information to the appropriate event handler.

### Transforming XML

XML can be transformed to a number of different formats. For example, an XML document can easily be converted to another XML document, HTML, CSV, or any of a number of different formats. This feature of XML is very important and allows a great deal of flexibility when presenting XML data. There are a number of Perl modules that support XML transformation and they'll be discussed in detail throughout the book.

> **Note**
>
> Remember, there is a difference between data and information. The term data can be used to describe an entire XML document (data = markup + information). Information, on the other hand, is the actual information contained in the XML data.

**Note**

A short XML primer is included in Appendix A, "What Is XML?" to help refresh your memory or give you an abbreviated introduction to XML.

## XML Parsers

Parsers come in many different forms. Some XML parsers don't require any programming, you just provide an input XML document, and the parser generates the output data. Other XML parsers provide Application Programming Interfaces (APIs) that allow the programmer to manipulate its functionality from within the application code. APIs are usually highly customizable and come with many different features. In Perl, a parser module provides an API to an XML parser engine. This API hides most of the details of the inner workings from the typical user, while providing a clean, easy-to-use, and well-defined interface.

Parsing an XML document involves reading the XML data and navigating through it while separating the contents of the XML document into meaningful components. Remember, XML data can come from a file, input stream (for example, a socket), a string, or just about any other possible data source. The most popular methods of parsing XML follow either the push model or the pull model. Each of these parsing methods is discussed in the following sections.

### Push Model of an XML Parser

The push model, as shown in Figure 2.1, is the core of the event-driven parsers. In the push model, special subroutines called *event handlers* are defined within your application. These event handlers are registered or tied to specific events and are automatically called by the XML parser when a particular event occurs. The push model was given its name because whenever a particular event is encountered, it pushes the event (and some event-specific data) to a predefined handler in the application. For example, you can define subroutines that are called when a start tag is encountered, when an end tag is encountered, and so forth. Using a little logic that we'll demonstrate, it is fairly straightforward to parse an XML document and extract its contents.

As you can see, this is a passive approach to parsing because your application waits for data to arrive. Basically, three steps are involved in this approach.

- Write the event handler subroutines.
- Parse the XML data.
- Wait for the event handlers to be called.

Of course, there is a little more to it, but that is basically what happens. It's important to understand the concept at a high level. This way, when we present the examples and discuss the code that actually performs each of these steps, you will have a good understanding of the process. Event-driven parsers and their underlying concepts are discussed in detail in Chapter 3, "Event-Driven Parser Modules."

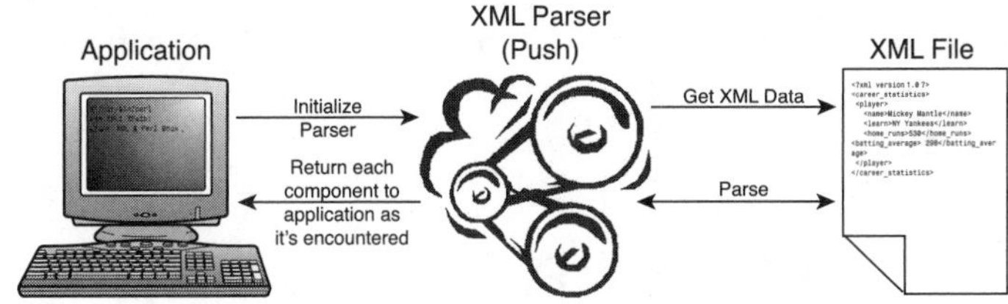


**Figure 2.1** Applications built using a push-based XML Parser play a passive role and receive data that is pushed from the XML parser.

## Pulling XML Parser Events to the Application

The pull model defines another parsing model. In this model, the application controls the parser and pulls the information from the parser as the parser iterates through the XML data. Figure 2.2 illustrates the pull XML parser model.

As opposed to the push model, the pull model requires the application to play a more active role in the parsing of the document. The pull model basically parses the XML data and holds it in a tree structure. In order to retrieve data, the application then must walk up and down through the tree and extract the desired sections of the XML data. The pull model is discussed in detail in Chapter 4, "Tree-Based Parser Modules."

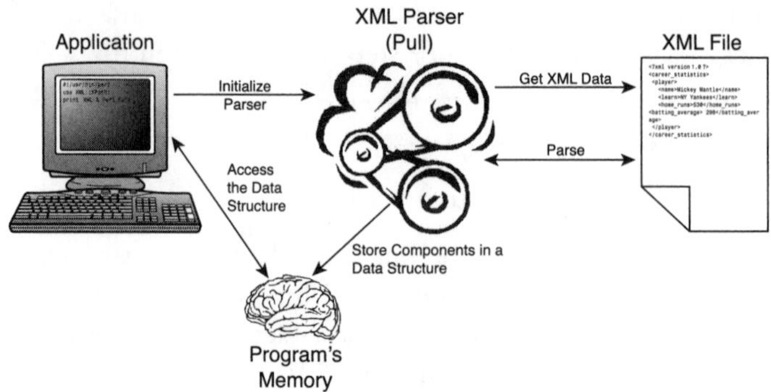


**Figure 2.2** Applications built using a pull-based XML parser play an active role in the parsing by pulling data from the XML document.

Together, these two paradigms form the basis of most XML parsers. We'll discuss the advantages and disadvantages of the push and pull methods throughout the book.

# XML Parser Paradigms

Now that we have discussed the low-level parser models, push and pull, let's look at the more commonly discussed models that are built on top of the push and pull concepts. The two major types of parsers are event-driven and tree-based parsers.

## Event-Driven XML Parsers

An event-driven parser is a model that can be closely associated with the push model. Event-driven parsers enable an application to define events for each recognized construct, and after that construct (event) is encountered, the parser calls the correct function in the application associated with that event. For example, we can define an event that is called whenever the opening tag (for example, `<name>`) of an element is encountered. Simple API for XML (SAX) is the most popular event-driven parser specification. It defines a standard way to access and manipulate a SAX-compliant parser. This is a very powerful model due to its speed and efficiency. We'll discuss event-driven modules in Chapter 3, "Event-Driven Parser Modules."

### Tree-Based XML Parsers

When we memorize some information (for example, a friend's telephone number), it's easier to remember it than it is to look it up in the telephone book. Unless we have amnesia, our memory serves as the fastest and most reliable source for retrieving data. If you look at the tree-based or pull parser model shown in Figure 2.2, you'll notice the parser has a brain of its own and, therefore, stores the parsed information in a data structure. After the information is stored in the memory of these data structures, it can be easily accessed from the application. One of the most popular tree-based XML parser models is called Document Object Model (DOM), which is a specification that defines the behaviors and data structures of DOM-compliant XML parsers. We'll talk more about DOM and other tree-based XML parsers in Chapter 4, "Tree-Based Parser Modules."

### XML Parsers Versus XML Processors

Try not to confuse XML parsers with XML processors. XML parsers are different from processors in that an XML parser is only one of the components of an XML processor. An XML processor may include several different components required to accomplish its task.

A perfect example of an XML processor is the eXtensible Stylesheet Language (XSL) Transformations (XSLT) processor. The XSLT processor is composed of many components, one of which is the actual XML parser itself. It uses the parsing component to decompose an XML document into meaningful parts so that other XSLT components can operate on the individual components. An XSLT processor converts requires two inputs: an XML document and an XSLT stylesheet. The XSLT stylesheet is an XML document that contains rules (called templates) that describe the format of the output document. The XSLT processor then applies these rules to the input XML document and generates the desired output. For example, we can start with an XML document, use an XSLT processor, and the end product could be an HTML document (for display on a web page), or even another XML document that is a subset of the original XML document. XSLT and other related topics will be discussed in Chapter 8, "XML Transformation and Filtering."

# Parsing an XML Document and Extracting Statistics

Now that you've got a good understanding of what it means to parse an XML document, let's take a look at a short example that uses one of the tools that were just discussed. For this example, we'll use the XML::Parser Perl module to parse a small XML document. Listing 2.1 shows a small XML document that contains statistics from two great baseball players. As you can see, the XML document is very simple. It has two `<player>` elements, and each `<player>` element has four child elements (`<name>`, `<team>`, `<home_runs>`, and `<batting_average>`). Granted, this is a small and simple XML document, but it is perfect for illustrating simple XML parsing. Our goal for this example is to parse this document and extract the statistics for each player.

Listing 2.1 **Career statistics for two Hall of Fame baseball players stored in an XML document. (Filename: ch2_baseball_stats.xml)**

```
<?xml version="1.0"?>
<career_statistics>
  <player>
      <name>Mickey Mantle</name>
      <team>NY Yankees</team>
      <home_runs>536</home_runs>
      <batting_average>.298</batting_average>
  </player>
  <player>
      <name>Joe DiMaggio</name>
      <team>NY Yankees</team>
      <home_runs>361</home_runs>
      <batting_average>.325</batting_average>
  </player>
</career_statistics>
```

We wrote a small application to parse this XML document. Don't worry about the source code yet, we'll start off slow and start showing Perl applications a little later in this chapter. For now, just focus on how an XML parser works, and don't be too concerned with all of the small details yet.

We used the XML::Parser Perl module to build an application to parse the XML document. The XML::Parser Perl module is an event based parser that will be discussed in Chapter 3, "Event-Driven Parser Modules." The output generated by the Perl XML parsing application is shown in the following:

```
career_statistics =

player =

name = Mickey Mantle
team = NY Yankees
home_runs = 536
batting_average = .298

player =

name = Joe DiMaggio
team = NY Yankees
home_runs = 361
batting_average = .325
```

Note that in the output, each element is printed out in the same order as the order that the opening tags appear in the XML document. As you look at the output listing, you're probably asking why the `<career_statistics>` and `<player>` elements are empty, right? Well, take a look at the original XML document in Listing 2.1 again. Notice that the original XML file really contains a `<career_statistics>` element that is made up of two child elements named `<player>`. Each `<player>` element is made up of four child elements: `<name>`, `<team>`, `<home_runs>`, and `<batting_average>`. So, when parsing the XML document, the `<career_statistics>` and `<player>` elements don't contain any character data themselves, but rather contain other elements—their child elements. After the `<name>`, `<team>`, `<home_runs>`, and `<batting average>` elements are encountered, the parser can extract the character data contained by each element. Of course, more complex scenarios exist in which elements contain attributes, character data, and child elements, but let's go one step at a time. You will have examples later that cover all these scenarios.

Now that we've given a quick introduction to parsing XML, the first question is, how do we do it? That's the easy part: use any number of Perl XML modules. It's only natural to try to use these two technologies together to solve complex problems. A large number of Perl modules are available that perform just about every conceivable task related to XML. As of this writing, there are nearly 500 Perl modules related to XML. We're going to explain the most popular modules, show you how to use them, and demonstrate them using real-world examples that can easily be extended to support more complex applications.

## Generating XML Documents

Where do XML documents come from? It's kind of like the famous question: Which came first, the chicken or the egg? You can't parse an XML document until you build one. The source data for an XML document can come from just about any imaginable source. For example, an XML document can be generated from a CSV file, a tab-delimited text file, the results of a database query, a Common Gateway Interface (CGI) web-based user input form that collects data from a user, Web services, and many, many other sources. You can see that there is an almost infinite number of data sources for XML documents.

Let's take a look at two methods of generating XML documents. First, an XML document can be created in a standard text editor or an XML-specific What You See Is What You Get (WYSIWYG) editor. This is called *static generation* because the XML document is created by typing the document into a text editor. The data in the file remains the same unless someone or something (that is, an application) modifies it. There isn't too much to it—you basically just type the contents of the XML file as you would type any other document. This is an option for very small XML files (for example, configuration files); however, it isn't practical for larger files. The larger and more complicated an XML document is, the greater the chance of error if the file is edited by hand.

XML documents can also be generated dynamically by an application. Dynamically generating XML is more interesting and applicable than statically generated documents, so let's take a more detailed look at this topic in the following section.

### Dynamically Generating XML Documents

Another method of generating an XML document is to dynamically generate the contents using an application (preferrably Perl based). Because XML is just plain text, an entire XML document can be easily contained within a Perl scalar. It also can be printed to any filehandle with a simple `print` command. Of course, plenty of modules are available that generate XML, which takes away some of complexities of doing everything yourself. We'll discuss these modules in Part III of this book, "Generating XML Documents Using Perl Modules." Some of the topics discussed include generating XML documents from text files, databases, and even other XML documents.

A good example to demonstrate dynamic XML file generation is a web form that is filled out by a user and then submitted to a Perl application running on the web server. This is certainly dynamic because we don't know what the user will enter as data. Assume that the web form shown in Figure 2.3 allows the user to fill out certain information and then submit the collected information to the server. The information provided by the user will be processed by a Perl script and used as input or source information for an XML document. An XML document will be generated containing the information provided by the user.

We won't get into too much detail here, but we will revisit this example in Chapter 5, "Generating XML Documents from Text Files." The purpose here is to provide a few high-level examples to illustrate the concepts instead of diving right into source code.

**User Input Form**

| | |
|---|---|
| **First Name** | John |
| **Last Name** | Smith |
| **Address** | 1155 Perl Drive |
| **City** | Los Angeles |
| **State** | California |
| **Zip Code** | 90102 |
| **Phone Number** | 818-555-1212 |

**Figure 2.3** Web-based HTML submission form used to collect data for our XML document.

When the Perl application receives the information from the form, it comes in a certain format. The Perl application can then parse this format to separate each field individually. Let's say the user fills in the required information and then submits the form. Now, inside our Perl application, we have the following data:

```
First Name: John
Last Name: Smith
Address: 1155 Perl Drive
City: Los Angeles
State: California
Zip: 90102
Phone Number: 818-555-1212
```

The Perl script can now process and modify the data and then generate an XML document containing this information. Listing 2.2 shows the submitted data in an XML document. This file now can be processed as an XML document. For example, now that the information submitted by the user is in XML, you have a variety of options. The XML document can be transformed to another format (using XSLT), searched (using Xpath), or sent to another application as a document that is based on an agreed-to format.

Listing 2.2 **Sample XML file generated from the web-based form input. (Filename: ch2_webform_input.xml)**

```
<?xml version="1.0"?>
<submission>
  <first_name>John</first_name>
  <last_name>Smith</last_name>
  <address>1155 Perl Drive.</address>
  <city>Los Angeles</city>
  <state>CA</state>
  <zip>90102</zip>
  <phone_number>818-555-1212</phone_number>
</submission>
```

This wasn't a very complicated example. As you can see, we've mapped the web form names (for example, first name, last name, and so forth) to element names inside the XML document for consistency. This is a good example of when you would dynamically generate XML.

Now that we have discussed XML file generation, we can proceed to more complex issues, such as searching XML data and transforming XML into other data formats.

# Searching XML Documents

Information storage is only useful if the information can be easily retrieved. Usually, information is retrieved from a relational database by sending commands (for example, Structured Query Language [SQL]) to the server. An XML document can be considered a facility for data storage, and therefore, can also be considered a rudimentary database. Just as SQL is the standard language for relational databases, the XML community has developed their own set of standards for retrieving information from an XML document. XPath is a standard that defines the syntax for addressing and fetching parts of an XML document.

**Note**

XPath and many other XML-related standards can be found on the web at `http://www.w3.org`.

Other XML standards exist, such as XML Query and XML Query Language (XQL), for querying XML documents. Each of these standards for querying XML documents uses its own syntax (though it might be similar) on top of the query engine.

Being able to extract data from an XML document can be very convenient. You can easily retrieve information from a certain part of the document by writing a query using XPath, XML Query, or XQL. Let's take a look at Figure 2.4, which shows (at a high level) just how XPath's query engine works.

As you can see in Figure 2.4, the application starts the query engine, initializes the query, and submits it to the engine for processing. The query engine then determines what is requested and goes to work to retrieve the requested information. After the data is located, it is returned to the application, which can proceed to process it. As you can see, the concept of the process is very simple and straightforward.

One area of XML processing that uses XPath quite extensively is XSLT. XPath is used to find portions of the XML document that match the criteria defined in the eXtensible Stylesheet Language (XSL) files (that is, which elements in the XML document will be extracted to create the output file).

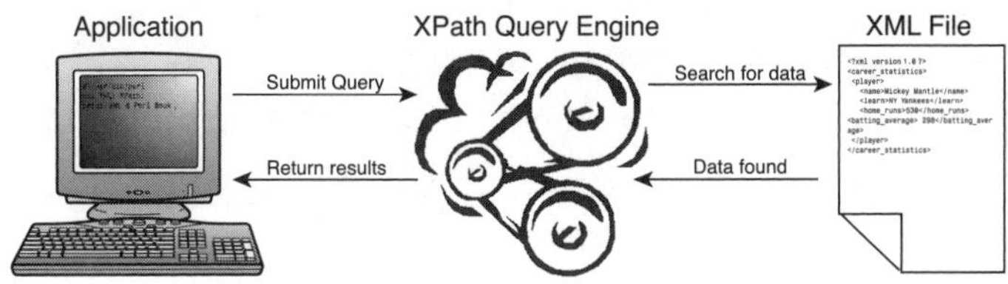


**Figure 2.4** XML XPath Query Engine.

## Transforming XML Documents

Now that we've covered parsing, generating, and searching an XML document, we get into another very important part of XML processing—XML transformation. You can transform, or in other words convert, an XML document to another format by applying various transformation techniques. You can transform the XML document to either another XML document, which might be a subset of the original document by filtering certain info, or you can transform to a whole different data format, like HTML, eXtensible HyperText Markup Language (XHTML), Wireless Markup Language (WML), CSV, and so forth.

Why would you want to convert our neatly formatted XML document to another format? We can read and understand the data as-is. Well the answer is, although as a technically savvy individual you took the time to learn XML and are now able to read it, most people would prefer their data represented in a user-friendly format.

One of the most popular methods of transforming XML to another format is to use the eXtensible Stylesheet Language for Transformations (XSLT) standard. An XSLT processor provides the interface needed to transform XML data. One of the processor's components is the XML parser itself, which is needed for the XSLT processor to understand and interact with XML. This makes sense if you think about it—the XSLT processor needs to parse the document to extract the information contained in the XML before it can format the contents. The processor requires an XSLT stylesheet to perform the transformation. An XSLT stylesheet is itself an XML document that contains embedded rules used to perform the transformation. An XSLT processor uses XPath and the rules contained in the XSLT stylesheet to transform the document. It searches through the XML data using XPath and tries to find the desired elements.

> **Note**
>
> We will come back to XML transformations and cover them in greater detail in Chapter 8, "XML Transformation and Filtering."

One of the most common (and easily demonstrated) transformations in use today is from XML to HTML. While the data is transferred and processed in a nicely formatted XML document, the XML document must be transformed into HTML to display in the browser with any type of formatting.

We don't want you to have to wait until Chapter 8 to see an example using an XSLT processor, so let's take a look at a simple example of transforming an XML document to HTML. To provide a common starting point, we'll reuse the XML document we discussed earlier, and it is presented here again as Listing 2.3 for your convenience. For this example, let's say that your task is to convert an XML report into HTML, so it can be displayed on a web page. Listing 2.3 shows the XML document we would like to convert and display in HTML.

Listing 2.3 **Career statistics for two Hall of Fame baseball players stored in an XML document. (Filename: ch2_baseball__stats.xml)**

```
<?xml version="1.0"?>
<career_statistics>
  <player>
      <name>Mickey Mantle</name>
      <team>NY Yankees</team>
      <home_runs>536</home_runs>
      <batting_average>.298</batting_average>
  </player>
  <player>
      <name>Joe DiMaggio</name>
      <team>NY Yankees</team>
      <home_runs>361</home_runs>
      <batting_average>.325</batting_average>
  </player>
</career_statistics>
```

If you recall, the previous XML file contains career statistics for two of the greatest baseball players ever to play the game. The data for each player includes the following elements: `<name>`, `<team>`, number of `<home runs>`, and career `<batting average>`.

As mentioned earlier, to perform the transformation, the XSLT processor requires two inputs: the XML document and an XSLT stylesheet. The XSLT stylesheet contains formatting information that determines both the content and format of the output HTML file. For example, if you wanted the text to be in a certain color or font, or if you want the information to be displayed in a table with particular column headings, this information would appear in the stylesheet. A sample XSLT stylesheet is shown in Listing 2.4.

Listing 2.4 **XSLT stylesheet used to generate an output HTML file. (Filename: ch2_baseball_stats.xslt)**

```
<?xml version="1.0"?>
<xsl:stylesheet xmlns:xsl=http://www.w3.org/1999/XSL/Transform
version="1.0">
<xsl:output omit-xml-declaration="yes"/>
<xsl:template match="career_statistics">
<html>
<body>
<h2>Baseball Players</h2>
   <table border="1">
<xsl:for-each select="player">
<tr>
   <td><xsl:value-of select="name"/></td>
   <td><xsl:value-of select="team"/></td>
   <td><xsl:value-of select="home_runs"/></td>
   <td><xsl:value-of select="batting_average"/></td>
</tr>
</xsl:for-each>
   </table>
</body>
</html>
</xsl:template>
</xsl:stylesheet>
```

When we apply our custom XSLT stylesheet to the original XML document, an HTML file is generated that contains the data from the XML file, presented in a customized view. Remember, XML contains only data with no information about the formatting, so we're free to format it as we see fit. That's one of the best features of XML—you can use several XSLT stylesheets to transform the same XML source document into different output HTML files. For example, let's say that your company's annual report is stored in XML and that you are responsible for generating different HTML versions of it. One version of the report would be used for internal purposes, and the other version would appear on the public web site. The internal version may contain proprietary information that shouldn't be displayed on the public web site. In order to generate different HTML versions of the annual report from a single XML document, just define one stylesheet for each target report. The XSLT stylesheet that generates the public version can easily filter out any proprietary information.

After applying the stylesheet in Listing 2.4 to the XML file, the XSLT processor generated the HTML output shown in Listing 2.5. Don't worry about the underlying transformation technology at this point; we just wanted to illustrate the capability of transforming XML into other formats. This is covered in detail in Chapter 8, "XML Transformation and Filtering."

Listing 2.5 **HTML document generated by using Perl and XSLT. (Filename: ch2_baseball_stats.html)**

```
<html>
<body>
<h2>Baseball Players</h2>
  <table border="1">
    <tr>
      <td>Name</td>
      <td>Teams</td>
      <td>Home Runs</td>
      <td>Batting Average</td>
    </tr>
    <tr>
      <td>Mickey Mantle</td>
      <td>NY Yankees</td>
      <td>536</td>
      <td>.298</td>
    </tr>
    <tr>
      <td>Joe DiMaggio</td>
      <td>NY Yankees</td>
      <td>361</td>
      <td>.325</td>
    </tr>
  </table>
</body>
</html>
```

Now that we have transformed the original file to HTML, it can easily be displayed in a web browser as shown in Figure 2.5. As you can see, the end result is a nicely formatted HTML table.

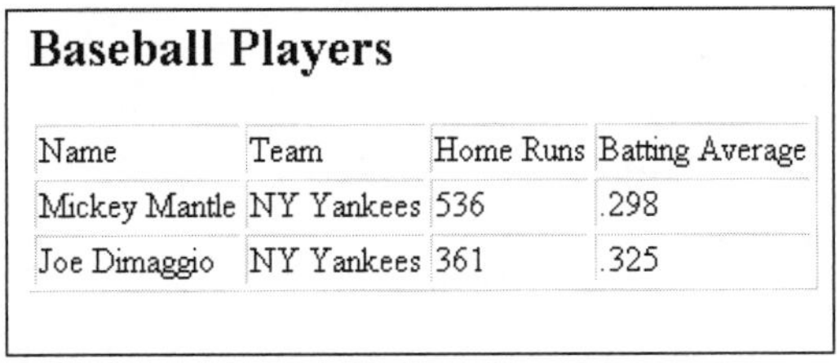

**Baseball Players**

| Name | Team | Home Runs | Batting Average |
|---|---|---|---|
| Mickey Mantle | NY Yankees | 536 | .298 |
| Joe Dimaggio | NY Yankees | 361 | .325 |

**Figure 2.5** HTML document generated by an XSLT transformation.

# Our First Perl XML Programs

This section presents two Perl programs (including source code) using several Perl XML modules. We will demonstrate some of the topics previously discussed (XML generation, parsing, and transformation) in Chapter 1, "Basics of XML Processing in Perl," and apply them to a simple, real-life application. We know that you've been patiently waiting for this moment. After all, you purchased this book to learn how to develop programs with Perl and XML, right? Well, since you asked for it, here it is.

> **Note**
>
> To run the programs discussed in this section, you need to install the following Perl modules:
>
> - XML::Simple
> - Data::Dumper
>
> For Perl module installation instructions please see Appendix B, "Perl Essentials."

# The Problem: Generating and Parsing an XML Document

The two most common XML programming tasks are XML document generation and XML document parsing. In this section, we will present two applications that demonstrate how to perform these tasks. Both of these tasks are commonly performed during XML processing and form the basis for more advanced applications throughout the book.

The first program reads a CSV file that contains user information and transforms it into XML. The second program parses the XML file that was generated by the first program, retrieves the user information, and transforms it into HTML for display in a web browser.

## Generating an XML Document

Let's assume you are given the task of converting the information in an electronic mailing list from CSV to XML because a new email application supports only XML input. The fields in the CSV file will be formatted as follows, with each user record on a separate line:

```
First Name, Last Name, Email Address
```

Simple enough? That's why we decided to use the Perl XML::Simple module. It's designed especially for simple tasks, although it can be used for more complex tasks. The rest of the book focuses on other Perl XML modules that are better suited for more difficult tasks. After you become familiar with the other XML modules, you'll be able to make a sound judgment and pick the right tool for the task at hand.

> **Note**
>
> Additional information about the XML::Simple Perl module can be found by typing **perldoc XML::Simple**. Also, XML::Simple will be discussed in greater detail in Chapter 4, "Tree-Based Parser Modules."

Now that you have an understanding of the program's requirements, you can really get your hands dirty. The CSV is a simple file with only three fields: first name, last name, and email address. The input CSV file is shown in Listing 2.6.

Listing 2.6 **The Input CSV file containing source data for XML document. (Filename: ch2_user_email.csv)**

```
Ilya,Sterin,isterin@cpan.org
Mark,Riehl,mark_riehl@hotmail.com
John,Smith,j.smith@xmlproj.com
```

Granted, this is a very small input file because it only has three records. However, the techniques used in this example can be applied to input data files with 3,000 or 30,000,000 records.

Now that we have the format of the input information, let's take a quick look at the required format of the output XML file. Let's assume that the output file is required to have the following format:

```
<users>
   <user>
      <first_name> </first_name>
      <last_name> </last_name>
      <email_address> </email_address>
   </user>
   ...
</users>
```

Note that we have a `<users>` element at the root of the document that is made up of multiple `<user>` elements. Each `<user>` element has one `<first_name>`, `<last_name>`, and `<email_address>` element.

The data for each user is stored in a predefined order: `<first_name>`, `<last_name>`, `<email address>`. Let's take a minute and list the steps that we would need to perform if we were doing this conversion by hand.

1. Read each line of the input file.
2. Parse the line into columns based on location of the delimiters.
3. Print each column surrounded by the proper start and end tags.

Because this is such a simple example, this is exactly how our program will work. Listing 2.7 shows the Perl program used to parse the CSV file and generate the desired output XML document. This example doesn't use any XML modules, it just parses the input file and then creates an XML document using the Perl `print` function. The example is explained in detail in the following sections.

Listing 2.7 **Perl application that converts the CSV input file to XML. (Filename: ch2_csv_to_xml_app.pl)**

```
use strict;

# Open the ch2_xml_users.csv file for input
open(CSV_FILE, "ch2_xmlusers.csv") ||
  die "Can't open file: $!";

# Open the ch2_xmlusers.xml file for output
open(XML_FILE, ">ch2_xmlusers.xml") ||
  die "Can't open file: $!";

# Print the initial XML header and the root element
print XML_FILE "<?xml version=\"1.0\"?>\n";
print XML_FILE "<users>\n";

# The while loop to traverse through each line in users.csv
while(<CSV_FILE>) {
    chomp;  # Delete the new line char for each line

   # Split each field, on the comma delimiter, into an array
    my @fields = split(/,/, $_);

print XML_FILE<<"EOF";
    <user>
       <first_name>$fields[0]</first_name>
       <last_name>$fields[1]</last_name>
       <email_address>$fields[2]</email_address>
    </user>
EOF
  }

```

```
31. # Close the root element
32. print XML_FILE "</users>";
33.
34. # Close all open files
35. close CSV_FILE;
36. close XML_FILE;
```

**1–9** The opening section of the program starts with the `use strict` pragma. This is a good practice in all Perl programs. The file ch2_xmlusers_csv is opened for input and ch2_xmlusers.xml is opened for output. After both files have been opened, we print the XML declaration and the opening tag for the `<users>` elements to the output file by using the `XML_FILE` filehandle.

```
1.  use strict;
2.
3.  # Open the ch2_xml_users.csv file for input
4.  open(CSV_FILE, "ch2_xmlusers.csv") ||
5.    die "Can't open file: $!";
6.
7.  # Open the ch2_xmlusers.xml file for output
8.  open(XML_FILE, ">ch2_xmlusers.xml") ||
9.    die "Can't open file: $!";10.
11. # Print the initial XML header and the root element
12. print XML_FILE "<?xml version=\"1.0\"?>\n";
13. print XML_FILE "<users>\n";
```

**Note**

In your program, `use strict` enforces error checking, and `use diagnostics` expands the diagnostics if the Perl compiler encounters an error or any questionable constructs.

**15–29** This portion of the program performs a majority of the work in this example. The input file (ch2_xmlusers.csv) is read line by line within the `while` loop, and each line is broken up into columns by the delimiter, which in our case is a comma. The columns are then printed to ch2_xmlusers.xml, surrounded by the appropriate tags. To print this example, we're using a Perl "Here" document, which allows us to print a block of text without having to use a print statement for each line. In this case, we're printing everything between `print XML_FILE<<"EOF"` and `EOF`. Note that variables are being evaluated inside this block. For additional information on Perl "Here" documents, please see perldoc perldata.

Because we know the order of the input columns (`first_name`, `last_name`, `email_address`), we can print the input contents directly to the output XML file. This procedure is repeated for each line (user) in the ch2_xmlusers.csv file, and a `<user>` element is created each time through the `while` loop.

```
15. # The while loop to traverse through each line in users.csv
16. while(<CSV_FILE>) {
17.      chomp;  # Delete the new line char for each line
18.
19.     # Split each field, on the comma delimiter, into an array
20.      my @fields = split(/,/, $_);
21.
22. print XML_FILE<<"EOF";
23.      <user>
24.         <first_name>$fields[0]</first_name>
25.         <last_name>$fields[1]</last_name>
26.         <email_address>$fields[2]</email_address>
27.      </user>
28. EOF
29.    }
```

**31–36** The final section of our Perl application just prints the closing root `</users>` tag to the output file. Note that the opening and closing `<user>` element tags were outside the `while` loop. The code inside the `while` loop creates each `<user>` element.

```
31. # Close the root element
32. print XML_FILE "</users>";
33.
34. # Close all open files
35. close CSV_FILE;
36. close XML_FILE;
```

The Perl application will generate the output that is shown in Listing 2.8.

Listing 2.8 **Generated XML file containing the data from the input CSV file. (Filename: ch2_xmlusers.xml)**

```
<?xml version="1.0"?>
<users>
   <user>
      <first_name>Ilya</first_name>
      <last_name>Sterin</last_name>
      <email_address>isterin@cpan.org</email_address>
   </user>
   <user>
      <first_name>Mark</first_name>
      <last_name>Riehl</last_name>
      <email_address>mark_riehl@hotmail.com</email_address>
   </user>
   <user>
      <first_name>John</first_name>
      <last_name>Smith</last_name>
      <email_address>j.smith@xmlproj.com</email_address>
   </user>
</users>
```

As you can see in Listing 2.9, the XML file that was generated by our program matches the required output file format. Don't worry, there are better ways to generate an XML file. We won't always be using the Perl `print` function to generate XML files. The goal was to illustrate the concept of generating an XML document using another file (in this case, CSV) as the input data source.

Now that we've generated our first XML file, how do we parse it? That is discussed in the next section.

## Parsing an XML Document

We've accomplished the first part of the application that showed the basics of generating a simple XML document. Now we can move on to the next task in which we transform the ch2_xmlusers.xml file in Listing 2.9 into an HTML file, so we can display the contents of the XML document in a browser.

> **Note**
>
> This chapter demonstrates the very basic concepts of XML generation, parsing, and transformation. Quite a few XML-related Perl modules are available to deal with each of these tasks. You'll see the benefits of the XML-related modules and when to use them (as well as when not to) as we move ahead and discuss more complicated examples.

Converting the input file from CSV to XML provides us with a document that is in a structured, clear, and easy-to-read format. Because XML is self-describing (because of the element names), anyone can look at the contents of an XML document and instantly see the layout of the data as well as the relationships between different elements. To display this information to someone not familiar with XML (or just for nicer formatting into tables), we need to convert it to another format. For this example, we have decided that we want this XML document to be displayed in a browser, so we must convert the XML document to HTML.

> **Note**
>
> A majority of the web browsers available today are able to display HTML in a consistent way. However, XML support among browsers isn't consistent and varies greatly among the most portable browsers (for example, some browsers will display XML whereas others require stylesheets). At the time of this writing, the most portable way to display an XML document with a browser is to convert the XML document to HTML.

To transform the XML document from XML to HTML, we need to parse it first. Using the XML::Simple module, this task is easily accomplished with its `XMLin` function, which reads XML from a file (string or an IO object), parses it, and returns a Perl data structure containing the information that was stored in XML. We can then traverse through the data structure, retrieve the required values, and print out the HTML file.

> **Additional XML::Simple Information**
>
> Note that there is also an `XMLout` function provided by XML::Simple. This function performs the reverse function of `XMLin` and returns XML based on the provided Perl data structure. Therefore, if `XMLout` is fed the same, unmodified data structure returned by `XMLin`, it will generate the original XML document. One potential issue is that the returned XML will be semantically alike, but not necessarily the same. This is due to the way Perl stores hashes, which is in no particular order. It's not necessarily a problem because many applications retrieve the data randomly and have no particular use for the element order, but it might pose a problem to applications that require a particular sequential order of elements (for example, sorted by a particular element). For additional information on XML::Simple, please see perldoc XML::Simple.

A number of attributes can be set to control XML::Simple's behavior. For example, we will use the `forcearray` attribute, which forces nested elements to be output as arrays, even if there is only one instance present. Also, we'll use the `keeproot` attribute, which causes the root element to be retained by XML::Simple (it is usually discarded).

Now that we have a high-level understanding of the XML::Simple module, let's take a detailed look at the program shown in Listing 2.9 that converts the input XML file to HTML.

Listing 2.9 **Program that converts an input XML file to HTML. (Filename: ch2_xml_to_html_app.pl)**

```
use strict;

# Load the XML::Simple module
use XML::Simple;

# Call XML::Simple's new constructor function to create an
# XML::Simple object and get the reference.
my $simple = XML::Simple->new();

# Read in ch2_xmlusers.xml and return a data structure.
# Note that forcearray and keeproot are both turned on
my $struct = $simple->XMLin("./ch2_xmlusers.xml", forcearray => 1,
➥keeproot => 1);

# Open ch2_xmlusers.html file for output
```

```
15.  # It will create it if it doesn't exist
16.  open(HTML_FILE, ">ch2_xmlusers.html") ||
17.    die "Can't open file: $!\n";
18.
19.  # Print the initial HTML tags
20.  print HTML_FILE "<html>\n<body>\n";
21.
22.  # The for loop traverses over each user.
23.  # $_ points to the user
24.  for (@{$struct->{users}->[0]->{user}}) {
25.    # Print the each field in the user structure
26.  print HTML_FILE <<"EOF";
27.    First Name: $_->{first_name}->[0]<br>
28.    Last Name: $_->{last_name}->[0]<br>
29.    Email Address: $_->{email_address}->[0]<br>
30.    ---------------------------------------<br>
31.  EOF
32.  }
33.
34.  # Print the ending HTML tags
35.  print HTML_FILE "</body><br></html>";
36.
37.  # Close ch2_xmlusers.html
38.  close (HTML_FILE);
```

**1–12** This initial block of the program starts with the standard `use strict` pragma. Because we're using the XML::Simple module, we must also include the `use XML::Simple` statement to load the XML::Simple module. After these initialization calls, we create a new XML::Simple object and then parse the XML file by calling the `XMLIn` function. The scalar `$struct` contains a reference to a data structure that contains the information from the XML file.

```
1.   use strict;
2.
3.   # Load the XML::Simple module
4.   use XML::Simple;
5.
6.   # Call XML::Simple's new constructor function to create an
7.   # XML::Simple object and get the reference.
8.   my $simple = XML::Simple->new();
9.
10.  # Read in ch2_xmlusers.xml and return a data structure.
11.  # Note that forcearray and keeproot are both turned on
12.  my $struct = $simple->XMLIn("./ch2_xmlusers.xml", forcearray => 1,
     ➥keeproot => 1);
```

**19–38** The second half of the program actually performs all the work. First, we open the output HTML file and print the initial required HTML tags. Then, we loop through an array of references to data structures that contain the information from the XML file. The information from the XML file is then printed to the HTML file in the proper order.

We're taking advantage of the "Here" document construct again. This way, we don't need multiple print statements. Note that each time through the `for()` loop corresponds to one row in the CSV file and one `<user>` element in the XML document. After looping through the array, we print the required closing tags to the HTML file. The resulting HTML file is shown in Listing 2.10.

Listing 2.10 **Contents of the dynamically generated HTML file. (Filename: ch2_xmlusers.html)**

```
<html>
<body>
First Name: Ilya<br>
Last Name: Sterin<br>
Email Address: isterin@cpan.org<br>
---------------------------------------<br>
First Name: Mark<br>
Last Name: Riehl<br>
Email Address: mark_riehl@hotmail.com<br>
---------------------------------------<br>
First Name: John<br>
Last Name: Smith<br>
Email Address: j.smith@xmlproj.com<br>
---------------------------------------<br>
</body>
</html>
```

This HTML document is shown in a browser in Figure 2.6. As you can see, we didn't apply any formatting to this document, just the required headers and footers so that it displays properly. Examples later in the book will demonstrate how to dynamically generate HTML documents containing tables of data.

```
First Name: Ilya
Last Name: Sterin
Email Address: isterin@cpan.org
--------------------------------------
First Name: Mark
Last Name: Riehl
Email Address: mark_riehl@hotmail.com
--------------------------------------
First Name: John
Last Name: Smith
Email Address: j.smith@xmlproj.com
--------------------------------------
```

**Figure 2.6** The ch2_xmlusers.html file displayed in a browser.

## Viewing the Contents of Data Structures

This section discusses a Perl module that allows us to visualize the data structure that is returned by the XML::Simple function `XMLin`. All we need is a simple script and the Perl Data::Dumper module. The Perl Data::Dumper module is very useful in situations like this, when we want to verify that we understand a particular data structure. It prints out the contents of a particular data structure in such a way that it enables us to see the hierarchy and relationships inside the data structure.

What we're going to do is follow the same steps of the last example: instantiate an XML::Simple object and then pass it the name of the input XML document (ch2_xmlusers.xml). The XML document will be parsed by the XML::Simple module and stored in a Perl data structure. At this point, we'll take a look at the contents of the Perl data structure by using the Perl Data::Dumper module. The Perl application that performs these steps is shown in Listing 2.11.

**Note**

For additional information the Perl Data::Dumper module, look at perldoc Data::Dumper.

Listing 2.11 **Perl application that uses the Data::Dumper module to visual a complex data structure. (Filename: ch2_data_dumper_app.pl)**

```
1.  use strict;
2.  use XML::Simple;
3.  use Data::Dumper;
4.
5.  my $simple = XML::Simple->new();
6.  my $struct = $simple->XMLin("./ch2_xmlusers.xml", forcearray => 1, keeproot
    ➥=> 1);
7.
8.  # Use Data::Dumper Dumper function to return a nicely
9.  # formatted stringified structure
10. print Dumper($struct);
```

**1–10** This program is basically the same as the last example with a few exceptions. Note that we need the `use Data::Dumper` pragma to load the Data::Dumper module. After creating a new XML::Simple object, we parse the XML document using the `XMLin` function. A Perl data structure that contains the parsed XML document stored in a Perl data structure and that is named `$struct` is returned.

All we need to do is pass the Perl data structure to the Dumper function that is provided by the Perl Data::Dumper module. That's all there is to it. The output is a nicely formatted report that can be used to study the data structure. The output from the Data::Dumper module is shown in Listing 2.12. Notice that the output from Data::Dumper is a mirror of the input XML file.

Listing 2.12 **Output from the Data::Dumper module showing the hierarchy of the parsed XML file from XML::Simple. (Filename: ch2_data_dumper_output.txt)**

```
$VAR1 = {
'users' => [
        {
          'user' => [
              {
                'first_name' => [
                                  'Ilya'
                                ],
                'email_address' => [
                                     'isterin@cpan.org'
                                   ],
                'last_name' => [
                                 'Sterin'
                               ]
              },
              {
                'first_name' => [
                                  'Mark'
```

```
                    ],
        'email_address' => [
                              'mark_riehl@hotmail.com'
                            ],
        'last_name' => [
                          'Riehl'
                        ]
      },
      {
        'first_name' => [
                           'John'
                         ],
        'email_address' => [
                              'j.smith@xmlproj.com'
                            ],
        'last_name' => [
                          'Smith'
                        ]
      }
           ]
   }
      ]
 };
```

As you can see, the Perl data structure follows the same structure as original XML document (which we would expect). We recommend using the Data::Dumper module often. It is useful in situations where you need to access data that is stored in a complex Perl data structure. By looking at the output from the Perl Data::Dumper module, it will be easier to write the code to access different parts of the data structure and extract the desired information.

## Summary

This chapter introduced XML processing and illustrated the many facets of XML processing—parsing, generation, and transformation. A brief introduction to each of these topics was presented in addition to several high-level examples. The examples were purposely made almost trivial to illustrate XML processing at a high level. Don't worry, the examples in the upcoming chapters become increasingly more difficult as we move on to more advanced topics.

For example, the next chapter, Chapter 3, "Event-Driven Parser Modules," focuses solely on event-driven parsers. Detailed examples for several of the more popular event driven parsers are provided.

# Exercise

1. Create a program using XML::Simple that will parse the following XML document shown below and convert it to a CSV formatted file. Using the same structure, change all first names to reflect only a first capitalized initial (for example, Ilya to I), then output this file to a new XML document.

```
<?xml version="1.0" ?>
- <users>
-   <user>
      <first_name>Ilya</first_name>
      <last_name>Sterin</last_name>
      <email_address>isterin@cpan.org</email_address>
    </user>
-   <user>
      <first_name>Mark</first_name>
      <last_name>Riehl</last_name>
      <email_address>mark_riehl@hotmail.com</email_address>
    </user>
-   <user>
      <first_name>John</first_name>
      <last_name>Smith</last_name>
      <email_address>j.smith@xmlproj.com</email_address>
    </user>
  </users>
```

For suggested solutions to this exercise, be sure to check out the web site: `http://www.xmlproj.com/book/chapter02`.

# II

# Parsing XML Documents Using Perl

# 3

# Event-Driven Parser Modules

## Chapter Roadmap

Now that we have covered some introductory material in the first two chapters, we're going to discuss XML parser modules. Remember, the purpose of an XML parser is to parse XML data. Why would we want to do that? So that we can extract the important information (that is, the information contained between start and end tags) contained in the XML data.

Note that I'm using the term *XML data* rather than *XML file*. That's because XML data can exist in a number of formats—an actual file stored on a hard disk, data sent across a Transmission Control Protocol (TCP) or User Datagram Protocol (UDP) socket, or in memory as a dynamically generated result of a database query. No matter where the XML data resides, eventually someone will need to parse it.

This chapter focuses on event-driven XML parser modules and how to easily develop Perl programs based on those modules. One of the modules that provides sequential event-driven access to XML data is XML::Parser. Because XML::Parser also incorporates other parsing models, I only demonstrate its stream style mode, which is in fact, the event-driven model. Other parsing models (for example, the DOM or tree-based parsers) are discussed in Chapter 4, "Tree-Based Parser Modules."

I also discuss the SAX (Simple API for XML) standard, which defines a common interface for event-driven parsers. Currently, there are two versions of the SAX standard—SAX 1 and SAX2. Both versions are discussed, as well as the differences between each of the versions. Several modules exist that conform to each version.

An important module that I discuss that conforms to the SAX1 version is XML::Parser::PerlSAX. The SAX2 modules are listed in the following:

- XML::SAX::PurePerl
- XML::SAX::Expat
- XML::LibXML
- XML::Xerces

Each module is discussed and I demonstrate how to use SAX as a common interface to these parsers. Finally, I discuss the differences between each module and when to use each module for a particular task.

This chapter focuses on solving problems using the event-driven parser modules. To do this, you'll need to install the following Perl modules:

- XML::Parser
- XML::Parser::PerlSAX
- XML::SAX
- XML::SAX::PurePerl
- XML::SAX::Expat
- XML::NameSpaceSupport (required by XML::SAX::Expat)
- XML::Xerces

**Note**

If you have any questions about Perl modules (for example, where to get them, how to install them, and so forth), please refer to Appendix B, "Perl Essentials."

## What Are the Major Approaches to XML Parsing?

Currently, there are two major methodologies behind XML parsing. First is a group of parsers built to conform to the Document Object Model (DOM) standard. Second is another group of parsers built to conform to the Simple API for XML (SAX) standard.

The DOM-based parsers generate a tree of objects in memory based on the structure and contents of the XML data. This enables you to walk through the tree and access information or access only a portion (or branch) of your XML data.

SAX-based parsers take a different approach to parsing—they are event-driven. An event-driven XML parser module searches through XML data and looks for particular patterns (for example, the start of an element, the end of an element, and so forth). If the pattern is found in the XML data, the parser calls a `callback` function and passes pertinent data as arguments to the function. Typically, a separate `callback` function is defined for each pattern in the XML data that we're interested in, which varies based on each particular application. I'll present examples that show how to define `callback` functions that match the different important patterns contained in XML data. A notional event-based parser is shown in Figure 3.1.

**Figure 3.1** Notional event-based XML parser.

## Advantages of Event-Driven Parsers

Event-driven parsers have several advantages over tree-based parsers.

An event-driven parser can handle huge amounts of XML data. Let's say that you need to parse XML data in a file that is hundreds of megabytes in size. The parser works through the file, reading each line, triggering events when they're needed. A DOM-based parser would need to read the entire file into memory at once, something that might be difficult on smaller PCs or workstations. So, for the same XML data, a DOM-based parser requires more memory. Depending on the size of the XML data, it can be impractical (or even impossible) to use a DOM-based parser.

Another advantage of an event-driven parser is the complete XML file doesn't need to be available to start parsing. That's because the event-driven parsers don't know anything about the XML data; for example, whether it is stored in a file or in memory. The only concern an event-driven parser has is to look for the relevant patterns and trigger the corresponding `callback` function. This is important if you're working in a client-server environment. An event-driven parser can parse XML data as it is read off a socket rather than waiting for the entire XML file to be delivered to the parser.

## Disadvantages of Event-Driven Parsers

Event-driven parsers have several disadvantages compared to DOM- or tree-based parsers.

Event-based parser applications are more difficult to develop than the equivalent DOM-based parser application. In an event-driven parser application, the data is pushed into the application by the parser, so the application must be prepared to accept and process the data using a series of event handler subroutines. The subroutines aren't difficult to develop, especially after you have a sample application to use as a template, but it does require some time and effort on your part. An application built using a DOM- or tree-based parser behaves a little differently in that the parser builds a tree, and it is the responsibility of the application to retrieve the data. So, the DOM-based parser handles the storage of the XML data (in the form of a tree), while an event-based parser application is required to store data based on parser-driven events.

Another disadvantage of an event-based parser is that it doesn't have the concept of an entire XML document nor of an XML document's hierarchical structure. Yes, this was listed as an advantage, and I consider it to be more of an advantage than a disadvantage, but there are times when you want to operate on an entire XML document. This is easy to do with a DOM- or tree-based parser because the entire document is already stored in memory. To do this in an event-based parser application, you would need to develop a custom data structure to store the data. This is not a big problem, but it does cause some additional work.

## What Is a Sequential Access Event-Driven XML Parser?

The topic of sequential access parsers is one of the most interesting concepts in the world of XML parsing. Because XML data is structured and appears in a particular order, these parsers enable us to access this data in the same order or sequence that was defined by the original XML data developer.

Most of the sequential parsers today are event-driven, and that is probably why confusion exists between the two concepts. A sequential access parser can be event-driven, but it doesn't have to be because it can conform to another model. In the event-driven model, when the sequential parser returns the chunks of XML data to the program, this data is passed to a user-defined function, which then processes the data. This function is called a `callback` function. A user can define a `callback` for each event (for example, each open tag, close tag, text, and so forth), and the parser will trigger the correct event when that construct (event) is encountered. Usually, data associated with the construct (for example, the element name) is passed into the `callback` function as an argument.

A sequential access event-driven XML parser starts at the top of the XML data and steps through the data line by line. For example, let's say that we have to parse the following XML data:

```
<?xml version="1.0"?>
<employees>
   <home_addresses>
      <name>Joseph Burns</name>
      <street>123 Main Street</street>
      <city>New York</city>
      <state>NY</state>
      <zip>10452</zip>
    </home_addresses>
</employees>
```

If we define a `callback` function that is called when an open tag for an element is encountered, then it would be called in the following order, once for each element: `<employees>`, `<home_addresses>`, `<name>`, `<street>`, `<city>`, `<state>`, and `<zip>`. Because the `callback` functions are called for each element in the same order as the elements appear in the XML data, this enables you to easily develop a Perl program to parse the XML data. It eliminates all the logic in your application that would be required if you didn't know the structure of the XML data.

These parsers are very fast and efficient because they simply read XML and return data to the program in chunks. The application then decides what to do with these chunks of data—process them or discard them—and enables the parser to proceed. These actions are performed until all the XML data is read, or until the program exits (due to an error or a user-defined command).

Now that we've discussed some of the theory behind XML parsers, let's take a look at some examples.

## XML::Parser Perl Module

The XML::Parser Perl module was originally written by Larry Wall and serves as a wrapper for James Clark's Expat parser's C libraries. Expat was one of the first XML parsers available, and it has proven itself over time to be very fast and powerful. Because Expat was one of the first XML parsers developed, it doesn't implement SAX, DOM, or XPath interfaces because the standards didn't exist or were immature and weren't yet widely accepted.

XML::Parser is also the underlying parser to several other parser implementations, but that is now changing with the development of the SAX2 interface and the XML::SAX module. As you will see, the XML::Parser Perl module is full of features that can accomplish just about any XML parsing task, and because of these numerous features, it is a very powerful tool for XML processing. The underlying Expat parser and the XML::Parser module are very stable because they have been around for quite some time.

### XML::Parser-Based Application

Let's create and examine a relatively small application. Assume that your company has outsourced desktop PC system administration to a support contractor. The support contractor stores all his information in a database and delivers reports to your company in XML. Your task is to develop a utility program that prints out a report for the non-technical personnel who are not yet familiar with the format of an XML document. This XML document can be very large, depending on the number of software packages that the company purchases. Because the reporting program will have to run on one of their standard desktop PCs (which in some cases might be an older, slower machine), we need to develop a resource-efficient program. This is the type of application where the stream-style processing in XML::Parser proves to be very beneficial.

In Chapter 1, "Basics of XML Processing in Perl," we discussed the steps required to build an XML-based application. Let's reuse those steps and apply them to the current example.

### Gather Requirements

As with any well-planned software application, we need to list our available data, the requirements, and the desired output data. Our goal for this example is to generate a report from XML data that contains our company's software inventory. For this simple example, let's assume that the XML data is generated by hand. Don't worry, all XML data isn't generated by hand. In Chapters 6, "Generating XML Documents from Databases," and 7, "Transforming Miscellaneous Data Formats to XML (and Vice-Versa)," we'll show you how to generate XML data from a number of input sources, including text files and relational databases.

To perform the proper inventory, we'll need the following information about each piece of software:

```
Name
Operating System
Number of Copies Purchased
Number of Copies Currently Being Used

Our output report should have the following format:
*Software Package Name *
Total Number of Packages: X
Total Number Available: Y
Value ($Z per piece): $Z * Total Number of Packages
```

### Describe the Format of the Stored Data

We know that we need to store a few pieces of information for each software package in our inventory. In the real world, a lot more data could be required for each piece of software (for example, licensing information, version number, patches or upgrades, and so forth); however, the pieces of information we have listed will suffice for our example.

We'll need to keep several points in mind while designing our format of the stored data. First, some of our data elements can have multiple child elements. For example, our base element will be the name of the software package. Some of our software packages are available for multiple operating systems, and the prices for each operating system could be different. Second, all our information (name, operating system name, total number of packages, total number of packages available) for each software package is required to appear at least once.

### Design a Document Type Definition or XML Schema

Now that we have the required data fields and the rules associated with the data (for example, each field is required to appear once for each base element), we can design a DTD and a schema to support our requirements. Remember, I discussed DTDs and schemas in Chapter 1. Both DTDs and schemas describe the content of XML data.

First, let's develop a DTD that supports our requirements. The root element of our DTD is called `software`, and it will be made up of multiple `distribution` elements. The root element is declared in the following section of the DTD:

```
<!ELEMENT software (distribution*)>
<!ELEMENT distribution (os*, price)>
<!ATTLIST distribution
name CDATA #REQUIRED
version CDATA #REQUIRED>
```

As you can see, we're saying that the `software` root element is made up of one or more `distribution` elements. Each `distribution` element is made up of an `os` element and a `price` element. Note that the `os` element can appear multiple times—this is required to support products that run on multiple operating systems. The `distribution` element also has two attributes—`name` and `version`. This enables each `distribution` element to be assigned a `name` and `version`. Note that the `*` after the `distribution` element indicates that the `distribution` element can appear one or more times.

The `os` element is similar to the `distribution` element in that it has two child elements (`total` and `out`) and an attribute (`name`).

```
<!ELEMENT os (total, out)>
<!ATTLIST os
name CDATA #REQUIRED>
<!ELEMENT total (#PCDATA)>
<!ELEMENT out (#PCDATA)>
```

Finally, the last child of the `distribution` element is the `price` element, which is defined by the following:

```
<!ELEMENT price (#PCDATA)>
```

All these individual portions of the DTD are combined to create the DTD shown in Listing 3.1.

Listing 3.1 **DTD for the software inventory XML document. (Filename: ch3_xml_parser_sw_inventory.dtd)**

```
<?xml version="1.0" encoding="UTF-8"?>
<!ELEMENT software (package*)>
<!ELEMENT package (operating_system*, price)>
<!ATTLIST package
```

```
  name CDATA #REQUIRED
  version CDATA #REQUIRED>
<!ELEMENT operating_system (licenses_purchased, licenses_in_use)>
<!ATTLIST operating_system
  name CDATA #REQUIRED>
<!ELEMENT licenses_purchased (#PCDATA)>
<!ELEMENT licenses_in_use (#PCDATA)>
<!ELEMENT price (#PCDATA)>
```

Now, let's build an XML schema based on the same set of data requirements. The corresponding XML schema is shown in Listing 3.2.

Listing 3.2 **XML schema for the software inventory XML file. (Filename: ch3_xml_parser_sw_inventory.xsd)**

```
<?xml version="1.0" encoding="UTF-8"?>
<xs:schema xmlns:xs="http://www.w3.org/2001/XMLSchema"
elementFormDefault="qualified">
   <xs:element name="licenses_in_use" type="xs:integer"/>
   <xs:element name="licenses_purchased" type="xs:integer"/>
   <xs:element name="operating_system">
      <xs:complexType>
         <xs:sequence>
            <xs:element ref="licenses_purchased"/>
            <xs:element ref="licenses_in_use"/>
         </xs:sequence>
         <xs:attribute name="name" type="xs:string" use="required"/>
      </xs:complexType>
   </xs:element>
   <xs:element name="package">
      <xs:complexType>
         <xs:sequence>
            <xs:element ref="operating_system" minOccurs="0"
            ➥maxOccurs="unbounded"/>
            <xs:element ref="price"/>
         </xs:sequence>
         <xs:attribute name="name" type="xs:string" use="required"/>
         <xs:attribute name="version" type="xs:string" use="required"/>
      </xs:complexType>
   </xs:element>
   <xs:element name="price" type="xs:string"/>
   <xs:element name="software">
      <xs:complexType>
         <xs:sequence>
            <xs:element ref="package" minOccurs="0" maxOccurs="unbounded"/>
         </xs:sequence>
      </xs:complexType>
   </xs:element>
</xs:schema>
```

Now that we have defined an XML DTD and an XML schema based on our requirements, let's build an XML file that conforms to the DTD and schema.

> **Note**
>
> Remember, you usually only use a DTD or a schema, not both at the same time. For the purpose of this example, I'm trying to demonstrate that they perform the same basic task—defining the structure and content of your XML data.

Now let's build an XML file that contains the software inventory information. Listing 3.3 shows an XML file that contains the software inventory in XML.

> **Note**
>
> The XML file should contain a reference to the corresponding DTD or schema.

Listing 3.3 **The software inventory data is stored in an XML file. (Filename: ch3_xml_parser_sw_inventory.xml)**

```
<?xml version="1.0"?>
<software_inventory>
   <package name="Dreamweaver" version="4">
      <operating_system name="Microsoft Windows">
         <licenses_purchased>15</licenses_purchased>
         <licenses_in_use>8</licenses_in_use>
      </operating_system>
      <operating_system name="Apple Mac OS">
         <licenses_purchased>10</licenses_purchased>
         <licenses_in_use>2</licenses_in_use>
      </operating_system>
      <price>299.99</price>
   </package>
   <package name="Microsoft Visual C++ Enterprise Edition" version="6">
      <operating_system name="Microsoft Windows">
         <licenses_purchased>15</licenses_purchased>
         <licenses_in_use>8</licenses_in_use>
      </operating_system>
      <price>1299.00</price>
   </package>
   <package name="XML Spy" version="4.2">
      <operating_system name="Microsoft Windows">
         <licenses_purchased>15</licenses_purchased>
         <licenses_in_use>8</licenses_in_use>
      </operating_system>
      <price>399.00</price>
   </package>
   <package name="Borland JBuilder Enterprise" version="6">
      <operating_system name="Microsoft Windows">
         <licenses_purchased>15</licenses_purchased>
```

```
            <licenses_in_use>8</licenses_in_use>
        </operating_system>
        <operating_system name="Apple Mac OS">
            <licenses_purchased>10</licenses_purchased>
            <licenses_in_use>2</licenses_in_use>
        </operating_system>
        <operating_system name="Linux">
            <licenses_purchased>10</licenses_purchased>
            <licenses_in_use>2</licenses_in_use>
        </operating_system>
        <operating_system name="Solaris Sparc">
            <licenses_purchased>10</licenses_purchased>
            <licenses_in_use>2</licenses_in_use>
        </operating_system>
        <price>2999.00</price>
    </package>
</software_inventory>
```

**Note**

As additional distributions are added to the inventory, the file in Listing 3.3 can be edited either manually or by another program. I will show you how to create a program that does just that in Chapter 6, "Generating XML Documents from Databases." For now, we'll just focus on parsing this file and generating a formatted report.

Before looking at the Perl application that generates the output report, let's take a minute and think about how we would manually perform this task.

1. Print out the heading for the report.
2. Read the XML document (shown in Listing 3.3) line by line (starting at the top).
3. Locate the package element and write out the desired information from each element. Also, add the number of licenses and the cost to our running totals, then repeat this step for each new package element that we find.
4. Print the summary information after reaching the end of the document.

As you'll see, the program in Listing 3.4 (ch3_xml_parser_app.pl) prints out a report from the information contained in the ch3_xml_parser_sw_ inventory.xml file by passing it as a command-line argument. Note that these are the steps that I just laid out. You may find that it is helpful to make a short list of the main steps in the process. In our application, we'll utilize XML::Parser's more commonly used functions and attributes to parse the XML document and generate the output report.

Now that we've defined our input data (in our XML file) and the output report format, let's take a look at a Perl program built upon XML::Parser that accomplishes this task. Our Perl program that uses the XML::Parser module to parse the input file is shown in Listing 3.4. I will walk through the program and explain each major section of the program.

Listing 3.4 **Program built using XML::Parser to parse the software inventory XML file. (Filename: ch3_xml_parser_app.pl)**

```
use strict;
use XML::Parser;

my $parser = XML::Parser->new(Style => 'Stream',
                              Handlers => {Init  => \&init,
                                           Start => \&start,
                                           Char  => \&char,
                                           End   => \&end,
                                           Final => \&final});

$parser->parsefile(shift);

#####################################
# These variables keep track        #
# of each distribution data, and    #
# are reset at each distribution.   #
#                                   #
my $dist_count = 0;                 #
my $dist_cost = 0;                  #
my $dist_out = 0;                   #
#####################################

#####################################
# These variables keep track        #
# of the totals which are           #
# accumulated throughout the      #
# parsing process                   #
#                                   #
my $total_count = 0;                #
my $total_cost = 0;                 #
my $total_out = 0;                  #
#####################################

my $curr_val = "";  ## Retains the text value
                    ## within the current node

my @os_avail = ();  ## An array of available
                    ## operating systems

sub init {
  my $e = shift;
```

```

  print "\n***** Software Inventory Report *****\n";
  print "------------------------------------\n\n";
}

sub start{
  my ($e, $tag, %attr) = @_;

  if ($tag eq "distribution") {
    print "*$attr{name} (version $attr{version})*\n";
  }
  elsif ($tag eq "os") {
    push($attr{name}, @os_avail);
  }
}

sub char {
  my ($e, $string) = @_;
  $curr_val = $string;
}

sub end {
  my ($e, $tag) = @_;

  if ($tag eq "price") {
    $dist_cost = $curr_val;
    $total_cost += $curr_val;
  }
  elsif ($tag eq "total") {
    $dist_count += $curr_val;
    $total_count += $curr_val;
  }
  elsif ($tag eq "out") {
    $dist_out += $curr_val;
    $total_out += $curr_val;
  }
  elsif ($tag eq "distribution") {
    print "Packages: $dist_count\n";
    print "Available: ".($dist_count - $dist_out)."\n";
    print "Value ($dist_cost per piece): \$".($dist_count*$dist_cost)."\n";
    print "------------------------------------\n\n";

    ## Empty the distribution variables
    $dist_count = 0;
    $dist_out = 0;
    @os_avail = ();
  }
}

sub final {
  my $e = shift;
```

*continues*

Listing 3.4 **Continued**

```
93.
94.     print "Total software packages: $total_count\n";
95.     print "Total software packages available: ".($total_count -
        ➥$total_out)."\n";
96.     print "Total cost for $total_count pieces of software: $total_cost\n";
97. }
```

### *Initialization*

**1–38** Our program starts with the standard `use strict` pragma, and then we utilize the `use` pragma to load the XML::Parser module. Next, we call the `new` function, which initializes the parser. Note that this call to `new` is very similar to a C++ constructor.

> **Note**
>
> Remember it's always a good idea to take advantage of the `use strict` Perl compiler pragma. The `use strict` pragma limits potentially unsafe code.

We pass two attributes to the `new` function, `Style` and `Handlers`. The `Style` attribute tells the parser which parsing style model we would like to use. The `Stream` value tells the parser to use the stream method of parsing, which is the event-driven model. Because we decided to use the event-driven model, we also need to use the `Handlers` attribute to pass the event handler functions. `Handlers` actually points to another hash, which contains the actual references to the subroutines that we will use to handle the predefined events. In this case, we assigned a handler subroutine to the `Init`, `Start`, `Char`, `End`, and `Final` events. All the subroutines that we defined (`init`, `start`, `char`, `end`, and `final`) are subroutines that we will define in our program, and each will be called by the XML::Parser module whenever the corresponding event is encountered. Now that the subroutines have been defined for each of the required handlers, and the parser has been initialized, we can start parsing the XML document. The XML::Parser module has three functions for parsing XML data: `parse`, `parsestring`, and `parsefile`. The first two functions are basically the same, expecting an input of XML data as a string. Note that the `parsestring` function is available only to provide backward compatibility for older applications. In our case, we'll use the `parsefile` subroutine because our XML data is in a standalone file.

> **Note**
>
> You are free to name your event handler subroutines anything that you choose. For ease of association, our subroutine names resemble the actual handlers. You can define any subroutine name as long as you assign the subroutine reference to the appropriate event handler. XML::Parser also provides the option of using predefined event handler names by using the `Handlers` facility. In this case, XML::Parser uses the following event handler names: `StartDocument`, `StartTag`, `Text`, `EndTag`, and `EndDocument`.

Because we are passing the XML document as a command-line argument, we use shift to retrieve the value from `@ARGV`. At this point, the process of parsing the XML document actually begins. XML::Parser parses through the whole document and calls event handlers to handle the encountered data while also verifying that the document is syntactically correct (that is, well-formed).

> **Note**
>
> You can use XML::Parser to check that XML data is well-formed by calling the proper parse method (that is, `parse` or `parsefile`) before setting any event handlers.

Next we declare and initialize eight different global data types that we'll use to keep track of the values through the calls to different handlers.

```
use strict;
use XML::Parser;

my $parser = XML::Parser->new(Style => 'Stream',
                              Handlers => {Init  => \&init,
                                           Start => \&start,
                                           Char  => \&char,
                                           End   => \&end,
                                           Final => \&final});

 $parser->parsefile(shift);

 ######################################
 # These variables keep track       #
 # of each distribution data, and   #
 # are reset at each distribution.  #
 #                                  #
 my $dist_count = 0;                #
 my $dist_cost = 0;                 #
 my $dist_out = 0;                  #
 ######################################

 ######################################
 # These variables keep track       #
 # of the totals which are          #
 # accumulated throughout the     #
 # parsing process                  #
```

*continues*

```
28.  #                                    #
29.  my $total_count = 0;                 #
30.  my $total_cost = 0;                  #
31.  my $total_out = 0;                   #
32.  ######################################
33.
34.  my $curr_val = "";  ## Retains the text value
35.                      ## within the current node
36.
37.  my @os_avail = ();  ## An array of available
38.                      ## operating systems
```

### init *and* start *Event Handlers*

**40–56** The `init` subroutine is called once before the actual parsing begins. In our example, we take advantage of this subroutine to generate a header for our report. The `start` subroutine is called once for the opening tag (for example, `<package>`). Note that three arguments are passed into the start subroutine:

- **`Expat` object**—This is the actual `Expat` object that was created with the initial call to `new`. We can use this object to gain access to object property values or object-specific functions.
- **Element name**—This scalar contains the name of the current element. If the XML::Parser module finds the opening tag for the package element (that is, `<package>`), then the element name `scalar` will contain the string "`package`".
- **Hash of attributes**—This argument is a hash of attributes for the current element. The data in the hash is stored in name-value pairs (for example, `version=>"4"`).

```
40.  sub init {
41.    my $e = shift;
42.
43.    print "\n***** Software Inventory Report *****\n";
44.    print "-----------------------------------\n\n";
45.  }
46.
47.  sub start{
48.    my ($e, $tag, %attr) = @_;
49.
50.    if ($tag eq "distribution") {
51.      print "*$attr{name} (version $attr{version})*\n";
52.    }
53.    elsif ($tag eq "os") {
54.      push($attr{name}, @os_avail);
55.    }
56.  }
```

### char *Event Handler*

**58–61** You have to be careful of the actions that are performed in this callback subroutine. Even though this is a short subroutine, it can be tricky.

The subroutine can be called multiple times for each encounter with character data. It is not recommended to use this subroutine for any action requiring a precise count of actions (for example, printing character, incrementing counters, and so forth). It is safe to use it to store the actual value of the characters, because regardless of how many times the handler is called, it will be passed the same value, and the outcome will be the same for all the calls made to it for the same character set. That is exactly what we do; we retain the value in `$curr_val` for later use.

```
58.  sub char {
59.    my ($e, $string) = @_;
60.    $curr_val = $string;
61.  }
```

> **Note**
> All the event handlers are passed the actual `Expat` object that was created when the new method is called.

### end *Event Handler and* final *Subroutine*

**63–97** The `end` handler is called whenever the parser encounters an end tag (for example, `</package>`) for an element. In this example, we use the end tag to notify the application that we've completed a particular element and to tabulate the required information. Note that we print out the summary information for that particular element and clear the values of any variables associated with that element.

The `final` subroutine is similar to the `init` subroutine in that it is only called once. However, as you may have guessed from the name, the `final` subroutine is called after the parsing has completed. In our example, we take advantage of the fact that this is the last subroutine called and use it to print out summary information.

```
63.  sub end {
64.    my ($e, $tag) = @_;
65.
66.    if ($tag eq "price") {
67.      $dist_cost = $curr_val;
68.      $total_cost += $curr_val;
69.    }
70.    elsif ($tag eq "total") {
71.      $dist_count += $curr_val;
72.      $total_count += $curr_val;
```

*continues*

```
  }
  elsif ($tag eq "out") {
    $dist_out += $curr_val;
    $total_out += $curr_val;
  }
  elsif ($tag eq "distribution") {
    print "Packages: $dist_count\n";
    print "Available: ".($dist_count - $dist_out)."\n";
    print "Value ($dist_cost per piece): \$".($dist_count*$dist_cost)."\n";
    print "-----------------------------------\n\n";

    ## Empty the distribution variables
    $dist_count = 0;
    $dist_out = 0;
    @os_avail = ();
  }
}

sub final {
  my $e = shift;

  print "Total software packages: $total_count\n";
  print "Total software packages available: ".($total_count -
  ➥$total_out)."\n";
  print "Total cost for $total_count pieces of software: $total_cost\n";
}
```

The output from our inventory report generator program is shown in Listing 3.5.

Listing 3.5 **Output software inventory report. (Filename: ch3_xml_parser_report.txt)**

```
***** Software Inventory Report *****
-----------------------------------------------

*Dreamweaver (version 4)*
Packages Purchased: 25
Packages Available: 15
Cost (299.99 per piece): $7499.75
-----------------------------------------------

*Microsoft Visual C++ Enterprise Edition (version 6)*
Packages Purchased: 15
Packages Available: 7
Cost (1299.00 per piece): $19485
-----------------------------------------------

*XML Spy (version 4.2)*
Packages Purchased: 15
Packages Available: 7
Cost (399.00 per piece): $5985
```

```
-------------------------------------------------

*Borland JBuilder Enterprise (version 6)*
Packages Purchased: 45
Packages Available: 31
Cost (2999.00 per piece): $134955
-------------------------------------------------

Total software packages purchased: 100
Total software packages available: 60
Total cost for 100 software packages: 4996.99
```

This example demonstrates how to use XML::Parser in the stream mode to parse an XML document and how to generate a report from the data contained in the XML document. We also defined the event handlers corresponding to the most important events. For additional information on the XML::Parser Perl module (including functions and attribute options), see the perldoc page that comes with its distribution.

# SAX1—Simple API for XML Version 1

What is the Simple API for XML (SAX)? SAX provides an event-based API to retrieve (that is, to parse) data from an XML document. What is the data in an XML document? Depending on the task at hand, you may need to extract an element name, the character data inside an element, an attribute associated with a particular element, or all the above. The SAX API is implemented by a large number of XML parsers, including Apache Xerces, MSXML from Microsoft, and the Oracle XML Parser.

## SAX1 Event Handling

How does the event handling inside a SAX processor work? The XML document is read sequentially (line by line), and the event-driven SAX processor calls a predefined subroutine (called an event handler in this case) whenever a particular condition (or set of conditions) is satisfied. The interface between the process and the event handlers is very user-friendly.

For example, we can set up event handlers that will be called by the SAX processor whenever it encounters any number of events. Here is a small subset of what the SAX processor considers to be an event:

- The start of an XML document
- The start tag of an element (<)
- The end tag of an element (</)
- The end of an XML document

Using the SAX approach provides several advantages to parsing XML documents.

- First, because you're reading the XML document sequentially, the data that you're parsing from the XML document is available as you process the file. This means that you don't need to wait for the entire file to be processed before you start seeing your results.
- Second, SAX works well with large files. Because the file is processed as it is being read, the entire file doesn't reside in memory all at once.
- Third, the SAX processor doesn't store any of the parsed data. What the application does with the event handler inside the application is up to you, the developer. All that the SAX processor does is call the event handler and pass in the proper data as a parameter. Some people would consider this a disadvantage compared to other parsing methods (for example, tree-based parsers); however, I consider this to be an advantage. It provides a lot of flexibility and enables (and almost forces) you to be a little creative while trying to parse a document. So, what you do inside of an event handler (what data you store, how you store it, and so forth) is up to you.

Now that we have a good understanding of SAX and *what* it does, let's take a look at an example of *how* it does it.

## XML::Parser::PerlSAX Perl Module

One of the more popular Perl SAX processors is XML::Parser::PerlSAX. XML::Parser::PerlSAX is a Perl SAX parser written by Ken MacLeod that was built using the XML::Parser module. The following example illustrates some of the SAX concepts that I discussed in the previous section and shows how to use XML::Parser::PerlSAX to parse an XML document.

### XML::Parser::PerlSAX-Based Application

Before we look at the XML document that we want to parse for this example, let's take a look at a DTD and XML schema that describes the XML document. Listing 3.6 shows the DTD for the course catalog file. As you can see, the root element is named `<course_catalog>` and it has two attributes—`school` and `term`. Note that `term` is an enumerated value that only allows four possible values. Each `<class>` element has one attribute (`name`) and two child elements (`<description>` and `<schedule>`). Note that each `<schedule>` element has the following child elements: `<room>`, `<day>`, `<start_time>`, `<end_time>`, and `<credits>`.

Listing 3.6 **DTD for the course catalog XML document. (Filename: ch3_course_catalog.dtd)**

```
<?xml version="1.0" encoding="UTF-8"?>
<!ELEMENT course_catalog (class+)>
<!ATTLIST course_catalog
   school CDATA #REQUIRED
   term (Fall | Winter | Spring | Summer) #REQUIRED>
<!ELEMENT school (#PCDATA)>
<!ELEMENT class (description, schedule+)>
<!ATTLIST class
   name CDATA #REQUIRED>
<!ELEMENT name (#PCDATA)>
<!ELEMENT description (#PCDATA)>
<!ELEMENT schedule ((room, day, start_time, end_time, credits))>
<!ELEMENT room (#PCDATA)>
<!ELEMENT day (#PCDATA)>
<!ELEMENT start_time (#PCDATA)>
<!ELEMENT end_time (#PCDATA)>
<!ELEMENT credits (#PCDATA)>
```

Listing 3.7 shows the XML schema for the course catalog XML document.

Listing 3.7 **XML schema for the course catalog XML document. (Filename: ch3_course_catalog.xsd)**

```
<?xml version="1.0" encoding="UTF-8"?>
<xs:schema xmlns:xs="http://www.w3.org/2001/XMLSchema"
elementFormDefault="qualified">
   <xs:element name="class">
      <xs:complexType>
         <xs:sequence>
            <xs:element ref="description"/>
            <xs:element ref="schedule" maxOccurs="unbounded"/>
         </xs:sequence>
         <xs:attribute name="name" type="xs:string" use="required"/>
      </xs:complexType>
   </xs:element>
   <xs:element name="course_catalog">
      <xs:complexType>
         <xs:sequence>
            <xs:element ref="class" maxOccurs="unbounded"/>
         </xs:sequence>
         <xs:attribute name="school" type="xs:string" use="required"/>
         <xs:attribute name="term" use="required">
            <xs:simpleType>
               <xs:restriction base="xs:NMTOKEN">
                  <xs:enumeration value="Fall"/>
                  <xs:enumeration value="Winter"/>
                  <xs:enumeration value="Spring"/>
                  <xs:enumeration value="Summer"/>
               </xs:restriction>
```

*continues*

Listing 3.7 **Continued**

```
            </xs:simpleType>
         </xs:attribute>
      </xs:complexType>
   </xs:element>
   <xs:element name="credits" type="xs:float"/>
   <xs:element name="day" type="xs:string"/>
   <xs:element name="description" type="xs:string"/>
   <xs:element name="end_time" type="xs:string"/>
   <xs:element name="name" type="xs:string"/>
   <xs:element name="room" type="xs:string"/>
   <xs:element name="schedule">
      <xs:complexType>
         <xs:sequence>
            <xs:element ref="room"/>
            <xs:element ref="day"/>
            <xs:element ref="start_time"/>
            <xs:element ref="end_time"/>
            <xs:element ref="credits"/>
         </xs:sequence>
      </xs:complexType>
   </xs:element>
   <xs:element name="school" type="xs:string"/>
   <xs:element name="start_time" type="xs:string"/>
</xs:schema>
```

The XML document that we want to process is shown in Listing 3.8. As you can see, it is a short, straightforward XML document containing the course catalog from a local university for the fall semester. Note that this document has data stored both in elements (as character data) and in attributes associated with particular elements.

Listing 3.8 **University course catalog stored in XML. (Filename: ch3_perlsax_catalog.xml)**

```
<?xml version="1.0" encoding="UTF-8"?>
<!—Filename: course_catalog_3-1.xml →
<course_catalog school="XML and Perl University" term="Fall">
   <class name="XML 101">
      <description>Hands on introduction to XML.</description>
      <schedule>
         <room>Lecture Hall 1</room>
         <day>Monday and Wednesday</day>
         <start_time>9:00 AM</start_time>
         <end_time>10:00 AM</end_time>
         <credits>2.0</credits>
      </schedule>
   </class>
   <class name="Perl 101">
      <description>Hands on introduction to Perl .</description>
```

```
        <schedule>
           <room>Lecture Hall 2</room>
           <day>Tuesday and Thursday</day>
           <start_time>1:00 PM</start_time>
           <end_time>3:00 PM</end_time>
           <credits>2.5</credits>
        </schedule>
     </class>
     <class name="Writing  for Engineers 101">
        <description>Covers the topic of technical writing.</description>
        <schedule>
           <room>Lecture Hall 3</room>
           <day>Monday and Friday</day>
           <start_time>1:00 AM</start_time>
           <end_time>3:00 PM</end_time>
           <credits>2.0</credits>
        </schedule>
     </class>
  </course_catalog>
```

As you can see, the root element of the document is named <course_catalog>. There are multiple occurrences of class elements, and each class element has several child elements—basically the important information associated with the class.

Let's say that you work for the university and your task is to parse the XML course catalog and generate a report that contains the pertinent information for each class. The output report should have the following format (repeating the class portion of the schedule once for each class):

```
School: <school name here> - <term> Semester Course Catalog
Class name: <class name here>
------------------
Description:
Room:
Day:
Start time:
End time:
```

### Developing the Application

Before we actually walk through the Perl program that parses the course catalog and generates our report, let's take a minute and think about how you would generate this report if you needed to do it by hand. To parse the document by hand, you would need to perform the following individual tasks:

1. Read the XML document (shown in Listing 3.8) line by line (starting at the top).
2. Locate the <course_catalog> element and write the desired attributes.

3. Look for the `<class>` elements that we're interested in, then find the schedule elements that belong to each class element.
4. Write out the element attributes and character data to a report.

Well, guess what? That's exactly how our report generator program will work! Remember, XML::Parser::PerlSAX is a sequential parser, so the document shown in Listing 3.8 will be processed one line at a time (as if you were reading it), starting at the first line in the document and finishing at the end of the document. As we're parsing the document, we'll need to check the element names in the document (returned inside the event handlers) against a list of the element names that are required to generate the output report.

Note that the `credits` element appears in our XML document; however, the number of credits for each class is not part of our output report. For this example, we can print out the results whenever we come across one of the elements (or attributes) in which we're interested. Depending on the required output, we don't have to print the results. For example, depending on our requirements, we might parse the results and store them in a database, display them in HTML as part of a web page, or just count the number of elements in an XML document that match a particular set of criteria. Don't worry, I'll cover all these parsing-related tasks (as well as a few others) in upcoming chapters, so let's take a look at the Perl application shown in Listing 3.9, which generates the required output report.

Listing 3.9 **Program that builds a course catalog report using XML::Parser::PerlSAX. (Filename: ch3_perlsax_app.pl)**

```
use strict;
use XML::Parser::PerlSAX;

# Instantiate a new parser object.
my $saxHandler = SaxHandler->new();
my $parser = XML::Parser::PerlSAX->new(Handler => $saxHandler);
my $inputXmlFile = "ch3_perlsax_catalog.xml";
my %parser_args = (Source => {SystemId => $inputXmlFile});
$parser->parse(%parser_args);

 exit;

 # Create a new package.
 package SaxHandler;
 use strict;

 my $current_element;

 sub new {
```

```
    my $type = shift;
    return bless {}, $type;
  }

  # start_element event handler
  sub start_element {
    my ($self, $element) = @_;

    my %atts = %{$element->{Attributes}};
    my $numAtts = keys(%atts);

    # Check to see if this element has attributes.
    if ($numAtts > 0) {
      my ($thisAtt, $key, $val);
      for $key (keys %atts) {
        $val = $atts{$key};

        if ($key eq 'school') {
           print "\nSchool: $val - ";
        }
        elsif ($key eq 'term') {
           print "$val Semester Course Catalog\n\n";
        }
        elsif ($key eq 'name') {
          print "Class name: $val\n";
          for (my $i = 0; $i < (12 + length($val)); $i++) {
            print "-";
          }
          print "\n";
        }
      }
    }
    $current_element = $element->{Name};
  }

  # characters event handler
  sub characters {
    my ($self, $character_data) = @_;

    my $text = $character_data->{Data};

    # Remove leading and trailing whitespace.
    $text =~ s/^\s*//;
    $text =~ s/\s*$//;

    if (length($text) ) {
      if (($current_element eq 'description') ) {
        print "Description: $text\n";
      }
      elsif ($current_element eq 'room') {
        print "Room: $text\n";
```

*continues*

Listing 3.9 **Continued**

```
71.         }
72.         elsif ($current_element eq 'day') {
73.           print "Day: $text\n";
74.         }
75.         elsif ($current_element eq 'start_time') {
76.           print "Start time: $text\n";
77.         }
78.         elsif ($current_element eq 'end_time') {
79.           print "End time: $text\n";
80.         }
81.       }
82.     }
83.
84.     # end_element event handler
85.     sub end_element {
86.       my ($self, $element) = @_;
87.
88.       if ($element->{Name} eq 'class') {
89.         print "\n";
90.       }
91.     }
92.
93.     # start_document event handler
94.     sub start_document {
95.         my ($self) = @_;
96.     }
97.
98.     # end_document event handler
99.     sub end_document {
100.        my ($self) = @_;
101.    }
```

I've listed the input XML file and the Perl program that parses the input file. Now, let's methodically walk through the Perl program, and I'll explain each of the event handlers, and then we'll see the report that is generated by our parsing program.

### *Initialization*

**1–22** This is the main portion of the program. First, we need to utilize the `use pragma` to identify which module we want to use. In this case, use XML::Parser::PerlSAX. In this code block, we create a new XML::Parser::PerlSAX parser object and pass in any required options (as key-value pairs or a single hash). Also, we identify the XML file to be parsed, and call the parse method that actually starts the parsing of the document. This portion of the program is basically responsible for initializing the parser and passing in any required options.

This code block is the beginning of the handler that is defined as an inline Perl package. This is a simple package that generates our output report.

```
1.   use strict;
2.   use XML::Parser::PerlSAX;
3.
4.   # Instantiate a new parser object.
5.   my $saxHandler = SaxHandler->new();
6.   my $parser = XML::Parser::PerlSAX->new(Handler => $saxHandler);
7.   my $inputXmlFile = "ch3_perlsax_catalog.xml";
8.   my %parser_args = (Source => {SystemId => $inputXmlFile});
9.   $parser->parse(%parser_args);
10.
11.   exit;
12.
13.   # Create a new package.
14.   package SaxHandler;
15.   use strict;
16.
17.   my $current_element;
18.
19.   sub new {
20.     my $type = shift;
21.     return bless {}, $type;
22.   }
```

#### start_element *Event Handler*

**24–53** This is the `start_element` event handler that is called by the parser each time the opening tag (for example, `<course_catalog>`) of an element is reached. In the `start_element` handler, we have access to the attributes associated with this element. As you can see from the example, we can receive a reference to a hash of attributes stored as key-value pairs. If we want to extract attributes in a particular order (for example, to satisfy the format of a particular report), we can loop through the hash of key-value pairs until we find the attribute that we're interested in. This enables us to skip over any attributes that aren't important to us.

XML::Parser::PerlSAX (and SAX in general) doesn't provide a method to identify the current element, so it is your responsibility to track your current location (that is, current element) within the XML document. One way to do this is to set a global variable equal to the current element (`$current_element = $element->{Name}`) in the `start_element` handler.

```
24.   # start_element event handler
25.   sub start_element {
26.     my ($self, $element) = @_;
27.
28.     my %atts = %{$element->{Attributes}};
29.     my $numAtts = keys(%atts);
```

*continues*

```
30.
31.     # Check to see if this element has attributes.
32.     if ($numAtts > 0) {
33.       my ($thisAtt, $key, $val);
34.       for $key (keys %atts) {
35.         $val = $atts{$key};
36.
37.         if ($key eq 'school') {
38.           print "\nSchool: $val - ";
39.         }
40.         elsif ($key eq 'term') {
41.           print "$val Semester Course Catalog\n\n";
42.         }
43.         elsif ($key eq 'name') {
44.           print "Class name: $val\n";
45.           for (my $i = 0; $i < (12 + length($val)); $i++) {
46.             print "-";
47.           }
48.           print "\n";
49.         }
50.       }
51.     }
52.     $current_element = $element->{Name};
53.   }
```

### characters *Event Handler*

**55–82** The `characters` event handler is called whenever the parser encounters the content of an element (that is, the data between a pair of start and end tags). One thing you need to do is remove the leading and trailing whitespace from the character data. This is because our XML document has extra newlines (at the end of every line) that have been inserted for human readability, but aren't required by XML or the parser. So, we need to remove the whitespace to eliminate confusion.

After removing the whitespace, we can search for particular element names using the `current_element` scalar that was defined inside the `start_element` handler. Note that we're explicitly searching for the element name because we don't want to include every element name. Did you notice that our original XML document included a `credits` element, but that we didn't need to include credits as part of the course catalog? Because we didn't try to match the `credit` element in the `characters` event handler, it won't show up in our generated report.

```
55.   # characters event handler
56.   sub characters {
57.     my ($self, $character_data) = @_;
58.
```

```
59.      my $text = $character_data->{Data};
60.
61.      # Remove leading and trailing whitespace.
62.      $text =~ s/^\s*//;
63.      $text =~ s/\s*$//;
64.
65.      if (length($text) ) {
66.        if (($current_element eq 'description') ) {
67.          print "Description: $text\n";
68.        }
69.        elsif ($current_element eq 'room') {
70.          print "Room: $text\n";
71.        }
72.        elsif ($current_element eq 'day') {
73.          print "Day: $text\n";
74.        }
75.        elsif ($current_element eq 'start_time') {
76.          print "Start time: $text\n";
77.        }
78.        elsif ($current_element eq 'end_time') {
79.          print "End time: $text\n";
80.        }
81.      }
82.    }
```

### end_element *Event Handler*

**84–91** The `end_element` event handler is called whenever the parser encounters the end tag of an element. For this particular example, we are only looking for the end tag of each `class` element, so that we can insert a newline between consecutive class elements.

```
84.    # end_element event handler
85.    sub end_element {
86.      my ($self, $element) = @_;
87.
88.      if ($element->{Name} eq 'class') {
89.        print "\n";
90.      }
91.    }
```

After running the XML::Parser::PerlSAX parser, you will see the output in Listing 3.10. As you can see, we've completed our initial task of generating a course catalog report based on the initial requirements.

Listing 3.10 **Output report generated by a program using the XML::Parser::PerlSAX module. (Filename: ch3_perlsax_report.txt)**

```
School: XML and Perl University - Fall Semester Course Catalog

Class name: XML 101
-------------------
Description: Hands on introduction to the exciting world of XML.
Room: Lecture Hall 1
Day: Monday and Wednesday
Start time: 9:00 AM
End time: 10:00 AM

Class name: Perl 101
--------------------
Description: Hands on introduction to the Perl language.
Room: Lecture Hall 2
Day: Tuesday and Thursday
Start time: 1:00 PM
End time: 3:00 PM

Class name: Writing  for Engineers 101
--------------------------------------
Description: Covers the topic of technical writing.
Room: Lecture Hall 3
Day: Monday and Friday
Start time: 1:00 AM
End time: 3:00 PM
```

## XML::Parser::PerlSAX Event Handlers

Because XML::Parser::PerlSAX is based on SAX1, it only supports a subset of the functions provided by SAX2. Occasions may arise when you need to use a SAX1-based parser; however, I would suggest using a SAX2-based parser for new projects. SAX2 adds additional functionality, and those additions are discussed in the next section.

**Note**

At the time of this writing, the Perl SAX specifications are due to be published by the Perl XML community. Unfortunately, we were unable to make the publishing deadline to include this content. Please check at the official Perl XML project home page (`http://www.xmlproj.com`) for additional information.

## SAX2

SAX2 is the successor to the SAX1 standard. Yes, it is a standard even though it is not published by W3C. It's an XML community standard and, therefore, is well-defined and easily adapted to your needs. SAX2 has become the preferred way to stream process XML.

The SAX1 standard was usable by many applications, but many programs required more information from the parser, and SAX1 did not address these issues. SAX2 was created to address these issues. It exposes more parsing information to the application and, therefore, fills in the gap of SAX1.

Most SAX development today has evolved around SAX2 specifications. Probably the only development you will see in the SAX1 arena is the actual upgrading and porting to the SAX2 interface. Perl's SAX2 XML development has currently accelerated thanks to its relatively small but very dedicated community of module developers. As you will see through the rest of this chapter, SAX2 modules are very easy to use considering the power and flexibility they offer.

### XML::SAX Perl Module

As the SAX standard evolved, several Perl modules were developed that provided a SAX interface to the XML parser. If you were to look on Comprehensive Perl Archive Network (CPAN) now, you would find a variety of XML modules as well as a few SAX parsers. Even though SAX is a well-defined standard, it becomes difficult to make sure the Perl module is compliant with the latest specifications and provides a common API. To help solve this dilemma, three very generous individuals (Matt Sergeant, Robin Berjon, and Kip Hampton) donated their valuable time to develop the next generation SAX facility, XML::SAX package.

> **Note**
>
> If you ever happen to run into one of the module developers, just scream "DAAHUUT!" and you'll feel right at home. It's the official saying of Perl XML module developers, which evolved from an IRC channel.

XML::SAX itself acts as a high-level interface to the SAX2-compliant parsers. XML::SAX module comes prepackaged with a few modules that provide different functionalities. They are the platform for SAX module and application development.

## XML::SAX::Base

If you are writing a SAX parser, driver, handler, or filter, this is the class you need to become familiar with to make your software compliant with Perl SAX2. XML::SAX::Base is a base class that can be inherited in your program. It eliminates a lot of redundancy and hassle in writing some of the common SAX handlers and routines. To inherit from it, you would simply insert the following line in your code.

```
use base qw(XML::SAX::Base);
```

This gives your program default SAX2 functions and properties. Now, when you develop your own handlers or any other functions that need customization, you can use the following template technique:

```
package MyHandler;
use base qw(XML::SAX::Base);
sub start_element {
my $self = shift;
#Do your processing here
$self->SUPER::start_element(@_);
}
```

For more information on XML::SAX::Base, please see the perldoc XML::SAX::Base documentation. If you are interested in developing SAX2 modules, you can find developer's documentation at `http://www.perlxml.net/sax`.

## XML::SAX::ParserFactory

If you are familiar with database processing in Perl and have used the DBI module, you'd see that the same problem existed in that world due to the diversity of databases and drivers necessary for accessing those databases. The DBI module solved that problem by providing a common interface to all the database-specific drivers. As a result of this effort, a majority of the databases in use today can be easily accessed and queried using the same API, so it has become the "Database Independent Interface." Using the same methodology, the XML::SAX::ParserFactory module was born. This object is used to return a SAX2 parser. Every time you install a SAX2-compliant parser, it registers itself in a configuration file named SAX.ini (which is installed with XML::SAX). This file is read by XML::SAX, from the most recently installed to the earliest installed parser.

XML::SAX::ParserFactory returns a parser of choice in three different ways.

- **Setting the $XML::SAX::ParserPackage variable.** It should be assigned the package name and can also contain the minimum version number.

  ```
  $XML::SAX::ParserFactory = "XML::LibXML::SAX::Parser (1.0)";
  ```

- **Using a `require_feature` function to set the features that the parser must support.** This method will query all parsers in SAX.ini and return the last installed parser that supports these feature(s) as shown in the following:

  ```
  use XML::SAX::ParserFactory;
  my $factory = XML::SAX::ParserFactory->new();
  $factory->require_feature (http://xml.org/sax/features/validation');
  ➥my $parser = $factory->parser(...);

  #or you can also specify this within the new function

  my $factory = XML::SAX::ParserFactory->new( RequiredFeatures => {
                      'http://xml.org/sax/features/validation' => 1,
                                              }
  ```

- **Creating a SAX.ini file and listing the requirement information in it**. Here is a sample line in SAX.ini:

  ```
  ParserPackage = XML::SAX::Expat (0.30)
  ```

  The information is written in foo = bar format. If you wanted a parser with certain features you can use this line:

  ```
  http://xml.org/sax/features/validation = 1
  ```

  The `XML::SAX::ParserFactory` object searches for the SAX.ini file in `@INC` and uses that if found.

- **If none of the above are specified, the parser will return the last installed SAX parser on the system.** XML::SAX comes bundled with XML::SAX::PurePerl and, therefore, you will always have this parser to fall back on in case no other parser is installed.

If the ParserFactory does not meet any of the above set criteria, it throws an exception.

You now see the significance of having the XML::SAX module and how it can benefit the SAX applications development. Let's take a look at how we can use this facility in a real application.

## XML::SAX::PurePerl Perl Module

XML::SAX::PurePerl is a SAX2 parser that is entirely written in Perl. Most of the other modules have C library dependencies that are usually hidden from the user. Why would it matter that the module is written entirely in Perl? Well, you could encounter a few situations where this would be very important.

What would happen if some crisis popped up and you needed to perform some XML parsing on a mission-critical web server that was currently live and servicing customers? Assume that the machine has Perl installed (of course), but doesn't have a C compiler—it has been removed to discourage any users from developing on the machine and also to free up disk space. Also, assume that you don't have administrative privileges on the machine, and that the system administrator is on vacation. If you think about it, this isn't an unrealistic situation, and something similar has probably happened to all of us. Also, a server such as this could reside in the company DMZ—physically in your building, but outside the corporate firewall. This would be the ideal situation to utilize the XML::SAX::PurePerl module. Because XML::SAX::PurePerl doesn't have the benefit of a C library, it is extremely slow for multi-user production environments. However, in a situation such as the one just described, performance probably isn't the most important measure of success. Sometimes, it is more important to get the job done than it is to get the job done quickly.

### XML::SAX::PurePerl Application

Let's take a look at an example using XML::SAX::PurePerl. Assume that your company uses a time reporting system and that every Friday it generates an XML file that contains the timecard information for all employees. In this example, we'll use the XML::PurePerl Perl module and generate the required summary report.

First, let's take a look at the DTD and XML schema for the XML document we'll need to process. The DTD is shown in Listing 3.11. As you can see, it basically contains all the information that might appear on a typical timecard. The root element is `<timecard_report>`, and it is made up of multiple `<employee>` elements. Each `<employee>` element has two attributes (`name` and `employee_num`) and a child element (`<project>`). The `project` element contains the `<project_number>` element and the `<hours_charged>` element.

Listing 3.11 **DTD for the timecard report XML document. (Filename: ch3_pureperl_timecard_report.dtd)**

```
<?xml version="1.0" encoding="UTF-8"?>
<!ELEMENT timecard_report (employee)*>
<!ELEMENT employee (project)*>
<!ATTLIST employee
   name CDATA #REQUIRED
   employee_num CDATA #REQUIRED>
<!ELEMENT project (project_number, hours_charged)>
<!ELEMENT project_number (#PCDATA)>
<!ELEMENT hours_charged (#PCDATA)>
```

The XML schema for the timecard report XML document is shown in Listing 3.12.

Listing 3.12 **XML schema for the timecard report XML document. (Filename: ch3_pureperl_timecard_report.xsd)**

```
<?xml version="1.0" encoding="UTF-8"?>
<xs:schema xmlns:xs="http://www.w3.org/2001/XMLSchema"
elementFormDefault="qualified">
   <xs:element name="employee">
      <xs:complexType>
         <xs:sequence minOccurs="0" maxOccurs="unbounded">
            <xs:element ref="project"/>
         </xs:sequence>
         <xs:attribute name="name" type="xs:string" use="required"/>
         <xs:attribute name="employee_num" type="xs:string" use="required"/>
      </xs:complexType>
   </xs:element>
   <xs:element name="hours_charged" type="xs:float"/>
   <xs:element name="project">
      <xs:complexType>
         <xs:sequence>
            <xs:element ref="project_number"/>
            <xs:element ref="hours_charged"/>
         </xs:sequence>
      </xs:complexType>
   </xs:element>
   <xs:element name="project_number" type="xs:string"/>
   <xs:element name="timecard_report">
      <xs:complexType>
         <xs:sequence minOccurs="0" maxOccurs="unbounded">
            <xs:element ref="employee"/>
         </xs:sequence>
      </xs:complexType>
   </xs:element>
</xs:schema>
```

As with the other examples, the XML document shown in Listing 3.13 isn't very complex, but it does have some of our data stored as both element attributes and as character data.

Listing 3.13 **Company timecard information in XML. (Filename: ch3_pureperl_timecard.xml)**

```
<?xml version="1.0" encoding="UTF-8"?>
<timecard_report>
   <employee name="Mark" employee_num="123">
      <project>
         <project_number>100-A</project_number>
         <hours_charged>19</hours_charged>
      </project>
      <project>
         <project_number>100-B</project_number>
         <hours_charged>21</hours_charged>
      </project>
   </employee>
   <employee name="Ilya" employee_num="129">
      <project>
         <project_number>101-A</project_number>
         <hours_charged>45</hours_charged>
      </project>
   </employee>
   <employee name="Alyse" employee_num="626">
      <project>
         <project_number>105-B</project_number>
         <hours_charged>43</hours_charged>
      </project>
   </employee>
   <employee name="Ed" employee_num="120">
      <project>
         <project_number>100-A</project_number>
         <hours_charged>10</hours_charged>
      </project>
      <project>
         <project_number>100-C</project_number>
         <hours_charged>12</hours_charged>
      </project>
   </employee>
</timecard_report>
```

Our task is to generate the report shown in Listing 3.14. Note that the report contains a repeating section for each employee, and that each employee can charge to multiple projects. Also, at the end of the report, we'll need to provide a project summary showing the total number of hours charged to each project.

Listing 3.14 **Contents of the output timecard report. (Filename: ch3_pureperl_report.txt)**

```
Timecard Report
---------------

Name: Mark
Employee Number: 123
Project Number: 100-A   Hours: 19
Project Number: 100-B   Hours: 21
Total Hours: 40

Name: Ilya
Employee Number: 129
Project Number: 101-A   Hours: 45
Total Hours: 45

Name: Alyse
Employee Number: 626
Project Number: 105-B   Hours: 43
Total Hours: 43

Name: Ed
Employee Number: 120
Project Number: 100-A   Hours: 10
Project Number: 100-C   Hours: 12
Total Hours: 22

Project Summary
---------------
Project 100-A charged a total of 29 hours
Project 100-B charged a total of 21 hours
Project 100-C charged a total of 12 hours
Project 101-A charged a total of 45 hours
Project 105-B charged a total of 43 hours
```

How do we do this? Please take a look at the program shown in Listing 3.15. It is similar to the XML::Parser::PerlSAX example; however, there are some important (and sometimes subtle) differences between the two approaches that you should know about.

Listing 3.15 **Program built using the XML::SAX::PurePerl module that will parse the input XML document containing weekly timecard information. (Filename: ch3_pureperl_app.pl)**

```
use strict;
use XML::SAX::ParserFactory;

$XML::SAX::ParserPackage = "XML::SAX::PurePerl";

my $handler = MyHandler->new();
```

*continues*

Listing 3.15 **Continued**

```
my $parser = XML::SAX::ParserFactory->parser(Handler => $handler);
my $inputXmlFile = shift || "ch3_pureperl.xml";
my %parser_args = (Source => {SystemId => $inputXmlFile});
$parser->parse(%parser_args);

package MyHandler;
my ($current_element, $total, %projectHours, $currentProj);

sub new {
  my $type = shift;
  return bless {}, $type;
}

# start_document event handler
sub start_document {
  my $key;

  print "\nTimecard Report\n";
  print "---------------\n";
}

sub start_element {
  my ($self, $element) = @_;

  # Set $current_element to the current element.
  $current_element = $element->{Name};

  my %atts = %{$element->{Attributes}};
  my $numAtts = keys(%atts);

  # Check to see if this element has attributes.
  if ($numAtts > 0) {
    print "\n";

    my ($thisAtt, $val);
    for my $key (keys %atts) {

      # Use this to look for a particular attribute.
      if ($atts{$key}->{Name} eq 'name') {
   print "Name: $atts{$key}->{Value}\n";
      }
      elsif ($atts{$key}->{Name} eq 'employee_num') {
   print "Employee Number: $atts{$key}->{Value}\n";
      }
    }
  }
}

# characters event handler
```

```
sub characters {
  my ($self, $characters) = @_;

  my $char_data = $characters->{Data};

  # Remove leading and trailing whitespace.
  $char_data =~ s/^\s*//;
  $char_data =~ s/\s*$//;

  if (length($char_data) ) {

    # Look for a particular element.
    if (($current_element eq 'project_number') ) {
      print "Project Number: $char_data\t";
      $currentProj = $char_data;
    }
    elsif ($current_element eq 'hours_charged') {
      if (exists ($projectHours{$currentProj}) ) {
      $projectHours{$currentProj} += $char_data;
      }
      else {
      $projectHours{$currentProj} = $char_data;
      }

      print "Hours: $char_data\n";

      # Increment the total hours here.
      $total += $char_data;
    }
  }
}

# end_element event handler
sub end_element {
  my ($self, $element) = @_;

  if ($element) {

    # We're at the end of an employee element, so
    # print out the total hours for this employee
    # and reset the scalar $total to 0.
    if (($element->{Name}) eq 'employee') {
      print "Total Hours: $total\n";
      $total = 0;
    }
  }
}

# end_document event handler
sub end_document {
  my $key;
```

*continues*

Listing 3.15 **Continued**

```
107.
108.     # Print out any summary information here.
109.     print "\nProject Summary\n";
110.     print "--------------\n";
111.     foreach $key (sort keys %projectHours) {
112.       print "Project $key charged a total of $projectHours{$key} hours\n"
113.     }
114.   }
```

Now that I have presented the Perl program built around the XML::SAX::PurePerl module, let's take a walk through the event handlers so that you understand what is happening in this example.

### XML::SAX::PurePerl Application Discussion

You will see a lot of similarity between the use of XML::Parser::PerlSAX and XML::SAX::PurePerl. First, as always, we start off with the `use strict` and `use diagnostics` pragmas—you should try to use both of these in all your Perl programs. For this example, we're going to do something a little different and use the XML::SAX::ParserFactory module. The XML::SAX::ParserFactory module acts as a front end for other modules and provides your application with a Perl SAX2 XML parser module. Whenever you install a SAX2 parser on your machine, it registers with XML::SAX and then is available to all applications by using XML::SAX::ParserFactory. The advantage of using the XML::SAX::ParserFactory module is that it provides a single interface to all your SAX2 parser modules.

> **Note**
> Please see perldoc XML::SAX::ParserFactory for additional information.

#### *Initialization*

**1–18** In the opening section of our program, we specify to the XML::Parser::Factory that we want to use the XML::SAX::PurePerl module. By doing this, the call to `XML::SAX::ParserFactory->parser()`returns an instance of the desired parser module—in our case, the PurePerl module. Now that we have an instance of the PurePerl module available to us in the `$parser` object, we can pass in any additional information that is required (for example, the name of the file containing the XML data) in a hash of key-value pairs.

The next section is the beginning of the inline package definition. As with the XML::Parser::PerlSAX module example, the purpose of this package is to assist us in parsing the XML document and generating the required output file. Note that we declare a hash named `projectHours`. We'll use this to store the project numbers and the number of hours charged to each project as key-value pairs.

```
1.  use strict;
2.  use XML::SAX::ParserFactory;
3.
4.  $XML::SAX::ParserPackage = "XML::SAX::PurePerl";
5.
6.  my $handler = MyHandler->new();
7.  my $parser = XML::SAX::ParserFactory->parser(Handler => $handler);
8.  my $inputXmlFile = shift || "ch3_pureperl.xml";
9.  my %parser_args = (Source => {SystemId => $inputXmlFile});
10.  $parser->parse(%parser_args);
11.
12.  package MyHandler;
13.  my ($current_element, $total, %projectHours, $currentProj);
14.
15.  sub new {
16.    my $type = shift;
17.    return bless {}, $type;
18.  }
```

### **start_document** *Event Handler*

**20–26** The `start_document` event handler is called once, so we use that to print out the heading for our report. The `start_element` event handler behaves exactly the same as the `start_element` handlers in the other parsers (that is, it is called when the parser encounters the opening [or start] tag for an element). One area of the start element that requires some explanation is attribute handling.

```
20.  # start_document event handler
21.  sub start_document {
22.    my $key;
23.
24.    print "\nTimecard Report\n";
25.    print "---------------\n";
26.  }
```

### start_element *Event Handler*

**28–53** In the `start_element` handler, you can see that there are two arguments. The first object is a reference to the current object (similar to a `*this` pointer in C++). The second argument is a reference to the attributes attached to the element. Note that the `start_element` is the only event handler that has access to the attributes. As you can see in the example, we can access the hash of attributes, treating it as any other hash containing key-value pairs. For our application, we need to find the values associated with the `Name` and `Employee Number` keys. We do this by looping through the hash and searching for the proper key name. After the required key is found, we print the value associated with the key.

```
28.  sub start_element {
29.    my ($self, $element) = @_;
30.
31.    # Set $current_element to the current element.
32.    $current_element = $element->{Name};
33.
34.    my %atts = %{$element->{Attributes}};
35.    my $numAtts = keys(%atts);
36.
37.    # Check to see if this element has attributes.
38.    if ($numAtts > 0) {
39.      print "\n";
40.
41.      my ($thisAtt, $val);
42.      for my $key (keys %atts) {
43.
44.        # Use this to look for a particular attribute.
45.        if ($atts{$key}->{Name} eq 'name') {
46.     print "Name: $atts{$key}->{Value}\n";
47.        }
48.        elsif ($atts{$key}->{Name} eq 'employee_num') {
49.     print "Employee Number: $atts{$key}->{Value}\n";
50.        }
51.      }
52.    }
53.  }
```

### characters *Event Handler*

**55–86** Similar to the other `characters` event handlers that we have seen so far, this event handler is called whenever the parser encounters character data for a particular element. Remember to remove both the leading and trailing whitespace—this is being performed by substitutions `s/^\s*//` and `s/\s*?//`. In this handler, we're looking for the `project_number` and `hours_charged` elements, and provided that they contain valid data, we're printing the contents. In this example, we were trying to explicitly match all the elements in the document. If there were additional elements in our input document (for example, an element containing the number of vacation hours used by an employee this calendar year), then it would have been skipped in the output report.

In this event handler, we set a global scalar named `$currentProj` to the name of the current project element. By doing this, we can assign the current project number and the cumulative number of hours charged to the project in our hash named `%projectHours`.

```
55.  # characters event handler
56.  sub characters {
57.    my ($self, $characters) = @_;
58.
59.    my $char_data = $characters->{Data};
60.
61.    # Remove leading and trailing whitespace.
62.    $char_data =~ s/^\s*//;
63.    $char_data =~ s/\s*$//;
64.
65.    if (length($char_data) ) {
66.
67.      # Look for a particular element.
68.      if (($current_element eq 'project_number') ) {
69.        print "Project Number: $char_data\t";
70.        $currentProj = $char_data;
71.      }
72.      elsif ($current_element eq 'hours_charged') {
73.        if (exists ($projectHours{$currentProj}) ) {
74.        $projectHours{$currentProj} += $char_data;
75.        }
76.        else {
77.        $projectHours{$currentProj} = $char_data;
78.        }
79.
80.        print "Hours: $char_data\n";
81.
82.        # Increment the total hours here.
83.        $total += $char_data;
84.      }
85.    }
86.  }
```

**end_element** ***Event Handler***

**88–102** As with the other `end_element` event handlers that we've discussed so far, this `end_element` event handler is called when the parser encounters the closing tag for an element. In this event handler, we use it to search for the end of an employee element. When we encounter the end of an employee element, it indicates that we've finished processing the current employee. So, we need to print out the total number of hours charged by the employee.

```
# end_element event handler
sub end_element {
  my ($self, $element) = @_;

  if ($element) {

    # We're at the end of an employee element, so
    # print out the total hours for this employee
    # and reset the scalar $total to 0.
    if (($element->{Name}) eq 'employee') {
      print "Total Hours: $total\n";
      $total = 0;
    }
  }
}
```

### end_document *Event Handler*

**104–114** The end_document event handler is called once when the parser reaches the end of the XML data (whether it is stored in a file or just as a block of XML data). This is the perfect location for printing out summary information or performing any other steps that need to be completed at the end of processing. In our case, we'll use the end_document handler to print out the contents of our projectHours hash that contains the project number and total hours stored as key-value pairs.

```
104.  # end_document event handler
105.  sub end_document {
106.    my $key;
107.
108.    # Print out any summary information here.
109.    print "\nProject Summary\n";
110.    print "---------------\n";
111.    foreach $key (sort keys %projectHours) {
112.      print "Project $key charged a total of $projectHours{$key} hours\n"
113.    }
114.  }
```

The output report generated by our application is shown in Listing 3.16. As you can see, the report is in the desired output format and contains all the required information.

Listing 3.16 **Output report in the desired format. (Filename: ch3_pureperl_report.txt)**

```
Timecard Report
---------------

Name: Mark
Employee Number: 123
```

```
Project Number: 100-A   Hours: 19
Project Number: 100-B   Hours: 21
Total Hours: 40

Name: Ilya
Employee Number: 129
Project Number: 101-A   Hours: 45
Total Hours: 45

Name: Alyse
Employee Number: 626
Project Number: 105-B   Hours: 43
Total Hours: 43

Name: Ed
Employee Number: 120
Project Number: 100-A   Hours: 10
Project Number: 100-C   Hours: 12
Total Hours: 22

Project Summary
---------------
Project 100-A charged a total of 29 hours
Project 100-B charged a total of 21 hours
Project 100-C charged a total of 12 hours
Project 101-A charged a total of 45 hours
Project 105-B charged a total of 43 hours
```

We just explored the use of XML::SAX with a SAX2 parser, XML::SAX::PurePerl. As I discussed, XML::SAX::PurePerl is a solid, reliable tool, but it has one weakness. XML::SAX::PurePerl can be slow because it is written purely in Perl and doesn't have the advantage of linked C libraries. A solution to this problem is discussed in the following section.

## XML::SAX::Expat Perl Module

When you are setting up a production environment and must depend on the stability and the speed of the parser, XML::SAX::Expat is the choice of professionals. It is built on top of XML::Parser, which has proven stability and speed. Basically, XML::SAX::Expat converts XML::Parser's streaming facility into a SAX2-compliant parser. Although the interface of any SAX2 parser is almost identical, let's take a look at another problem/solution scenario using XML::SAX::Expat.

### XML::SAX::Expat-Based Application

In a production environment, computer resources are critical. Ideally, we want applications to run as efficiently (in terms of both memory usage and speed) as possible. Although SAX parsers do not require a lot of memory, we always want to minimize the number of helper or miscellaneous processes running on a server so that the available resources are freed for mission-critical applications.

Let's say that we're working for a busy online retailer and it is the holiday season. All the incoming orders are stored in an XML file. Our task is to parse the XML file containing the orders and generate shipping labels for the warehouse workers.

### XML::SAX::Expat Application Discussion

The incoming orders are stored in a simple XML document based on the format of the DTD shown in Listing 3.17. As you can see, the DTD has a root element named `<shipping_orders>` and a child element named `<online_order>`. Each `<online_order>` element has the following child elements: `<name>`, `<address>`, `<phone>`, `<item>`, `<item_number>`, `<credit_card>`, and `<order_number>`. Note that the `<item>` element can be repeated multiple times for each order (in case the customer orders more than one item).

Listing 3.17 **DTD for the shipping order's XML document. (Filename: ch3_expat_shipping_order.dtd)**

```
<?xml version="1.0" encoding="UTF-8"?>
 (Agile Communications, Inc.) —>
<!ELEMENT shipping_orders (online_order*)>
<!ELEMENT online_order (name, address, phone, item*, credit_card, order_number)>
<!ELEMENT name (#PCDATA)>
<!ELEMENT address (#PCDATA)>
<!ELEMENT phone (#PCDATA)>
<!ELEMENT item (item_number, quantity, item_description)>
<!ELEMENT item_number (#PCDATA)>
<!ELEMENT quantity (#PCDATA)>
<!ELEMENT item_description (#PCDATA)>
<!ELEMENT credit_card (#PCDATA)>
<!ELEMENT order_number (#PCDATA)>
```

The XML schema for the same XML document is shown in Listing 3.18.

Listing 3.18 **XML schema for the XML shipping order's XML document. (Filename: ch3_expat_shipping_order.xsd)**

```
<?xml version="1.0" encoding="UTF-8"?>
<xs:schema xmlns:xs="http://www.w3.org/2001/XMLSchema"
elementFormDefault="qualified">
   <xs:element name="address" type="xs:string"/>
   <xs:element name="credit_card" type="xs:string"/>
   <xs:element name="item">
      <xs:complexType>
         <xs:sequence>
            <xs:element ref="item_number"/>
            <xs:element ref="quantity"/>
            <xs:element ref="item_description"/>
         </xs:sequence>
      </xs:complexType>
   </xs:element>
   <xs:element name="item_description" type="xs:string"/>
   <xs:element name="item_number" type="xs:string"/>
   <xs:element name="name" type="xs:string"/>
   <xs:element name="online_order">
      <xs:complexType>
         <xs:sequence>
            <xs:element ref="name"/>
            <xs:element ref="address"/>
            <xs:element ref="phone"/>
            <xs:element ref="item" minOccurs="0" maxOccurs="unbounded"/>
            <xs:element ref="credit_card"/>
            <xs:element ref="order_number"/>
         </xs:sequence>
      </xs:complexType>
   </xs:element>
   <xs:element name="order_number" type="xs:string"/>
   <xs:element name="phone" type="xs:string"/>
   <xs:element name="quantity" type="xs:integer"/>
   <xs:element name="shipping_orders">
      <xs:complexType>
         <xs:sequence>
            <xs:element ref="online_order" minOccurs="0" maxOccurs="unbounded"/>
         </xs:sequence>
      </xs:complexType>
   </xs:element>
</xs:schema>
```

So, what we need to do is write a program using XML::Parser::Expat that can parse the XML document and generate the required shipping labels as shown in Listing 3.19.

Listing 3.19 **XML document that contains online order transactions. (Filename: ch3_expat_shipping_order.xml)**

```
<?xml version="1.0" encoding="UTF-8"?>
<!DOCTYPE shipping_orders SYSTEM "ch3_online_order.dtd">
<shipping_orders>
<online_order>
      <name>Joe DiMaggio</name>
   <address>161st St and River Ave, Bronx, NY 10452 </address>
      <phone>111-222-3333</phone>
      <item>
         <item_number>112</item_number>
         <quantity>6</quantity>
         <item_description>Baseball bat</item_description>
      </item>
      <credit_card>2214</credit_card>
      <order_number>1</order_number>
   </online_order>
   <online_order>
      <name>Mickey Mantle</name>
      <address>111 Hastings Street, Spavinaw, OK 74366</address>
      <phone>222-333-4444</phone>
      <item>
         <item_number>209</item_number>
         <quantity>6</quantity>
         <item_description>Baseballs</item_description>
      </item>
      <item>
         <item_number>220</item_number>
         <quantity>1</quantity>
         <item_description>Baseball glove</item_description>
         </item>
      <credit_card>2415</credit_card>
      <order_number>2</order_number>
   </online_order>
   <online_order>
      <name>Yogi Berra</name>
      <address>100 Arch Way, St. Louis MO 63101</address>
      <phone>333-444-5555</phone>
      <item>
         <item_number>122</item_number>
         <quantity>1</quantity>
         <item_description>NY Yankee Hat</item_description>
      </item>
      <credit_card>2150</credit_card>
      <order_number>3</order_number>
   </online_order>
   <online_order>
```

```
        <name>Phil Rizzuto</name>
        <address>1112 18th St, Brooklyn NY, 10452</address>
        <phone>555-666-7777</phone>
        <item>
           <item_number>994</item_number>
           <quantity>1</quantity>
           <item_description>Pair of shoes</item_description>
           </item>
        <item>
           <item_number>332</item_number>
           <quantity>1</quantity>
           <item_description>Sunglasses</item_description>
        </item>
        <credit_card>1588</credit_card>
        <order_number>4</order_number>
     </online_order>
  </shipping_orders>
```

Our shipping label should be in the following format:

```
Order Number:
Cut mailing label along perforated marks
---------------------------------------
Mail To:
[NAME GOES HERE]
[ADDRESS GOES HERE]
---------------------------------------
Phone:

Please ship the below items:

Item Number:
Number of items ordered:
Description:
Credit card (last 4 digits):
```

As you can see, the fields are all in the same order that they appear in our XML file. This is the benefit of SAX parsing because the tree is traversed in the order that elements appear, enabling SAX to only cache the current construct in memory (thus using minimal resources). If you wanted to use this data in a different format, you have two options. Either reorder your XML document, or maintain your own cache and state and release it whenever needed. For applications relying heavily on these features, there are other solutions, which I will discuss in Chapter 4.

Let's now take a look at the Perl application shown in Listing 3.20. This Perl application utilizes the SAX2 parser XML::SAX::Expat Perl module and generates the formatted output that is required.

Listing 3.20 **XML::SAX::Expat-based program to generate shipping labels. (Filename: ch3_expat_online_order_app.pl)**

```
use strict;
use XML::SAX::ParserFactory;

# Set the current package.
$XML::SAX::ParserPackage = "XML::SAX::Expat";

# Instantiate new handler and parser objects.
my $handler = MyHandler->new();
my $parser = XML::SAX::ParserFactory->parser(Handler => $handler);

# Parse the document name that was passed in off the command line.
$parser->parse_uri($ARGV[0]);

package MyHandler;

my $current_element;
my $text;

sub new {
  my $self = shift;
  return bless {}, $self;
}

# start_element handler
sub start_element {
  my ($self, $element) = @_;

  my %atts = %{$element->{Attributes}};
  my $current_element = $element->{Name};

  if ($current_element eq "online_order") {
    print "Order Number: $atts{'{}number'}->{Value}\n";
    print "Cut mailing label along perforated marks\n";
    print "-----------------------------------------\n";
    print "Mail To:\n";
  }

}

# characters handler
sub characters {
  my ($self, $character_data) = @_;

  $text = $character_data->{Data};
}

# end_element handler
sub end_element {
```

```
  my ($self, $element) = @_;

  my $current_element = $element->{Name};
  if ($current_element eq "name") {
    print "$text\n";
  }
  elsif ($current_element eq "address") {
    print "$text\n";
    print "----------------------------------------\n";
  }
  elsif ($current_element eq "phone") {
    print "Phone: $text\n\n";
    print "Please ship the below items:\n";
  }
  elsif ($current_element eq "item_number") {
    print "\nItem Number: $text\n";
  }
  elsif ($current_element eq "quantity") {
    print "Number of items ordered: $text\n";
  }
  elsif ($current_element eq "item_description") {
    print "Description: $text\n";
  }
  elsif ($current_element eq "credit_card") {
    print "Credit card (last 4 digits): $text\n";
  }
  elsif ($current_element eq "online_order") {
    print "\n";
  }
}
```

Again, we accomplished our task using simple event handlers that are mostly made up of conditional statements. Isn't this stuff easy? Listing 3.21 shows the output from running this program at the command prompt with the filename of the XML document shown in Listing 3.19 as the command-line argument.

Listing 3.21 **Output report that contains order and shipping information. (Filename: ch3_expat_online_order_report.txt)**

```
Order Number: 1234
Cut mailing label along perforated marks
----------------------------------------
Mail To:
Joe DiMaggio
161st St and River Ave, Bronx, NY 10452
----------------------------------------
Phone: 111-222-3333

Please ship the below items:

Item Number: 112
```

*continues*

Listing 3.21 **Continued**

```
Number of items ordered: 6
Description: Baseball bat
Credit card (last 4 digits): 2214

Order Number: 1235
Cut mailing label along perforated marks
-----------------------------------------
Mail To:
Mickey Mantle
111 Hastings Street, Spavinaw, OK 74366
-----------------------------------------
Phone: 222-333-4444

Please ship the below items:

Item Number: 209
Number of items ordered: 6
Description: Baseballs

Item Number: 220
Number of items ordered: 1
Description: Baseball glove
Credit card (last 4 digits): 2415

Order Number: 1236
Cut mailing label along perforated marks
-----------------------------------------
Mail To:
Yogi Berra
100 Arch Way, St. Louis MO 63101
-----------------------------------------
Phone: 333-444-5555

Please ship the below items:

Item Number: 122
Number of items ordered: 1
Description: NY Yankee Hat
Credit card (last 4 digits): 2150

Order Number: 1237
Cut mailing label along perforated marks
-----------------------------------------
Mail To:
Phil Rizzuto
1112 18th St, Brooklyn NY, 10452
-----------------------------------------
Phone: 555-666-7777
```

```
Please ship the below items:

Item Number: 994
Number of items ordered: 1
Description: Pair of shoes, size 9.5

Item Number: 332
Number of items ordered: 1
Description: Sunglasses
Credit card (last 4 digits): 1588
```

This time we use the `parse_uri` function, which enables us to simply pass it the file name of the file we want to open and parse. This is just an alternative to providing a hash as we did in the XML::Parser::PerlSAX and XML::SAX::PurePerl examples. The `parse_uri` also accepts optional attributes as a second argument. See the SAX2 reference at the end of this chapter for more information.

The `MyHandler` class defines three handlers: `start_element`, `characters`, and `end_element`. In our experience, these are the most widely used handlers, and the majority of XML processing applications can be written just using these three. The SAX2 API defines a variety of different handlers that can be used to gain a better control of your application, if such precision is needed.

## XML::Xerces Perl Module

The XML::Xerces Perl module provides a Perl API to the Xerces XML parser developed by the Apache Software Foundation. This is the same organization that develops and distributes the Apache web server. If you're familiar with their products, then you know that the Apache Foundation has a well-deserved reputation for developing commercial-quality open source software that strictly follows the required standards. One of their most popular products is the Apache web server, which is the most widely used web server on the Internet.

The Apache Xerces XML parser is another well-designed product. Xerces is very popular for several reasons. First, it follows the XML standards very strictly. Xerces follows the XML 1.0 specification and the related standards (for example, DOM 1.0, DOM 2.0, SAX 1.0, SAX 2.0, namespaces, and schemas). Second, it is available for a number of languages. Xerces parsers are available in Java, C++, and of course Perl. Third, Xerces is available on a number of platforms. Chances are, it is available for your platform. If for some reason you can't find a Xerces binary for your platform, the source code is available.

The XML::Xerces Perl module was developed by Jason Stewart and provides a Perl wrapper around the Xerces C library. One of the benefits of the XML::Xerces parser is that it is a validating parser. A validating parser ensures that the input XML document contains all the required elements and attributes that are defined in either the DTD or XML schema. If the XML document doesn't comply with the accompanying DTD or schema, the XML::Xerces parser will issue a warning. In this section, we'll take a look at an XML::Xerces example that uses the SAX2 API.

## XML:Xerces Perl Module Application

This example demonstrates how to use the XML::Xerces Perl module to parse an XML document and generate a report. For this example, we'll design an XML document that contains information collected during Automated Teller Machine (ATM) transactions. The XML document should contain basic information, such as customer name, account number, transaction type, and money amount.

The output report for this application presents all the transactions for a day in an easy-to-read format. Also, it counts the total number of transactions for the day and the sum amount of money deposited and withdrawn from the ATM.

### Developing the Application

The first step in the application development is to define the input data format. For this example, we have developed the DTD shown in Listing 3.22.

Listing 3.22 **DTD for the XML ATM transaction log. (Filename: ch3_xerces_atm_log.dtd)**

```
<?xml version="1.0" encoding="UTF-8"?>
<!ELEMENT atm_log (transaction)+>
<!ATTLIST atm_log date CDATA #REQUIRED>
<!ELEMENT transaction (name,account,amount)>
<!ATTLIST transaction type (withdrawal | deposit) #REQUIRED>
<!ELEMENT name (#PCDATA)>
<!ELEMENT account (#PCDATA)>
<!ELEMENT amount (#PCDATA)>
```

As you can see, this is a straightforward DTD. The `<atm_log>` is the root element and it has one attribute named `date`, which contains the date that the ATM log was collected. The `<atm_log>` element contains multiple `<transaction>` elements. Each of the `<transaction>` elements contains a `<name>`, `<account>`, and `<amount>` element and a `transaction_type` attribute. Note that the `transaction_type` attribute has only two valid values, `withdrawal` or `deposit`. The corresponding XML schema is shown in Listing 3.23.

Listing 3.23 **XML schema for the XML ATM transaction log. (Filename: ch3_xerces_atm_log.xsd)**

```
<?xml version="1.0" encoding="UTF-8"?>
<xs:schema xmlns:xs="http://www.w3.org/2001/XMLSchema"
elementFormDefault="qualified">
   <xs:element name="account" type="xs:string"/>
   <xs:element name="amount" type="xs:float"/>
   <xs:element name="atm_log">
      <xs:complexType>
         <xs:sequence maxOccurs="unbounded">
            <xs:element ref="transaction"/>
         </xs:sequence>
         <xs:attribute name="date" type="xs:string" use="required"/>
      </xs:complexType>
   </xs:element>
   <xs:element name="name" type="xs:string"/>
   <xs:element name="transaction">
      <xs:complexType>
         <xs:sequence>
            <xs:element ref="name"/>
            <xs:element ref="account"/>
            <xs:element ref="amount"/>
         </xs:sequence>
         <xs:attribute name="type" use="required">
            <xs:simpleType>
               <xs:restriction base="xs:NMTOKEN">
                  <xs:enumeration value="withdrawal"/>
                  <xs:enumeration value="deposit"/>
               </xs:restriction>
            </xs:simpleType>
         </xs:attribute>
      </xs:complexType>
   </xs:element>
</xs:schema>
```

The input XML document based on the DTD shown in Listing 3.22 is presented in Listing 3.24. As you can see, we have four transaction elements in the XML document.

Listing 3.24 **Input XML file containing the ATM transaction log. (Filename: ch3_atm_log.xml)**

```
<?xml version="1.0" encoding="UTF-8"?>
<!DOCTYPE atm_log SYSTEM "ch3_atm_log.dtd">
<atm_log date="6/14">
   <transaction type="withdrawal">
      <name>Mark Rogers</name>
      <account>11-22-33</account>
      <amount>100.00</amount>
   </transaction>
```

*continues*

Listing 3.24 **Continued**

```
   <transaction type="deposit">
      <name>Joseph Burns</name>
      <account>11-23-22</account>
      <amount>500.00</amount>
   </transaction>
   <transaction type="withdrawal">
      <name>Kayla Burns</name>
      <account>22-34-55</account>
      <amount>250.00</amount>
   </transaction>
   <transaction type="deposit">
      <name>Joe Reilly</name>
      <account>11-33-44</account>
      <amount>1000.00</amount>
   </transaction>
</atm_log>
```

### XML::Xerces Application Discussion

The XML::Xerces Perl program is shown in Listing 3.25. In the next few sections, I'll discuss the important points in the application.

Listing 3.25 **XML::Xerces Perl application. (Filename: ch3_xerces_sax2_app.pl)**

```
use strict;
use XML::Xerces;

my $file = "ch3_atm_log.xml";
my ($deposit_count, $withdrawal_count);

package EventHandler;
use strict;
use vars qw(@ISA);
 @ISA = qw(XML::Xerces::PerlContentHandler);

 my ($trans_type, $total_deps, $total_withdrawals, $current_element);

 sub start_document {
     print "ATM Summary Report\n";
 }

 sub start_element {
   my ($self,$uri,$localname,$qname,$attrs) = @_;
   my $attVal;

   $current_element = $localname;

   if ($attrs->getLength > 0) {

```

```
       if ($localname eq "atm_log") {
      $attVal = $attrs->getValue("date");
      print "Date: $attVal\n\n";
      print "-------------------\n";
       }

       if ($localname eq "transaction") {
      $trans_type = $attrs->getValue("type");
       }
  }
}

sub characters {
  my ($self,$str,$len) = @_;
  $self->{chars} += $len;

  if ($current_element eq "name") {
      print "Name: $str\n";
  }

  if ($current_element eq "account") {
      print "Account Number: $str\n";
  }

  if ($current_element eq "amount") {

      if ($trans_type eq "deposit") {
     $total_deps += $str;
     ++$deposit_count;
      }
      elsif ($trans_type eq "withdrawal") {
     $total_withdrawals += $str;
     ++$withdrawal_count;
      }
      print "Amount: \$$str\n";
  }
}

sub end_element {
  my ($self,$uri,$localname,$qname) = @_;

  if ($localname eq "transaction") {
      print "-------------------\n";
  }
}

sub end_document {
    my $total_transactions = $deposit_count + $withdrawal_count;
    my $output_dep = sprintf("%.2f", $total_deps);
    my $output_wd = sprintf("%.2f", $total_withdrawals);

```

*continues*

Listing 3.25 **Continued**

```
    print "Total of $total_transactions processed today\n\n";

    print "Transaction Summary\n";
    print "Received: $deposit_count deposits\n";
    print "Total Value of Deposits: \$$output_dep\n\n";

    print "Received: $withdrawal_count withdrawals\n";
    print "Total Value of Withdrawals: \$$output_wd\n";
}

package main;
my $parser = XML::Xerces::XMLReaderFactory::createXMLReader();

eval {
    $parser->setFeature("http://xml.org/sax/features/validation", 1);
};

if ($@) {
    if (ref $@) {
   die $@->getMessage();
    } else {
   die $@;
    }
 }

 my $error_handler = XML::Xerces::PerlErrorHandler->new();
 $parser->setErrorHandler($error_handler);

 my $event_handler = EventHandler->new();
 $parser->setContentHandler($event_handler);

 eval {
   $parser->parse (XML::Xerces::LocalFileInputSource->new($file));
 };

 if ($@) {
     if (ref $@) {
    die $@->getMessage();
     } else {
    die $@;
     }
 }

 exit;
```

### *Initialization*

**1–5** The initialization section of the program contains the standard `use strict` pragma. Because we are using the XML::Xerces module, we need to load the module by using the `use XML::Xerces` pragma. The input XML document filename is hard coded to the `$inputXml` scalar; however, the program can be easily modified to accept another means of input (for example, a command-line argument, configuration file, and so forth).

```
1.  use strict;
2.  use XML::Xerces;
3.
4.  my $file = "ch3_atm_log.xml";
5.  my ($deposit_count, $withdrawal_count);
```

### **start_document** *and* **start_element** *Event Handlers*

**14–36** The `start_document` event handler is used in this case to print the report heading. Remember, the `start_document` handler is called only once per XML document (when the parser first starts parsing the XML document), so it is the ideal event handler to use when you need something to happen only once per XML document. In our case, the one-time event is printing the report heading. Note that the `start_document` event handler doesn't receive any arguments when called by the parser.

```
14.  sub start_document {
15.      print "ATM Summary Report\n";
16.  }
17.
18.  sub start_element {
19.    my ($self,$uri,$localname,$qname,$attrs) = @_;
20.    my $attVal;
21.
22.    $current_element = $localname;
23.
24.    if ($attrs->getLength > 0) {
25.
26.        if ($localname eq "atm_log") {
27.       $attVal = $attrs->getValue("date");
28.       print "Date: $attVal\n\n";
29.       print "-------------------\n";
30.        }
31.
32.        if ($localname eq "transaction") {
33.       $trans_type = $attrs->getValue("type");
34.        }
35.    }
36.  }
```

The `start_element` handler is called whenever the parser encounters the start of an element. Several arguments are passed into the subroutine. The standard arguments are

- **`$self`**—Contains the element object.
- **`$uri`**—Contains the URI of the namespace for this element.
- **`$localname`**—Contains the element name.
- **`$qname`**—Contains the XML qualified name for this element. The qualified name has a `namespace:element_name` format.
- **`$attrs`**—Contains any attributes associated with this element.

One of the first actions inside the `start_element` handler is to set the global scalar `$current_element` to the local scalar `$localname`. We'll use this to track the current element inside other event handlers.

Next, we are processing attributes. First, we use the `getLength` method to determine the number of attributes associated with the current element. If the element has attributes, then we know we are currently processing either the `<atm_log>` root element or one of the `<transaction>` elements (because they are the only elements in our XML document that have attributes).

If the element is the root element `<atm_log>`, we are extracting the date attribute and using the value to finish printing the report header. On the other hand, if we're processing a transaction element, we're extracting and storing the transaction type. Remember, the only valid transaction types are withdrawal or deposit. So, we set a global scalar named `$trans_type` equal to the current transaction type. This is similar to the global scalar that we set to the current element and will be used to accumulate results.

#### characters *Event Handler*

**38–62** The `characters` event handler receives three arguments when it is called. The input arguments are

- **`$self`**—Contains the element object.
- **`$str`**—Contains the character data for the current element.
- **`$len`**—Contains the length of the character data.

In the `characters` event handler, we're checking the value of the `$current_element` scalar that was set in the `start_element` handler. After we find the current element that we're looking for, we can print the name of the element and the element contents.

When we encounter an <amount> element, we're looking at the value of the `$trans_type` scalar (which was set in the `start_element` handler). Because we are responsible for adding up the number of withdrawals and deposits, we need to know the type of the current transaction. If the current transaction type is a deposit, we increment the number of deposits processed and add the amount to the total amount deposited. If the current transaction type is a withdrawal, then we increment the number of withdrawals and the amount to the total amount withdrawn.

```
38.   sub characters {
39.     my ($self,$str,$len) = @_;
40.     $self->{chars} += $len;
41.
42.     if ($current_element eq "name") {
43.         print "Name: $str\n";
44.     }
45.
46.     if ($current_element eq "account") {
47.         print "Account Number: $str\n";
48.     }
49.
50.     if ($current_element eq "amount") {
51.
52.         if ($trans_type eq "deposit") {
53.        $total_deps += $str;
54.        ++$deposit_count;
55.         }
56.         elsif ($trans_type eq "withdrawal") {
57.        $total_withdrawals += $str;
58.        ++$withdrawal_count;
59.         }
60.         print "Amount: \$$str\n";
61.     }
62.   }
```

### end element *and* end document *Event Handlers*

**64–85** The `end_element` event handler receives the following arguments when it is called:

- **`$self`**—Contains the element object.
- **`$uri`**—Contains the URI of the namespace for this element.
- **`$localname`**—Contains the element name.
- **`$qname`**—Contains the XML qualified name for this element. The qualified name has a `namespace:element_name` format.

Note that these arguments are similar to those passed to the `start_element` event handler. The only difference is that the `end_element` event handler doesn't receive attributes.

```
64.   sub end_element {
65.     my ($self,$uri,$localname,$qname) = @_;
66.
67.     if ($localname eq "transaction") {
68.         print "-------------------\n";
69.     }
70.   }
71.
72.   sub end_document {
73.       my $total_transactions = $deposit_count + $withdrawal_count;
74.       my $output_dep = sprintf("%.2f", $total_deps);
75.       my $output_wd = sprintf("%.2f", $total_withdrawals);
76.
77.       print "Total of $total_transactions processed today\n\n";
78.
79.       print "Transaction Summary\n";
80.       print "Received: $deposit_count deposits\n";
81.       print "Total Value of Deposits: \$$output_dep\n\n";
82.
83.       print "Received: $withdrawal_count withdrawals\n";
84.       print "Total Value of Withdrawals: \$$output_wd\n";
85.   }
```

The only thing that we're doing inside the `end_element` event handler is checking the name of the element being processed. If we are processing the end tag of a `<transaction>` element, then we're printing out a separator line that appears in the output report.

The `end_document` event handler (as the name implies) is called once at the end of the document. That makes it an ideal location to print any summary information. We're using it to print the results that we've accumulated while processing the XML document.

### *Parser Initialization*

**87–120** This block contains the `main` package that instantiates a parser object and sets the appropriate options.

```
87.   package main;
88.   my $parser = XML::Xerces::XMLReaderFactory::createXMLReader();
89.
90.   eval {
91.       $parser->setFeature("http://xml.org/sax/features/validation", 1);
92.   };
93.
94.   if ($@) {
95.       if (ref $@) {
```

```
96.        die $@->getMessage();
97.         } else {
98.        die $@;
99.         }
100.    }
101.
102.    my $error_handler = XML::Xerces::PerlErrorHandler->new();
103.    $parser->setErrorHandler($error_handler);
104.
105.    my $event_handler = EventHandler->new();
106.    $parser->setContentHandler($event_handler);
107.
108.    eval {
109.      $parser->parse (XML::Xerces::LocalFileInputSource->new($file));
110.    };
111.
112.    if ($@) {
113.         if (ref $@) {
114.       die $@->getMessage();
115.         } else {
116.       die $@;
117.         }
118.    }
119.
120.    exit;
```

First, the new parser object is created on line 88:

```
my $parser = XML::Xerces::XMLReaderFactory::createXMLReader();
```

After the object is created, we set the appropriate options. The first option we set is to report all validation errors. In this case, the parser would generate a warning to notify us if the input XML document didn't follow the DTD or XML schema. For example, let's say that our XML document contained an element that wasn't defined in the original DTD or XML schema. Let's say that the XML document contains multiple transaction elements followed by an <atm_location> element (which isn't defined in our DTD):

```
<?xml version="1.0" encoding="UTF-8"?>
<!DOCTYPE atm_log SYSTEM "ch3_atm_log.dtd">
<atm_log date="6/14">
   <transaction type="withdrawal">
      <name>Mark Rogers</name>
      <account>11-22-33</account>
      <amount>100.00</amount>
   </transaction>
…
   <atm_location>Grocery store</atm_location>
</atm_log>
```

By turning on the validation option, we'll get the following error from the XML::Xerces Perl module:

```
ERROR:
FILE: /home/mriehl/book/ch3_atm_log.xml
LINE:   24
COLUMN: 7
MESSAGE: Unknown element 'atm_location' at ch3_xerces_sax2.pl
```

A number of other features can be used, depending on your situation. For example, you can enable schema constraint checking; the downside is that it may be time consuming or memory intensive. Please see the Apache XML::Xerces documentation for additional features.

As you can see, we're using Perl `eval` blocks to catch any run-time exceptions that may be returned by the parser. If you're not familiar with the Perl `eval` statement, it is similar to a "try block" in either C++ or Java. For additional information on the Perl `eval` function, see `perldoc -f eval`.

Next we register an error handler. If we don't register an error handler in our application, all error events will be silently ignored except for fatal errors. Because we would like to be notified of any possible errors, we are setting an error handler.

After setting an error handler, we instantiate an event handler (defined in our EventHandler package) and parse the XML document. The XML::Xerces parser calls the event handlers whenever the corresponding events are encountered (for example, `start_element`, `end_element`, and so forth).

The XML::Xerces Perl application is a report that is shown in Listing 3.26. As you can see, the report summarizes the contents of the input XML document, counts the number of deposits and withdrawals, and sums the totals of the deposits and withdrawals.

Listing 3.26 **Output report containing a summary of ATM transactions. (Filename: ch3_xerces_report.txt)**

```
ATM Summary Report
Date: 6/14

--------------------
Name: Mark Rogers
Account Number: 11-22-33
Amount: $100.00
--------------------
Name: Joseph Burns
Account Number: 11-23-22
Amount: $500.00
--------------------
```

```
Name: Kayla Burns
Account Number: 22-34-55
Amount: $250.00
-------------------
Name: Joe Reilly
Account Number: 11-33-44
Amount: $1000.00
-------------------
Total of 4 processed today

Transaction Summary
Received: 2 deposits
Total Value of Deposits: $1500

Received: 2 withdrawals
Total Value of Withdrawals: $350
```

## Summary

This chapter contained simple examples that used the Perl `print` command to generate reports after parsing XML documents. The purpose of this chapter was to show you how to use the sequential Perl XML parser modules. The examples in this chapter provide you with a series of templates (one for each of the major sequential XML Perl parser modules) that can be easily extended to do just about anything you want with the parsed data. Remember, sometimes the difficult part is parsing the data (that is, getting it to a point where you can send it to a report using a Perl `print` statement).

Now that you actually have access to the data contained inside the XML documents (that is, the contents of the output reports), it would be easy to push the parsed data into a database table using the Perl DBI, display the results on a web page in an HTML table using XSLT, or even generate another XML document. All these topics (and more) are covered in the upcoming chapters. You may have been under the impression that parsing the XML document would be difficult and confusing (which is understandable). However, as I have just demonstrated, it probably wasn't as difficult as you first thought. A lot of people have spent a great deal of time working on these modules to make them as simple as possible, and they've done a great job!

## Exercises

1. Modify the course catalog XML document (and the corresponding DTD or XML schema) to include classes for each semester for an entire year (Fall, Winter, Spring, and Summer). Then, modify the PerlSAX application shown in Listing 3.9 to print out a report similar to the report shown in Listing 3.10 for each semester.
2. Modify the XML ATM log DTD to support multiple days of transactions. Then, modify the Xerces application shown in Listing 3.25 to generate a report that provides a summary for each day and totals the deposits and withdrawals over the entire time period.

For suggested solutions to this exercise, be sure to check out the web site: `http://www.xmlproj.com/book/chapter3`.

## Relevant Links

Apache XML Project: `http://xml.apache.org`
SAX: `http://www.saxproject.org/`

# 4

# Tree-Based Parser Modules

## Chapter Roadmap

This chapter focuses on solving problems using the tree-based XML parser modules. In Chapter 3, "Event-Driven Parser Modules," we discussed the concept of an event-based parser. If you remember, some of the event-based parsers discussed in Chapter 3 were based on the SAX standard while others were not. We have a similar situation again in this chapter. While all the modules discussed in this chapter can be considered tree-based, not all the XML parser modules are based on the Document Object Model (DOM) standard. We'll discuss the concept of a tree-based parser, then the non-DOM-compliant XML parser modules, and finally the DOM and the DOM-compliant modules.

To run all the examples discussed in this chapter, you need to install the following Perl modules:

- XML::Simple
- XML::Twig
- XML::DOM
- XML::LibXML
- XML::Xerces

> **Note**
>
> If you have any questions about Perl modules (for example, where to get them, how to install them, and so forth), please refer to Appendix B, "Perl Essentials."

## What Is a Tree-Based XML Parser?

During the last chapter, we discussed event-based XML parsers. An event-based XML parser defines subroutines that are triggered whenever the XML parser encounters a particular construct. This chapter discusses an alternative to event-based XML parsing called tree-based XML parsing.

A tree-based XML parser takes a different approach to the task of parsing an XML document. Contrary to the passive event-based approach where the application defines event handlers and waits for the handler to be triggered, the tree-based approach to XML parsing is more active. In the tree-based approach, the entire XML document is parsed and the entire document is stored in memory in a structure similar to a tree. To access a particular portion of the XML document, the application must actively retrieve it. As you can see, this is the opposite approach to an event-based parser where an event handler would need to be defined and would then wait until the parser encountered the corresponding construct.

As an example of how a tree-based parser works, let's assume that your client contacts are stored in an XML document such as this:

```
<?xml version="1.0" encoding="UTF-8"?>
<contacts>
   <client>
      <name>Mark</name>
      <phone>111-222-3333</phone>
   </client>
   <client>
      <name>Joseph</name>
      <phone>222-333-4444</phone>
   </client>
</contacts>
```

The tree-based parser would take the XML document as input and generate a tree structure in memory that contains the data. Figure 4.1 shows a high level view of a tree-based parser. As you can see, the parser takes an XML document as input and generates a tree structure containing the contents of the XML elements.

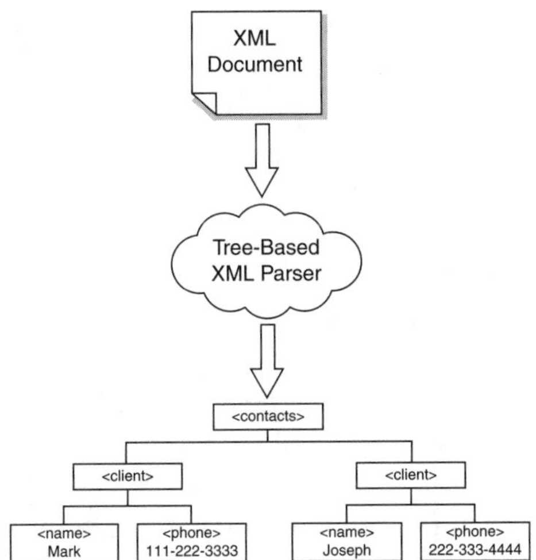


**Figure 4.1** Notional tree-based XML parser.

Tree-based XML parsers have a few differences from event-based parsers, which can be considered advantages (depending on your situation). First, a program built using a tree-based XML parser module is usually smaller in size than a program built with an event-based parser. This is due to the fact that you don't have to generate event handlers to extract the information from the XML data. Also, you don't need to store information extracted from the XML data for later processing (the tree-based parser stores the data for you). Second, tree-based parsers provide random access to the XML data. Let's say you need to access the last element in an XML document. Using an event-based parser, you'll need to handle events for every element in the document, searching for the element in which you're interested. If you're looking for a particular element with a tree-based parser, you can directly access the element as soon as the XML document has been parsed.

## Tree-Based XML Parser Modules

Tree-based XML parsing is one of two most popular ways of parsing XML, along with stream-based parsing, which was discussed in Chapter 3. The Document Object Model (DOM) standard defines a standard way to parse and represent the XML data in a tree-based parser. Tree-based parsers are also called *in-memory parsers*, because unlike stream-based parsers, which iterate over each piece of data and keep very minimal state information, tree-based parsers iterate over the XML document and create an in-memory representation of it for later use. You can then use Perl's standard facilities to access the information in the data structure. The next few sections discuss non-DOM-compliant tree-based XML parsers.

## XML::Simple Perl Module

Back in Chapter 2, "Now Let's Get Our Hands Dirty," you saw a small example using the XML::Simple Perl module to parse a document. In this section, we'll discuss another example using the XML::Simple Perl module and explain the XML::Simple API and some of the more useful options.

The XML::Simple Perl module was written by Grant McClean. As an XML parser module, it is (as you may have guessed from the name) very simple to use. XML::Simple provides an easy-to-use API and is built on the XML::Parser module discussed in Chapter 3. It is ideal to use for small XML documents, such as configuration files, and in any other situation when you don't need any additional features, just a simple, easy-to-use XML parser. Let's take a look at an example of how to use the XML::Simple Perl module.

### XML::Simple Perl Module Example

Some of our work involves working with databases, usually through the Perl Database Interface (DBI). The Perl DBI provides a consistent, database-independent interface to an application, regardless of the database that is being used. This means that a database application using the Perl DBI can use a consistent interface for a number of databases. This is a powerful capability that enables you to develop a very flexible application. The same application (with literally a one line change) can access an Oracle database, a Microsoft SQL Server database, or the open-source MySQL database. Using the Perl DBI and an XML parser or generator module provides a strong foundation for a number of applications.

> **Note**
>
> We will be discussing the Perl DBI in Chapter 6, "Generating XML Documents from Databases." If you can't wait until Chapter 6 for this discussion of the Perl DBI, take a look at the official Perl DBI page `http://dbi.perl.org`.

The reason that I mentioned the Perl DBI is that for it to operate properly, you need to pass in some initial configuration information. I usually store this information in an external XML document, and the XML::Simple Perl module is ideally suited for these types of situations. For example, to open a connection to a database using the Perl DBI, you need the following information:

- Database username
- Database password
- Database server IP address (or Domain Name Server [DNS] resolvable hostname)
- DBI driver name
- Database name
- Database port

It's usually a good idea to store this type of configuration information outside your application. Storing this configuration information external to the application eliminates the need for a user to look through source code and change hard-coded values. Now that you know what information we need in the configuration file, let's take a look at a DTD configuration file shown in Listing 4.1.

Listing 4.1 **Configuration file DTD. (Filename: ch4_simple_config.dtd)**

```
<?xml version="1.0" encoding="UTF-8"?>
<!ELEMENT db_config_information (db_user, db_server+)>
<!ELEMENT db_user (username, password)>
<!ELEMENT username (#PCDATA)>
<!ELEMENT password (#PCDATA)>
<!ELEMENT db_server (server_ip, db_driver, port)>
<!ATTLIST db_server hostname CDATA #IMPLIED
                    os CDATA #IMPLIED>
<!ELEMENT server_ip (#PCDATA)>
<!ELEMENT db_driver (#PCDATA)>
<!ELEMENT port (#PCDATA)>
```

As you can see, this is a very simple DTD that contains configuration information. Note that the DTD supports multiple database servers for each user. If this were a longer configuration file (for example, a few hundred lines), using XML instead for the configuration file format would clearly be an advantage. By storing the configuration information in XML, you can easily verify that the configuration file is well-formed and valid. This assures you that all the required information is present and reduces the amount of error checking that is required by the application. Listing 4.2 shows the XML schema for the configuration file.

Listing 4.2 **XML schema that describes the application configuration file. (Filename: ch4_simple_config.xsd)**

```
<?xml version="1.0" encoding="UTF-8"?>
<xs:schema xmlns:xs="http://www.w3.org/2001/XMLSchema"
elementFormDefault="qualified">
   <xs:element name="db_config_information">
      <xs:complexType>
         <xs:sequence>
            <xs:element ref="db_user"/>
            <xs:element ref="db_server" minOccurs="0" maxOccurs="unbounded"/>
         </xs:sequence>
      </xs:complexType>
   </xs:element>
   <xs:element name="db_driver" type="xs:string"/>
   <xs:element name="db_server">
      <xs:complexType>
         <xs:sequence>
            <xs:element ref="server_ip"/>
            <xs:element ref="db_driver"/>
            <xs:element ref="port"/>
         </xs:sequence>
         <xs:attribute name="hostname" type="xs:string"/>
         <xs:attribute name="os" type="xs:string"/>
      </xs:complexType>
   </xs:element>
   <xs:element name="db_user">
      <xs:complexType>
         <xs:sequence>
            <xs:element ref="username"/>
            <xs:element ref="password"/>
         </xs:sequence>
      </xs:complexType>
   </xs:element>
   <xs:element name="password" type="xs:string"/>
   <xs:element name="port" type="xs:positiveInteger"/>
   <xs:element name="server_ip" type="xs:string"/>
   <xs:element name="username" type="xs:string"/>
</xs:schema>
```

We've shown the DTD and the XML schema, now let's take a look at the XML configuration file that is shown in Listing 4.3. It contains user and database server information required to establish Perl DBI connections. As you can see, this configuration file contains information for the username "`mark`", and shows my connection information for two servers named "`rocket`" and "scooter". Associated with each server is an IP address (<server_ip>), a driver name (<db_driver>), and a port number (<port>).

Listing 4.3 **XML configuration file. (Filename: ch4_simple_config.xml)**

```
<?xml version="1.0" encoding="UTF-8"?>
<!DOCTYPE db_config_information SYSTEM "ch4_simple_config.dtd">
<db_config_information>
   <db_user>
      <username>mark</username>
      <password>mark's password</password>
   </db_user>
   <db_server hostname="rocket" os="Linux">
      <server_ip>192.168.1.10</server_ip>
      <db_driver>MySQL</db_driver>
      <port>3306</port>
   </db_server>
   <db_server hostname="scooter" os="Microsoft Windows">
      <server_ip>192.168.1.50</server_ip>
      <db_driver>ODBC</db_driver>
      <port>3379</port>
   </db_server>
</db_config_information>
```

Tree-based parsers are easier to understand when you can see how the data is stored after it has been parsed. This makes it much easier to access the particular elements that you are interested in retrieving. Figure 4.2 shows a graphical representation of the XML configuration file as it is stored in memory after parsing by the XML::Simple Perl module. As you should expect, we have one root element (<config_information>) that has three child elements (<db_user>, <db_server[0]>, and <db_server[1]>). Note the index next to each <db_server> element. This is used to indicate multiple occurrences of elements with the same name.

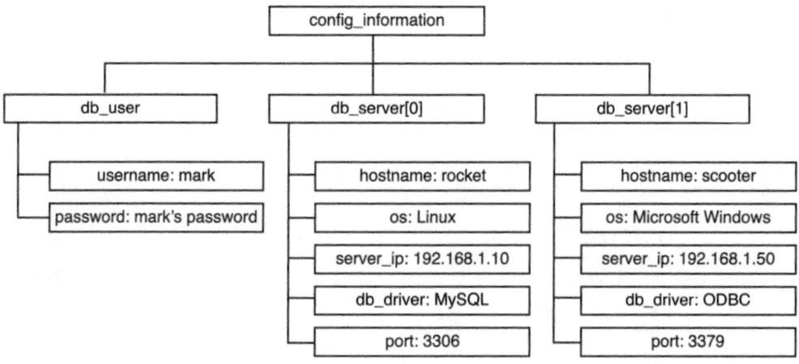


**Figure 4.2** Tree representation of the XML configuration file.

Now let's take a look at the Perl program in Listing 4.4. This program was built with the XML::Simple module and parses the XML configuration file that was shown earlier in Listing 4.3.

Listing 4.4 **Configuration file parser built with the XML::Simple Perl module. (Filename: ch4_simple_app.pl)**

```
1.  use strict;
2.  use XML::Simple;
3.
4.  # Parse the input XML document
5.  my $root = XMLin("./ch4_simple_config.xml", forcearray=>1);
6.
7.  # Print config info.
8.  print "Configuration Information\n";
9.  print "User: $root->{db_user}->[0]->{username}->[0]\n";
10. print "Password: $root->{db_user}->[0]->{password}->[0]\n\n";
11.
12. # Print info about the first server (note indexes = 0).
13. print "Server #1\n";
14. print "Hostname: $root->{db_server}->[0]->{hostname}\n";
15. print "Hostname: $root->{db_server}->[0]->{os}\n";
16. print "IP Address: $root->{db_server}->[0]->{server_ip}->[0]\n";
17. print "DB Driver: $root->{db_server}->[0]->{db_driver}->[0]\n";
18. print "Port: $root->{db_server}->[0]->{port}->[0]\n\n";
19.
20. # Print info about the second server (note indexes = 1).
21. print "Server #2\n";
22. print "Hostname: $root->{db_server}->[1]->{hostname}\n";
23. print "Hostname: $root->{db_server}->[1]->{os}\n";
24. print "IP Address: $root->{db_server}->[1]->{server_ip}->[0]\n";
25. print "DB Driver: $root->{db_server}->[1]->{db_driver}->[0]\n";
26. print "Port: $root->{db_server}->[1]->{port}->[0]\n";
```

### *Initialization and Parsing*

**1–5** The first section of this program contains the usual `use` pragma statement (`use strict`) that we include in all our programs. Because we're using the XML::Simple Perl module, we need to load the XML::Simple Perl module with the `use XML::Simple` pragma.

As mentioned earlier, XML::Simple is built on top of the XML::Parser Perl module that we discussed in Chapter 3. We don't need a `use XML::Parser` pragma because this is already handled for us inside the XML::Simple Perl module. The XML::Simple Perl module exports two functions: `XMLin()` and `XMLout()`. As you may have guessed from the names, the `XMLin()` function is used to parse XML data while the `XMLout()` function is used to generate XML data. Because we're concerned with parsing, we'll be using the `XMLin()` function.

The `XMLin()` function parses XML data and returns a reference to a data structure that contains the information stored in the XML document. This function can accept an input filename, an undefined filename, or just a string containing XML data. In our example, we have provided the name of an input XML document named ch4_simple_config.xml. If `undef` is provided as the filename, the XML::Simple module will look for an XML document in the current directory with the same name as the program. For example, if your parsing program was named `foo.pl` and you didn't provide an input filename or string containing XML data, then the XML::Simple module would look for a file named `foo.xml` and try to parse it. XML::Simple will also accept a scalar containing an XML string as an input. This is helpful if XML data is being dynamically generated, saving you the trouble of writing the XML data to a file and then opening the file.

In this example, `$root` is a reference to a data structure that contains all the information stored in the XML configuration file. Now that the XML document has been parsed, the information is stored for us in this data structure, and we just need to go and retrieve it.

```
1.  use strict;
2.  use XML::Simple;
3.
4.  # Parse the input XML document
5.  my $root = XMLin("./ch4_simple_config.xml", forcearray=>1);
```

***Retrieving the Parsed Information***

**7–26** How do we retrieve the parsed information that is stored in the data structure? I'll show you in this section of the example.

Because this is a relatively short and flat XML document (that is, not a lot of nested elements), we're going to explicitly extract all the information. If this XML configuration were longer or contained multiple elements (for example, multiple `<db_user>` elements), we would need to loop through each occurrence of the same element. Note that the DTD or the XML schema would need to be changed to support multiple `<db_user>` elements.

In our program, the scalar `$root` is a reference to a data structure similar to the one shown in Figure 4.1. As you can see, we need to walk up and down the tree and retrieve our data. It may seem a bit confusing at first, but after you're comfortable with Perl references and nested data structures, it will seem like second nature.

```
7.  # Print config info.
8.  print "Configuration Information\n";
9.  print "User: $root->{db_user}->[0]->{username}->[0]\n";
10. print "Password: $root->{db_user}->[0]->{password}->[0]\n\n";
```

*continues*

```

# Print info about the first server (note indexes = 0).
print "Server #1\n";
print "Hostname: $root->{db_server}->[0]->{hostname}\n";
print "Hostname: $root->{db_server}->[0]->{os}\n";
print "IP Address: $root->{db_server}->[0]->{server_ip}->[0]\n";
print "DB Driver: $root->{db_server}->[0]->{db_driver}->[0]\n";
print "Port: $root->{db_server}->[0]->{port}->[0]\n\n";

# Print info about the second server (note indexes = 1).
print "Server #2\n";
print "Hostname: $root->{db_server}->[1]->{hostname}\n";
print "Hostname: $root->{db_server}->[1]->{os}\n";
print "IP Address: $root->{db_server}->[1]->{server_ip}->[0]\n";
print "DB Driver: $root->{db_server}->[1]->{db_driver}->[0]\n";
print "Port: $root->{db_server}->[1]->{port}->[0]\n";
```

**Note**

For additional information about Perl references and nested data structures, see the perldoc perlref page.

The index in each reference indicates a particular occurrence of an element. For example, the statement

```
$root->{db_user}->[0]->{username}->[0]
```

refers to the following portion of the input XML document:

```
<db_user>
   <username>mark</username>
```

This line refers to the first (and only in this case) `<username>` element that is a child of the `<db_user>` element. There is one subtle item to notice about the statement that refers to one of the element attributes

```
$root->{db_server}->[0]->{hostname}
```

that refers to the following portion of the XML document:

```
<db_server hostname="rocket" os="Linux">
```

Did you notice how we don't need an index after the `hostname` element? Because `hostname` is an attribute of the `db_server` element, it can only appear once. If you try to use an index, you will create an error because Perl will incorrectly try to interpret the reference as a reference to an array. Therefore, you don't need the index to extract the attribute value.

### *XML::Simple Perl Program Output*

Listing 4.5 shows the output that is generated by the XML::Simple Perl program. As desired, we've extracted the contents of the XML document and printed the information that was contained in each element. In a real application, instead of printing out the contents of the input XML document, you could create a hash to store the key-value pairs for further processing. For example, `$hashname{username}` would contain "`mark`", and `$hashname{password}` would contain "`mark's password`".

Listing 4.5 **Output generated by the XML::Simple-based program. (Filename: ch4_simple_output.txt)**

```
Configuration Information
User: mark
Password: mark's password

Server #1
Hostname: rocket
IP Address: 192.168.1.10
DB Driver: MySQL
Port: 3306

Server #2
Hostname: scooter
IP Address: 192.168.1.50
DB Driver: ODBC
Port: 3379
```

The XML::Simple module is ideal to use in situations such as this when you need to parse small- to medium-sized XML documents. As I have demonstrated, the API for the XML::Simple module is very easy to use for tasks similar to our example. However, cases when you should choose other modules may arise, especially when you need to deal with larger XML documents. We'll discuss one of those cases in the next section.

> **Note**
>
> For additional XML::Simple module information (including all the possible options), please take a look at the available online documentation by using perldoc XML::Simple.

## XML::Twig Perl Module

The XML::Twig Perl module by Michel Rodriguez is similar to the XML::Simple Perl module in that it is built on top of the XML::Parser module. However, that is where the similarities end. XML::Twig is a tree-based parser, but it gives you more flexibility compared to other tree-based parsers by providing two important characteristics found in other parsers.

First, the XML::Twig Perl module is similar to a SAX-based module because it can be configured to have a small memory requirement. This is important when working with large XML documents, especially if you're only interested in a small subset of the elements. Second, the XML::Twig Perl module provides an API that it similar to XPath in retrieving elements and attributes. This is important because it isn't a module proprietary scheme of accessing elements and attributes.

When it comes to parsing XML data, the XML::Twig Perl module supports three modes of operation.

- The first XML::Twig mode can be utilized if a document is small (that is, the XML document would easily fit into memory). It parses the XML document into a tree that resides entirely in memory.
- The second XML::Twig mode is used if the XML document is too large to parse entirely in memory. When operating in this mode (the XML::Twig perldoc refers to this processing as "chunk by chunk"), the XML document is parsed piece by piece (similar to the event-based approach to XML parsing), and then the parsed section of the document is discarded.
- Finally, XML::Twig also enables you to parse only a particular section of the XML document without loading the entire document into memory.

Because I just demonstrated how the XML::Simple module parses small, simple, documents, the next example focuses on how to use the XML::Twig Perl module to parse a subset of a larger, more complex XML document.

### XML::Twig Example

One of the most useful capabilities of the XML::Twig module is the capability to parse only a portion of an XML document. When would you use this capability? Let's say for this example that you work for a large online retailer and that your catalog is stored in XML. Your task is to generate a report for a particular portion of the catalog. For a large catalog, it isn't unrealistic that the XML document could be several hundred megabytes (MB) in size. While it is physically possible to use a standard tree-based parser on a document this size, it isn't recommended. Remember, an XML document in memory will be many times the size it occupies on disk. You could use a SAX-based parser; however, for some applications it may be more work than you need to do (or, in some situations, have time to do). One possible option is to use the XML::Twig module to process only a portion of an XML document.

First, before we get into the program that performs the task, let's start with the format of the XML document. Remember, this is a catalog in XML format for a large online retailer. As you can imagine, in addition to being very large, an XML document that supports these requirements would be fairly complex. This document would have a large number of nested elements. Listing 4.6 shows the DTD that is being used by the online retailer. As you can see, the DTD is fairly simple; however, you can see that there are several levels of nesting, similar to what you might expect if you were visiting an online retailer.

Listing 4.6 **DTD that describes the online retailer catalog. (Filename: ch4_twig_retail.dtd)**

```
<?xml version="1.0" encoding="UTF-8"?>
<!ELEMENT catalog (department*)>
<!ELEMENT department (category*)>
<!ATTLIST department name CDATA #REQUIRED>
<!ELEMENT category (product*)>
<!ATTLIST category name CDATA #REQUIRED>
<!ELEMENT product (name, sku, description, price)>
<!ELEMENT name (#PCDATA)>
<!ELEMENT sku (#PCDATA)>
<!ELEMENT description (#PCDATA)>
<!ELEMENT price (#PCDATA)>
```

Listing 4.7 shows the XML schema that describes the format of our XML catalog.

Listing 4.7 **XML schema that describes the online retailer catalog. (Filename: ch4_twig_retail.xsd)**

```
<?xml version="1.0" encoding="UTF-8"?>
<xs:schema xmlns:xs="http://www.w3.org/2001/XMLSchema"
elementFormDefault="qualified">
   <xs:element name="catalog">
      <xs:complexType>
         <xs:sequence>
            <xs:element ref="department" minOccurs="0" maxOccurs="unbounded"/>
         </xs:sequence>
      </xs:complexType>
   </xs:element>
   <xs:element name="category">
```

*continues*

Listing 4.7 **Continued**

```
      <xs:complexType>
         <xs:sequence>
            <xs:element ref="product" minOccurs="0" maxOccurs="unbounded"/>
         </xs:sequence>
         <xs:attribute name="name" type="xs:string" use="required"/>
      </xs:complexType>
   </xs:element>
   <xs:element name="department">
      <xs:complexType>
         <xs:sequence>
            <xs:element ref="category" minOccurs="0" maxOccurs="unbounded"/>
         </xs:sequence>
         <xs:attribute name="name" type="xs:string" use="required"/>
      </xs:complexType>
   </xs:element>
   <xs:element name="description" type="xs:string"/>
   <xs:element name="name" type="xs:string"/>
   <xs:element name="price" type="xs:string"/>
   <xs:element name="product">
      <xs:complexType>
         <xs:sequence>
            <xs:element ref="name"/>
            <xs:element ref="sku"/>
            <xs:element ref="description"/>
            <xs:element ref="price"/>
         </xs:sequence>
      </xs:complexType>
   </xs:element>
   <xs:element name="sku" type="xs:string"/>
</xs:schema>
```

Now that you understand the structure of the XML document based on the DTD and XML schema, let's take a look at the sample XML document shown Listing 4.8. As you can see, we have two departments (`electronics` and `print`) represented in the XML document, and each of the departments has at least one category represented. Our task for this example is to generate a report that shows all products, regardless of department or category. As mentioned earlier, this may seem like a big task, especially if the file is several hundred megabytes (or even several gigabytes) in size. However, you'll soon see that this is a simple task with the XML::Twig Perl module.

Listing 4.8 **Online retailer catalog in XML. (Filename: ch4_twig_retail.xml)**

```
<?xml version="1.0" encoding="UTF-8"?>
<!DOCTYPE catalog SYSTEM "xml-twig.dtd">
<catalog>
   <department name="electronics">
      <category name="personal computers">
         <product>
            <name>Computer hard drive</name>
            <sku>1112819</sku>
            <description>120 GB hard drive</description>
            <price>$100.00</price>
         </product>
         <product>
            <name>Rewritable CDs</name>
            <sku>11291119</sku>
            <description>Box of 10</description>
            <price>$5.00</price>
         </product>
      </category>
      <category name="software">
         <product>
            <name>Microsoft Windows</name>
            <sku>11299938</sku>
            <description>Operating system</description>
            <price>$29.99</price>
         </product>
      </category>
   </department>
   <department name="print">
      <category name="books">
         <product>
            <name>XML and Perl</name>
            <sku>9987298</sku>
            <description>The XML and Perl book.</description>
            <price>$39.99</price>
         </product>
      </category>
   </department>
</catalog>
```

There are several ways to solve this problem, but one of the easiest solutions would be to use XML::Twig to parse only a portion of the XML document. For this example, we're only interested in the product elements, and the program shown in Listing 4.9 does just that. Let's walk through the program and see how it works.

Listing 4.9 **XML::Twig-based program to parse a portion of an XML document. (Filename: ch4_twig_app.pl)**

```
1.  use strict;
2.  use XML::Twig;
3.
4.  # Instantiate the parser object and set the
5.  # subroutine to be called.
6.  my $twig = new XML::Twig(twig_handlers => {product =>\&print_products});
7.  $twig->parsefile( "ch4_twig_retail.xml");
8.
9.  # Handler subroutine
10. sub print_products {
11.   my($t, $elt)= @_;
12.
13.   # Retrieve the element contents here.
14.   my $name = $elt->first_child('name')->text;
15.   my $sku = $elt->first_child('sku')->text;
16.   my $description = $elt->first_child('description')->text;
17.   my $price = $elt->first_child('price')->text;
18.
19.   # Print the results here.
20.   print "------------------------------------\n";
21.   print "Name = $name\n";
22.   print "SKU = $sku\n";
23.   print "Description = $description\n";
24.   print "Price = $price\n\n";
25.
26.   # Free the memory
27.   $t->purge;
28. }
```

### *Standard Pragmas*

**1–2** As you can see, this is a very short example which illustrates the power of the XML::Twig Perl module. The first section of the program includes the standard pragma statement that we see at the top of our programs (`use strict`). Also, we include the `use XML::Twig` pragma to load the XML::Twig module.

```
1.  use strict;
2.  use XML::Twig;
```

### *Parsing and Extracting Information*

**4–28** This section of the program does all the work for us. First, we call `new` and create a new XML::Twig object. The `twig_handlers` argument to the constructor is a hash that consists of key=>value pairs. In this case, the key is the element name that we want to parse, and the value is a reference to a subroutine that acts like an event handler in a SAX-based parser (that is, it is called whenever we encounter one of the specified elements). So, we've created a subroutine named `print_products` that is called whenever we encounter a `<product>` element. After setting up the initial handler, we call the `parsefile` method to parse the XML document.

As the document is parsed, the subroutine `print_products` is called each time XML::Twig encounters a `<product>` element. The subroutine receives the twig object and the element as arguments. As you can see, we can easily extract the element text by using the `first_child` method. Don't forget to call the `purge` method to free up any memory associated with the element that was just parsed; otherwise, this would cause a memory leak. It may not be an issue when parsing a small XML document such as our example, but it would cause a problem if you were parsing a large XML document.

```
# Instantiate the parser object and set the
# subroutine to be called.
my $twig = new XML::Twig(twig_handlers => {product =>\&print_products});
$twig->parsefile( "ch4_twig_retail.xml");

# Handler subroutine
sub print_products {
  my($t, $elt)= @_;

  # Retrieve the element contents here.
  my $name = $elt->first_child('name')->text;
  my $sku = $elt->first_child('sku')->text;
  my $description = $elt->first_child('description')->text;
  my $price = $elt->first_child('price')->text;

  # Print the results here.
  print "---------------------------------\n";
  print "Name = $name\n";
  print "SKU = $sku\n";
  print "Description = $description\n";
  print "Price = $price\n\n";

  # Free the memory
  $t->purge;
 }
```

The output of the XML::Twig-based application is shown in Listing 4.10. As you can see, I've retrieved all the `<product>` elements.

Listing 4.10 **Output report from the XML::Twig application. (Filename: ch4_twig_report.txt)**

```
------------------------------------
Name = Computer hard drive
SKU = 1112819
Description = 120 GB hard drive
Price = $100.00

------------------------------------
Name = Rewritable CDs
SKU = 11291119
Description = Box of 10
Price = $5.00

------------------------------------
Name = Microsoft Windows
SKU = 11299938
Description = Operating system
Price = $29.99

------------------------------------
Name = XML and Perl
SKU = 9987298
Description = The XML and Perl book.
Price = $39.99
```

**Parsing Multiple Elements**

Of course, we could have set up several subroutines as handlers and parsed several elements from the document. However, we decided to keep things simple and extract every occurrence of just the product elements.

We've only scratched the surface of the XML::Twig Perl module. For example, you can also use the XML::Twig Perl module to build an XML filter that can modify only selected elements in an XML document. As you can see, the XML::Twig Perl module provides much more capability than we discussed. I wanted to demonstrate a particular situation where I felt the XML::Twig Perl module is well suited. Take the time to read through the XML::Twig Perl module documentation. You may see additional uses for the module in your daily work.

The tree-based parser modules that we've discussed each have their own way of doing things, showing again that there is more than one way to solve a problem using Perl. In the next few sections, we're going to discuss tree-based parsers that follow the DOM standard.

**Note**

For additional XML::Twig Perl module information (including all the possible options), please take a look at the available online documentation by using perldoc XML::Twig or see `http://www.xmltwig.com`. The XML::Twig Perl module happens to be one of the best documented modules (that is, the perldoc pages contain lots of examples).

## What Is the Document Object Model?

The DOM is a platform and programming language independent standard that was developed to provide a programming API that supports both HTML and XML documents. The DOM was originally developed as a specification to enhance the portability of JavaScript scripts and Java applications between different web browsers. Early members of the DOM working group had a lot of hands-on experience with Standard General Markup Language (SGML), and they influenced the direction of the standard development. Thanks to all their hard work, the DOM developers have built an API that allows us to add, delete, retrieve, and modify the contents of XML and HTML documents. Of course, this chapter focuses strictly on XML documents.

**Note**

For additional information on the DOM, please see `http://www.w3.org/DOM/`.

One important concept to keep in mind is that the DOM is programming language independent. It specifies the structure of a document and methods for accessing the document, but doesn't specify any implementation details—they're left up to the individual developers. The remainder of this chapter focuses on the DOM-based Perl XML parser modules.

## DOM-Based XML Parser Modules

The XML::DOM Perl module is a Perl implementation of the W3C DOM Level 1 specification that was written by T. J. Mather. XML::DOM is an extension of the XML::Parser Perl module that parses XML data (either files or strings). It generates a hierarchical data structure containing the contents of the XML document. The API provided by the XML::DOM Perl module to access the hierarchical data is directly based on the requirements in the W3C specification. In addition, the XML::DOM Perl module has also added several additional methods that aren't required by the standard. Most of these additions have been added as helper methods that make the module a little easier to use.

This module is one of the more widely used XML parsing modules. As a result of its widespread use, this module is very stable, very well documented, and is considered by many to be the de facto XML parsing module for Perl.

**Note**

For additional information on the W3C DOM Level 1 specification, please see `http://www.w3.org/TR/REC-DOM-Level-1/`.

### XML::DOM Perl Module Example

Now that you've had an introduction to the XML::DOM Perl module, let's take a look at an example to see how we might be able to use it as the basis for an application.

Let's assume that your company is one of several organizations involved with monitoring network traffic on an experimental network. During a test period, a network sniffer records all the Internet Protocol (IP) packets transmitted during the course of the testing period. The network sniffer parses the IP packets, extracts the pertinent information, and stores the contents of the IP packets in the form of an XML document. XML was selected as the format for the message traffic to facilitate data exchange among the different organizations involved with the testing. Our task is to use the XML::DOM module to generate a report from the recorded data in a particular format.

During the testing, we don't need to store all the fields in each IP packet, just those that are important for data analysis. Listing 4.11 shows the DTD that was developed to support these requirements. As you can see, this is a simple DTD that is basically made up of multiple `<packet>` elements. Note that each `<packet>` element has a unique sequence identification number that is an attribute with an `ID` type. The `ID` attribute type requires that each `seqnum` attribute is unique throughout the XML document.

Listing 4.11 **DTD that defines the format of the network sniffer log. (Filename:ch4_dom_netlog.dtd)**

```
<?xml version="1.0" encoding="UTF-8"?>
<!ELEMENT sniffer_data (packet*)>
<!ELEMENT packet (protocol, timestamp, source, dest)>
<!ATTLIST packet seqnum ID #REQUIRED>
<!ELEMENT protocol (#PCDATA)>
<!ELEMENT timestamp (#PCDATA)>
<!ELEMENT source (#PCDATA)>
<!ELEMENT dest (#PCDATA)>
```

The XML schema that describes the same XML document is shown in Listing 4.12.

Listing 4.12 **XML schema that defines the format of the network sniffer log. (Filename: ch4_dom_netlog.xsd)**

```
<?xml version="1.0" encoding="UTF-8"?>
<xs:schema xmlns:xs="http://www.w3.org/2001/XMLSchema"
elementFormDefault="qualified">
   <xs:element name="dest" type="xs:string"/>
   <xs:element name="packet">
      <xs:complexType>
```

```
        <xs:sequence>
            <xs:element ref="protocol"/>
            <xs:element ref="timestamp"/>
            <xs:element ref="source"/>
            <xs:element ref="dest"/>
        </xs:sequence>
        <xs:attribute name="seqnum" type="xs:ID" use="required"/>
    </xs:complexType>
</xs:element>
<xs:element name="protocol" type="xs:string"/>
<xs:element name="sniffer_data">
    <xs:complexType>
        <xs:sequence>
            <xs:element ref="packet" minOccurs="0" maxOccurs="unbounded"/>
        </xs:sequence>
    </xs:complexType>
</xs:element>
<xs:element name="source" type="xs:string"/>
<xs:element name="timestamp" type="xs:positiveInteger"/>
</xs:schema>
```

A sample XML document that contains the recorded network traffic is shown in Listing 4.13. As you can see, each `<packet>` element has a unique sequence number and several required elements (`<protocol>`, `<timestamp>`, `<source>`, and destination hostname (`<dest>`)). In a real-world application, the timestamp could be the standard Unix epoch timestamp (seconds since January 1, 1970), the number of seconds since midnight, or relative to the beginning of the test period.

Listing 4.13 **Network traffic sniffer log in XML. (Filename: ch4_dom_netlog.xml)**

```
<?xml version="1.0" encoding="UTF-8"?>
<!DOCTYPE sniffer_data SYSTEM "netlog2.dtd">
<sniffer_data>
    <packet seqnum="tx_1">
        <protocol>SMTP</protocol>
        <timestamp>1</timestamp>
        <source>scooby</source>
        <dest>smtp_server</dest>
    </packet>
    <packet seqnum="tx_2">
        <protocol>FTP</protocol>
        <timestamp>4</timestamp>
        <source>shaggy</source>
        <dest>ftp_server</dest>
    </packet>
    <packet seqnum="tx_3">
        <protocol>SNMP</protocol>
        <timestamp>7</timestamp>
        <source>sys_admin</source>
```

*continues*

Listing 4.13 **Continued**

```
      <dest>gateway</dest>
   </packet>
   <packet seqnum="tx_4">
      <protocol>DNS</protocol>
      <timestamp>8</timestamp>
      <source>casper</source>
      <dest>dns_server</dest>
   </packet>
   <packet seqnum="tx_5">
      <protocol>HTTP</protocol>
      <timestamp>9</timestamp>
      <source>casper</source>
      <dest>web_server</dest>
   </packet>
   <packet seqnum="tx_6">
      <protocol>SSH</protocol>
      <timestamp>11</timestamp>
      <source>speedracer</source>
      <dest>accounting</dest>
   </packet>
   <packet seqnum="tx_7">
      <protocol>SMTP</protocol>
      <timestamp>13</timestamp>
      <source>scooby</source>
      <dest>smtp_server</dest>
   </packet>
   <packet seqnum="tx_8">
      <protocol>SMTP</protocol>
      <timestamp>13</timestamp>
      <source>scooby</source>
      <dest>smtp_server</dest>
   </packet>
</sniffer_data>
```

Now that we've seen the data, we need to create a program that generates an output report summarizing the data. The report should have the following format:

```
Sequence Number:
Protocol:
Timestamp:
Source Hostname:
Destination Hostname:
```

A sample section of the report for the first `<packet>` element in the XML document would contain the following information:

```
Sequence Number: tx_1
Protocol: SMTP
Timestamp: 1
Source Hostname: Scooby
Destination Hostname: smtp_server
```

In addition, we want to keep a count of how many packets we see on the network for each protocol. The Perl program to parse and summarize the network traffic log is shown in Listing 4.14.

Listing 4.14 **XML::DOM-based program to parse and summarize the network sniffer log. (Filename: ch4_dom_app.pl)**

```
use strict;
use XML::DOM;

# Declare a few variables.
my ($packet, %protoCount, $nodeName, @pktInfoArray, $pktInfo);

# Instantiate a new XML::DOM parser.
my $parser = XML::DOM::Parser->new();

# Parse the input XML document.
my $doc = $parser->parsefile ("ch4_dom_netlog.xml");
my $root = $doc->getDocumentElement();

# Retrieve an array of all nodes.
my @packetArray = $root->getChildNodes();

# Loop through the array.
foreach $packet (@packetArray) {
  if ($packet->getNodeType() == ELEMENT_NODE) {
     print "Seqnum: " . $packet->getAttribute("seqnum") . "\n";
     @pktInfoArray = $packet->getChildNodes();

     foreach $pktInfo (@pktInfoArray) {

       if ($pktInfo->getNodeType() == ELEMENT_NODE) {
          $nodeName = $pktInfo->getNodeName();
          $nodeName =~ s/(\w+)/\u\L$1/g;

          print "$nodeName";

          if ($pktInfo->getNodeName() eq "protocol") {
             if ($protoCount{$pktInfo->getFirstChild()->getData}) {
                $protoCount{$pktInfo->getFirstChild()->getData}++;
             }
             else {
                $protoCount{$pktInfo->getFirstChild->getData} = 1;
             }
          }
          print " : " . $pktInfo->getFirstChild()->getData . "\n";
       }
    }
    print "\n";
  }
```

*continues*

Listing 4.14 **Continued**

```
44. }
45.
46. my ($key);
47. print "\n---------------------------\n";
48. print "Protocol Summary\n";
49. foreach $key (keys %protoCount) {
50.    print "$key\t$protoCount{$key}\n";
51. }
```

### *Standard Pragmas*

**1–5** The opening section of our program contains our standard `use` pragma (`use strict`). Because we're using the XML::DOM module, we'll need to include the `use XML::DOM` pragma as well. A few of our global scalars, arrays, and hashes are also declared in this opening block.

```
1.  use strict;
2.  use XML::DOM;
3.
4.  # Declare a few variables.
5.  my ($packet, %protoCount, $nodeName, @pktInfoArray, $pktInfo);
```

### *Initialization and Parsing*

**7–12** This section of the program performs the initialization for the parser module and actually parses the document. There are several important steps that take place in this portion of the program.

The first step in the Perl program is to create a new XML::DOM parser object, which is named `$parser`. We need a parser object, so we can call the `parsefile` method. Second, we call the `parsefile` method, which parses the XML document specified in the argument and then returns an XML::DOM::Document object that we have named `$doc`. This XML::DOM::Document object has a tree structure consisting of node objects. The `getDocumentElement` method provides us with direct access to the node that is the root element of the entire document. The `getChildNodes()` method returns an array of all nodes that are children of the current node. All elements in the document are children of the root element, so we now have access to all elements in the XML document.

```
7.  # Instantiate a new XML::DOM parser.
8.  my $parser = XML::DOM::Parser->new();
9.
10. # Parse the input XML document.
11. my $doc = $parser->parsefile ("ch4_dom_netlog.xml");
12. my $root = $doc->getDocumentElement();
```

### *Extracting the Parsed Information*

**14–51** The array @packetArray contains all the <packet> elements in our XML document. We'll need to loop through the array using a foreach() loop to access the individual packet elements.

At the first if() statement on line 19, we need to check and verify that the current <packet> is an element. Note that the ELEMENT_NODE type is a constant by the XML::DOM Perl module. Based on the design of our XML document, each time through the outermost foreach() loop, we'll see another packet element. This can be easily verified by the getNodeType method. It returns the current node type (for example, element, attribute, cdata, and so forth).

```
14.  # Retrieve an array of all nodes.
15.  my @packetArray = $root->getChildNodes();
16.
17.  # Loop through the array.
18.  foreach $packet (@packetArray) {
19.    if ($packet->getNodeType() == ELEMENT_NODE) {
20.       print "Seqnum: " . $packet->getAttribute("seqnum") . "\n";
21.       @pktInfoArray = $packet->getChildNodes();
22.
23.       foreach $pktInfo (@pktInfoArray) {
24.
25.         if ($pktInfo->getNodeType() == ELEMENT_NODE) {
26.            $nodeName = $pktInfo->getNodeName();
27.            $nodeName =~ s/(\w+)/\u\L$1/g;
28.
29.            print "$nodeName";
30.
31.            if ($pktInfo->getNodeName() eq "protocol") {
32.               if ($protoCount{$pktInfo->getFirstChild()->getData}) {
33.                  $protoCount{$pktInfo->getFirstChild()->getData}++;
34.               }
35.               else {
36.                  $protoCount{$pktInfo->getFirstChild->getData} = 1;
37.               }
38.            }
39.            print " : " . $pktInfo->getFirstChild()->getData . "\n";
40.         }
41.      }
42.      print "\n";
43.    }
44.  }
45.
46.  my ($key);
47.  print "\n--------------------------\n";
48.  print "Protocol Summary\n";
49.  foreach $key (keys %protoCount) {
50.     print "$key\t$protoCount{$key}\n";
51.  }
```

> **Note**
> A full listing of the valid predefined constants can be found in the XML::DOM perldoc.

After we verify that we've received an element back from the array, we're at a packet node in the DOM tree. First, we retrieve the packet's only attribute (named `seqnum`) by using the `getAttribute()` method.

Now that we've retrieved the `seqnum` attribute from the `<packet>` element node, we're ready to retrieve the child nodes of the packet element using the `getChildNodes()` method. The `@pktInfoArray` array contains all the nodes that are children of the `<packet>` element. So, the `@pktInfoArray` array contains `<protocol>`, `<timestamp>`, `<source>`, and `<dest>` elements. Looping through the array, we use the `getNodeName()` method to retrieve the name of the current node, and then the `getFirstChild()->getData()` method to retrieve the character data stored in the element. While looping through all the elements, we're also counting the number of occurrences of each protocol type and accumulating the results in a hash named `%protoCount`.

The output report generated by the XML::DOM-based Perl program is shown in Listing 4.15.

Listing 4.15 **Output from the XML::DOM parsing program. (Filename: ch4_dom_report.txt)**

```
Seqnum: tx_1
Protocol : SMTP
Timestamp : 1
Source : scooby
Dest : smtp_server

Seqnum: tx_2
Protocol : FTP
Timestamp : 4
Source : shaggy
Dest : ftp_server

Seqnum: tx_3
Protocol : SNMP
Timestamp : 7
Source : sys_admin
Dest : gateway

Seqnum: tx_4
Protocol : DNS
Timestamp : 8
Source : casper
Dest : dns_server
```

```
Seqnum: tx_5
Protocol : HTTP
Timestamp : 9
Source : casper
Dest : web_server

Seqnum: tx_6
Protocol : SSH
Timestamp : 11
Source : speedracer
Dest : accounting

Seqnum: tx_7
Protocol : SMTP
Timestamp : 13
Source : scooby
Dest : smtp_server

Seqnum: tx_8
Protocol : SMTP
Timestamp : 13
Source : scooby
Dest : smtp_server


----------------------------
Protocol Summary
SNMP  1
FTP   1
DNS   1
SMTP  3
SSH   1
HTTP  1
```

**Note**

For additional information on the XML::DOM Perl (including all the possible options), please take a look at the available online documentation by using perldoc XML::DOM.

## XML::LibXML

XML::LibXML is a Perl interface to the libxml2 C library developed for the Gnome project. The XML::LibXML Perl module was developed by Matt Sergeant and Christian Glahn while the libxml2 C library was developed by Daniel Velliard. XML::LibXML conforms to the DOM2 standard.

Unlike several of the tree-based parsers that we have discussed so far in this chapter (for example, XML::Simple, XML::Twig), the XML::LibXML Perl module isn't built on top of XML::Parser. If you remember our original discussion back in Chapter 3 about XML::Parser, you'll recall that it doesn't implement actual DOM, SAX, or XPath interfaces. XPath is discussed a little later in Chapter 8, "XML Transformation and Filtering."

Both XML::Parser and all the Perl modules built upon it are severely limited regarding support for standards. However, libxml2 was developed after the DOM, SAX, and XPath standards were mature, so fortunately for us, libxml2 supports the DOM, SAX, and XPath APIs. Depending on your task at hand, you'll have access to all three APIs in the same module. The advantage of having a DOM and SAX API in the same Perl module is that you can take advantage of a DOM tree and SAX events. For example, you can walk up and down an in-memory tree and generate SAX events.

### XML::LibXML Example

Now that you have an understanding of the capabilities of the XML::LibXML module, let's take a look at an example. Assume that your company has purchased new accounting software to manage all the company billing records. Unfortunately, the new software isn't compatible with the old software (not an unrealistic example). Let's say that the old software can dump the current customer information into an XML document; however, the new accounting package can't accept XML data as input. Instead, it expects to see the data in a particular text-based format. Your task is to develop a parser to read the XML document and generate the required report.

Our first task is to review the input XML document format. Listing 4.16 shows the DTD for the XML document that contains our accounts receivable information.

Listing 4.16 **DTD that describes the accounts receivable information. (Filename: ch4_libxml_customers.dtd)**

```
<?xml version="1.0" encoding="UTF-8"?>
<!ELEMENT customer_data (customer*)>
<!ELEMENT customer (name, balance, due_date)>
<!ATTLIST customer account_number ID #REQUIRED>
<!ELEMENT name (#PCDATA)>
<!ELEMENT balance (#PCDATA)>
<!ELEMENT due_date (#PCDATA)>
```

As you can see, this is a fairly simple DTD that contains multiple occurrences of the <customer> element. Our example is based on a simple <customer> element that only contains the <name>, <balance>, and <date> child elements. In a real world application, we would expect a customer element to contain a few more child elements. For example, you could expect to see elements such as an account number, mailing address, telephone number, credit card number, and possibly even a transaction history. However, the same capabilities of the XML::LibXML module that will apply to this simple example can easily be extended to apply to a more complex example. An XML schema that describes our XML document is shown in Listing 4.17.

Listing 4.17 **Accounts receivable schema. (Filename: ch4_libxml_customers.xsd)**

```
<?xml version="1.0" encoding="UTF-8"?>
<!—W3C Schema generated by XML Spy v4.2 U (http://www.xmlspy.com)—>
<xs:schema xmlns:xs="http://www.w3.org/2001/XMLSchema"
elementFormDefault="qualified">
   <xs:element name="balance" type="xs:float"/>
   <xs:element name="customer">
      <xs:complexType>
         <xs:sequence>
            <xs:element ref="name"/>
            <xs:element ref="balance"/>
            <xs:element ref="due_date"/>
         </xs:sequence>
         <xs:attribute name="account_number" type="xs:ID" use="required"/>
      </xs:complexType>
   </xs:element>
   <xs:element name="customer_data">
      <xs:complexType>
         <xs:sequence>
            <xs:element ref="customer" minOccurs="0" maxOccurs="unbounded"/>
         </xs:sequence>
      </xs:complexType>
   </xs:element>
   <xs:element name="due_date" type="xs:date"/>
   <xs:element name="name" type="xs:string"/>
</xs:schema>
```

Now that we understand the format of our input XML document, let's take a look at a sample XML document that is shown in Listing 4.18. Remember, XML data is not always in a standalone file. It can just as easily be stored in a Perl scalar variable, or sent to an application through a file handle (socket). Our sample data has information for six customers. Note that each <customer> element has a unique account_number attribute.

Listing 4.18 **Accounts receivable data in XML. (Filename: ch4_libxml_customers.xml)**

```
<?xml version="1.0" encoding="UTF-8"?>
<!DOCTYPE customer_data SYSTEM "ch4_libxml_customers.dtd">
<customer_data>
   <customer account_number="cid_1">
      <name>Joseph Burns</name>
      <balance>19.95</balance>
      <due_date>May 5</due_date>
   </customer>
   <customer account_number="cid_2">
      <name>Kayla Burns</name>
      <balance>29.95</balance>
      <due_date>May 12</due_date>
   </customer>
   <customer account_number="cid_3">
      <name>Roger Smith</name>
      <balance>100.25</balance>
      <due_date>May 19</due_date>
   </customer>
   <customer account_number="cid_4">
      <name>James Kennedy</name>
      <balance>0.00</balance>
      <due_date>N/A</due_date>
   </customer>
   <customer account_number="cid_5">
      <name>Margaret Pelligrino</name>
      <balance>0.00</balance>
      <due_date>N/A</due_date>
   </customer>
   <customer account_number="cid_6">
      <name>Joseph Jones</name>
      <balance>1000.00</balance>
      <due_date>May 22</due_date>
   </customer>
</customer_data>
```

Assume that the new accounting software requires input in the following format:

```
Account Number:
Customer Name:
Balance:
Due Date:
```

A sample of the report using only the first `<customer>` element in the XML document would contain the following information:

```
Account Number: cid_1
Customer Name: Joseph Burns
Balance: 19.95
Due Date: May 5
```

The XML::LibXML-based program used to generate the required output from the input XML document is shown in Listing 4.19. Let's work our way through the example and explain each of the sections.

Listing 4.19 **XML::LibXML-based program used to parse the accounts receivable data. (Filename: ch4_libxml_app.pl)**

```
use strict;
use XML::LibXML;

my $file = "ch4_libxml_customers.xml";

# Instantiate a new XML::LibXML parser.
my $parser = XML::LibXML->new();

# Parse the XML document.
my $tree = $parser->parse_file($file);
my $root = $tree->getDocumentElement;

# Retrieve an array of all customers.
my @customers = $root->getElementsByTagName('customer');

my $total;

print "Accounts Receivable Report\n";
print "-------------------------\n";

# Loop through the array of all customers.
foreach my $customer (@customers) {
  my $account_num = $customer->getAttribute('account_number');
  print "Account Number: $account_num\n";

  my @name = $customer->getElementsByTagName('name');
  my $thisName = $name[0]->getFirstChild->getData();
  print "Customer Name: $thisName\n";

  my @balance = $customer->getElementsByTagName('balance');
  my $thisBalance = $balance[0]->getFirstChild->getData();
  print "Balance: \$$thisBalance\n";
  $total += $thisBalance;

  my @due_date = $customer->getElementsByTagName('due_date');
  my $thisDueDate = $due_date[0]->getFirstChild->getData();
  print "Due Date: $thisDueDate\n\n";
}

print "--------------------------\n";
print "Total Due: \$$total\n";
```

### Standard Pragmas

**1–2** Similar to all our examples, the opening section contains the recommended pragma (`use strict`). Because we're using the XML::LibXML module, we need the pragma `use XML::LibXML` to load the XML::LibXML module.

```
1.  use strict;
2.  use XML::LibXML;
```

### Parsing the XML Data with XML::LibXML

**4–11** The initial calls to XML::LibXML are similar to those of other parsers. The first step in parsing an XML document with XML::LibXML is to create a new XML::LibXML object by calling the constructor with the function `new()`.

The XML::LibXML supports three types of input for the XML data: as a Perl scalar, as a file handle (for example, a socket connection), and as a standalone file. Depending on the location of the XML data (that is, in a file, scalar, or filehandle), you'll need to call the appropriate method to parse the XML data. In our case, the XML data is contained in a file named customers.xml, so we use the `parse_file()` method.

After calling the `parse_file()` method, the document has been parsed, and an XML::LibXML::Document DOM object named `$tree` was returned. Now that we have a handle to the DOM object through the `$tree` scalar, we can call the method `getElementsByTagName()`. This method returns an array containing all occurrences of a particular element, and in our case, we want all the `<customer>` elements.

```
4.  my $file = "ch4_libxml_customers.xml";
5.
6.  # Instantiate a new XML::LibXML parser.
7.  my $parser = XML::LibXML->new();
8.
9.  # Parse the XML document.
10. my $tree = $parser->parse_file($file);
11. my $root = $tree->getDocumentElement;
```

### Retrieving the Parsed Information

**13–41** Now that we have all the customer elements (stored in the `@customer` array), we can loop through all the elements and extract the child elements and attributes that we need to generate our report. The first thing that we do is extract the `account_number` attribute from each element by using the following method:

```
my $account_num = $customer>getAttribute('account_number');
```

All the other required information (that is, the character data) contained in the other elements is extracted using the following method:

```
my @name = $customer->getElementsByTagName('name');
```

This method returns an array of XML::LibXML::Node objects representing all occurrences of the <name> element for the current <customer> element. Because there is only one <name> element for each <customer> element, we're always going to be interested in the first element in the array (identified by `index[0]`). Up until this point, we're manipulating objects that contain the character data. To extract the character data in the elements, we need to use the following method:

```
my $thisName = $name[0]->getFirstChild->getData();
```

Note that we're accessing the first element of the `@name` array (because there is only one element in the array in our case). This method of creating the object array and accessing the character data is repeated for each child element of the <customer> element.

One other task that we're performing as part of the report generation is to keep a running total of the accounts receivable. This was easily accomplished with a variable that was declared outside the `for()` statement that loops through all the <customer> elements. We then increment the total for the individual total of each customer.

```
# Retrieve an array of all customers.
my @customers = $root->getElementsByTagName('customer');

my $total;

print "Accounts Receivable Report\n";
print "-------------------------\n";

# Loop through the array of all customers.
foreach my $customer (@customers) {
  my $account_num = $customer->getAttribute('account_number');
  print "Account Number: $account_num\n";

  my @name = $customer->getElementsByTagName('name');
  my $thisName = $name[0]->getFirstChild->getData();
  print "Customer Name: $thisName\n";

  my @balance = $customer->getElementsByTagName('balance');
  my $thisBalance = $balance[0]->getFirstChild->getData();
  print "Balance: \$$thisBalance\n";
  $total += $thisBalance;

  my @due_date = $customer->getElementsByTagName('due_date');
  my $thisDueDate = $due_date[0]->getFirstChild->getData();
```

*continues*

```
    print "Due Date: $thisDueDate\n\n";
}

print "--------------------------\n";
print "Total Due: \$$total\n";
```

The accounts receivable report generated by the XML::LibXML Perl program is shown in Listing 4.20.

> **Note**
>
> If you ever need to track billing records and calculate billing cycles, there are a number of Perl modules that will make that job much easier. A potentially useful module is the Date::Calc Perl module. It performs all types of calculations based on the Gregorian calendar. For example, let's say you need to calculate dates based on 90-day billing cycles—this module can calculate the next billing date.

Listing 4.20 **Output accounts receivable report generated by the XML::LibXML-based Perl program. (Filename: ch4_libxml_report.txt)**

```
Accounts Receivable Report
--------------------------
Account Number: cid_1
Customer Name: Joseph Burns
Balance: $19.95
Due Date: May 5

Account Number: cid_2
Customer Name: Kayla Burns
Balance: $29.95
Due Date: May 12

Account Number: cid_3
Customer Name: Roger Smith
Balance: $100.25
Due Date: May 19

Account Number: cid_4
Customer Name: James Kennedy
Balance: $0.00
Due Date: N/A

Account Number: cid_5
Customer Name: Margaret Pelligrino
Balance: $0.00
Due Date: N/A

Account Number: cid_6
Customer Name: Joseph Jones
Balance: $1000.00
Due Date: May 22

Total Due: $1150.15
```

> **Note**
> For additional XML::LibXML module information (including all the possible options), please take a look at the available online documentation by using perldoc XML::LibXML.

## Summary

In this chapter, I discussed the tree-based XML parsing approach. You are now familiar with stream-based and tree-based approaches, as well as the advantages and disadvantages of each approach. Most XML application development utilizes one or both of these parsing concepts. Based on our discussions, you should now be able to make a sound judgment about which module to use in a particular situation.

## Exercises

1. Modify the XML::Twig example shown in Listing 4.9 to also parse the `<department_name>` elements and include them as part of the output report. Is it easy to retrieve another element earlier in the path?
2. Find or build a large XML document (at least several MB) and use the Perl Benchmark module to compare parsing times of the various DOM modules. If we needed to extract only a portion of an XML document, is the XML::Twig XPath like mode much faster? How much faster?

For suggested solutions to this exercise, be sure to check out the web site: `http://www.xmlproj.com/book/chapter4`.

## Relevant Links

W3 DOM Standard: `http://www.w3.org/DOM/`
XML::Twig Page: `http://www.xmltwig.com/`

# III

# Generating XML Documents Using Perl Modules

# 5

# Generating XML Documents from Text Files

## Chapter Roadmap

This chapter focuses on generating XML documents from a number of data sources. So far, you have learned how to parse and process XML, but I haven't discussed the actual source of XML data. How do you create or generate an XML document? In this chapter, I will discuss several approaches to generating XML documents. During the course of this discussion, I will present examples of programs that generate XML data from a number of sources. I'll show how to generate XML using simple print statements as well as using Perl modules. The XML::Writer Perl module is used as a primary writer module; however, the XML::Handler::YAWriter Perl module is also presented as a potential alternative to the XML::Writer Perl module.

To run the examples presented in this chapter, you'll need to install the following Perl modules:

- XML::Writer
- XML::Handler::YAWriter

**Note**

Remember, if you have any questions about Perl modules (for example, where do you get them, how do you install them, and so forth), please refer to Appendix B, "Perl Essentials."

## Introduction to XML Generation

One of the fundamental skills you will use when working with XML is generating an XML document. Before any XML processor can operate on an XML document, someone, somewhere (and it might be you) will need to create the XML document. Two methods of generating XML documents exist: static generation and dynamic generation. Each will be discussed in the following paragraphs.

The static approach to generating an XML document typically refers to the manual process of writing the XML document in an editor. This file is initially created and remains the same until someone or something modifies it. Small and simple XML documents can be easily written using just a plain text editor, as long as you are familiar with the XML syntax. For the larger more complex files, this approach is very cumbersome and error prone. For these reasons alone, you should utilize an XML generation tool. Several currently available commercial and open source tools enable you to create XML documents using a What You See Is What You Get (WYSIWYG) interface. These tools are helpful because they point out errors immediately in your XML files (for example, missing end tags, missing required elements, and so forth). One commercial tool used during the development of this book is XML Spy (`http://www.xmlspy.com`). XML Spy is a suite of tools that have been designed to support all aspects of XML work (for example, editing, DTD development, XML schema development, and XSLT stylesheets).

The dynamic approach to generating XML documents is commonly used. Dynamically generated XML documents are created by an application. This technique is usually employed when a program generates an XML file based on a data source (for example, user-supplied input on a web page, CSV input file, results of a database query, and so forth). Or, an application can be used to convert the contents of a text file to XML.

The XML standard defines many rules that must be followed whenever you create XML documents. Both static and dynamically generated XML documents must follow these rules. To simplify the production of XML documents, several Perl modules have been developed to support this task. Let's take a look at the different methods of generating XML documents.

# Different Methods of Generating XML Data

As I mentioned earlier, there are two types of XML data—static XML documents and dynamically generated XML documents. Two approaches to generating XML data also exist. I call them the "crazy" approach and the "lazy" approach.

> **Note**
>
> Remember, XML data can consist of a standalone file or XML data in memory (for example, dynamically generated XML data that is sent across a network).

## Using the Perl *print* Function to Generate XML Data

The crazy approach refers to using Perl's `print` function to print out all parts of the XML document. Because an XML document is just plain text, it can be easily generated using the standard Perl `print` function. In the next few sections, we'll take a closer look at the advantages and disadvantages to this approach.

### Advantages of Using the Perl *print* Function

A few (but not too many) advantages exist for using the Perl `print` function to generate your XML documents.

- It's simple. Just use the Perl `print` function to generate XML documents.
- It can be performed very quickly with basic Perl skills. Perl's `print` function is quick and easy to use for short, simple XML documents.
- Your application will not have external module dependencies. One possible situation when this could be important is in the case of a production server. Let's say that you're working on the server; however, because it's the production server, you're restricted from installing any modules.

#### Disadvantages of Using the Perl *print* Function

As you will soon see, there are more disadvantages than advantages to using this approach.

- In this case, the user may be responsible for escaping attribute values and character data (not a problem if you use a "Here" document). The first line of an XML document contains `<?xml version="1.0"?>`. If you use the Perl `print` function to generate XML data, then you're required to escape any quotation marks. For example, `version="1.0"` must be escaped to `version=\"1.0\"` because it appears inside of a `print` statement.
- This method doesn't perform any checks to verify that the resulting XML document is well-formed. So, it is your responsibility to make sure that the generated XML document is well-formed. The user is responsible for verifying that there is an end tag that matches each start tag. This can begin to get confusing if you have a complicated, nested XML document.
- The user is responsible for generating the constructs for different types of markup (for example, tags, comments, and processing instructions).
- The resulting program can be difficult to maintain or modify (especially if the application is passed on to another developer).

If you're going to be generating anything other than the simplest XML documents, I strongly suggest using an XML writer module.

### Using a Perl Module to Generate XML Data

The second method of generating data, which I call the lazy approach (also considered the smarter approach), is the easier approach of the two. How do you do it? Simply use a Perl module that was designed specifically for the task. The module takes care of the standard syntax and only expects you to pass it data. In this situation, your only responsibility is to determine what information should appear in the XML data, while the Perl module manages the XML-related tasks (for example, verifying matching start and end tags).

A major advantage of using a Perl module to generate XML data is that it abstracts (and almost hides) the difficult standards-related tasks from the user.

The lazy programmer is the one who takes the easiest approach to finishing the task—using a writer module. Although an XML writer module may be considered by some to be overkill for generating a simple XML document, it definitely provides a cleaner, more general approach to generating XML data. Let's take a look at a few advantages and disadvantages associated with using a Perl module to generate XML data.

### Advantages of an XML-Generating Module

The following are some advantages of using the Perl module:

- Modules perform some error checking to verify that generated XML data is well-formed (for example, it matches start and end tags). Typically, the module will generate an error if you forget a closing tag or improperly try to nest elements.
- Long-term maintenance is easier.
- The source code is shorter, cleaner, and easier to understand if you build an application based on a module.

### Disadvantage of an XML-Generating Module

The big disadvantage here is that some time will be required to become familiar with the module, but most module APIs are usually very straightforward.

I've discussed a few reasons why you would want to use a Perl module to assist you in generating XML data. Several Perl modules exist that have been specifically developed to generate XML data. In the next section, you'll take a look at examples that demonstrate each of the approaches to generating XML data that we just discussed.

# Examples of XML Document Generation

In this section, I'm going to present a few examples that demonstrate the different approaches to generating XML data. While going through the examples, try to keep the advantages and disadvantages of each approach in mind. First, let's take a look at generating an XML document by using the Perl `print` function.

## Using the Perl *print* Function

No, don't worry; if you are reading this section, you are not necessarily crazy, but rather enjoy exploring things. Using Perl's `print` function to generate XML data can be time saving, and at other times, time consuming. It all depends on the task. Just follow the famous advice, "Use the right tool for the right job," and make the right choice.

If your requirement is to simply generate a relatively small XML file, then it won't be time consuming. If you don't mind explicitly typing every XML construct in your Perl code, then a simple Perl program based on the `print` function might just be your answer. Any other task will most likely greatly benefit from the use of a specialized XML writer module. For example, a small application configuration file might be a good candidate for manual generation.

Remember, first and foremost, an XML document is really just a text file that follows a strict set of rules for defining structure and content. You can take advantage of this fact, and you can use the standard Perl `print` function to generate an output XML document. Let's say that you are responsible for generating the simple XML document for configuring a Perl DBI-based application. You parsed this XML document back in Chapter 4, "Tree-Based Parser Modules," using the XML::Simple Perl module; however, let's take a look at how to generate it using the Perl `print` function. The XML document is shown in Listing 5.1.

Listing 5.1 **XML document containing DBI configuration information. (Filename: ch5_dbi_config.xml)**

```
<?xml version="1.0" encoding="UTF-8"?>
<!DOCTYPE db_config_information SYSTEM "ch5_dbi_config.dtd">
<db_config_information>
   <db_user>
      <username>mark</username>
      <password>mark's password</password>
   </db_user>
   <db_server hostname="rocket" os="Linux">
      <server_ip>192.168.1.10</server_ip>
      <db_driver>MySQL</db_driver>
      <port>3306</port>
   </db_server>
   <db_server hostname="scooter" os="Microsoft Windows">
      <server_ip>192.168.1.50</server_ip>
      <db_driver>ODBC</db_driver>
      <port>3379</port>
   </db_server>
</db_config_information>
```

As you can see, this is a very simple XML document, and you can easily generate it using the standard Perl `print` function. The Perl program that was used to generate the XML document is shown in Listing 5.2.

Listing 5.2 **Perl program used to generate a Perl DBI configuration file in XML. (Filename: ch5_dbi_config_app.pl)**

```
1.   use strict;
2.
3.   # Open the output file.
4.   open (OUTPUT, "> ch5_dbi_config.xml")
5.     or die "Can't open ch5_dbi_config.xml file for writing: $!\n";
6.
7.   # Start the Perl "Here" document.  Everything until the
8.   # EOF is printed by the single print statement.
9.   print OUTPUT <<EOF;
10.
11.   <?xml version="1.0" encoding="UTF-8"?>
12.   <!DOCTYPE db_config_information SYSTEM "xml-simple.dtd">
13.   <db_config_information>
14.      <db_user>
15.         <username>mark</username>
16.         <password>mark's secret password</password>
17.      </db_user>
18.      <db_server hostname="rocket" os="Linux">
19.         <server_ip>192.168.1.10</server_ip>
20.         <db_driver>MySQL</db_driver>
21.         <port>3306</port>
22.      </db_server>
23.      <db_server hostname="scooter" os="Microsoft Windows">
24.         <server_ip>192.168.1.50</server_ip>
25.         <db_driver>ODBC</db_driver>
26.         <port>3379</port>
27.      </db_server>
28.   </db_config_information>
29.   EOF
30.
31.   close (OUTPUT);
```

## Example Discussion

**1–5** As you can already see, the program shown in Listing 5.2 is very simple. The top of the Perl program contains the standard pragma (`use strict`). Note that we don't need an additional `use` module pragmas because we're only using the standard Perl `print` function. Then, we open the output file named `ch5_dbi_config.xml` that will contain the generated XML data.

```
1.   use strict;
2.
3.   # Open the output file.
4.   open (OUTPUT, "> ch5_dbi_config.xml")
5.     or die "Can't open ch5_dbi_config.xml file for writing: $!\n";
```

**7–31** In this section of the program, we take advantage of a little-known Perl construct called a "Here" document. It can save a lot of time and greatly simplify the structure of your program. Basically, everything between the two occurrences of the terminating string (in our case, "`EOF`") is printed, so all you need to do is insert your XML document between the `EOF` as you would like it printed. Note that you basically have to type the entire XML document inside the "Here" blocks.

One advantage of the "Here" document is that you don't need to have a print statement on each line. One disadvantage is that you can't have comments inside of a "Here" block—the comments will show up inside the output file. Here are the four steps to using this construct:

First, following the "<<" symbol, we specify a string to terminate all the quoted characters. In our case, the string that signifies the end of the block is "`EOF`". Note that we're sending the output to the OUTPUT filehandle.

Second, all lines following the current line down to (but not including) the terminating line are considered part of the output string. So, we basically just insert the entire contents of our XML document. There isn't a limit to the size of the output string, so this output string could span several pages (if required).

Third, we'll need to identify the end of the output block. So, we insert `EOF` on a line all by itself. Note that the ending tag for a "Here" document (in our case, `EOF`) must appear flush against the left margin, and it can't have any trailing spaces or tabs. When you run this program, it prints everything that is contained between the two `EOF` statements.

Keep this syntax in mind; it comes in handy in a number of situations. If we didn't use the "Here" document syntax, we would have needed a `print` function on each line of the program. In addition to causing your hands to ache after typing all those print statements, all those print statements would cause your program to be very cluttered and prone to error.

**Note**

You can find additional information on the Perl "Here" documents by looking at perldoc perldata.

## Using the Perl XML::Writer Module

XML::Writer is an XML writer Perl module that was developed by David Megginson (`http://www.megginson.com/`) to address some of the problems associated with using the standard Perl `print` function to generate XML data. Most of the problems usually appear when trying to generate complex XML documents using only the standard Perl `print` function. I will show you how the XML::Writer module simplifies the task of generating an XML document and provides support for generating more complex documents by handling potentially error-prone aspects of XML document generation. Basically, this module addresses just about all the disadvantages related to using the Perl `print` function.

For example, the module generates escape characters for both attribute values and character data. XML::Writer builds all the required markup text (for example, tags, comments, and processing instructions). In addition, the XML::Writer module executes several checks to verify that the generated XML document is well-formed (for example, that all start tags have corresponding end tags) and simplifies your code. As you can see, the XML::Writer module does a lot of behind-the-scenes work for you. This enables you to concentrate on other parts of the application.

## XML::Writer Perl Module Example

Probably the best way to illustrate the capabilities of the XML::Writer module is to start with an example. Let's first look at an example that generates the short, XML configuration file that was shown in Listing 5.1. Yes, this is the same task performed in the previous example (Listing 5.2) using the Perl `print` function. Now, I'll show you how easy it is to use the XML::Writer module.

Listing 5.3 **Program that demonstrates basic XML::Writer functionality. (Filename: ch5_xml_writer_app.pl)**

```
use strict;
use XML::Writer;
use IO::File;

# Open the output XML document.
my $output = new IO::File(">ch5_dbi_config_writer.xml");

# Instantiate a new XML::Writer object.
my $writer = new XML::Writer(OUTPUT => $output, DATA_MODE=>1,
                             DATA_INDENT=>4);

 # Start generating the XML document.
 $writer->xmlDecl("UTF-8");
 $writer->doctype("db_config_information", "", "xml-simple.dtd");
 $writer->startTag("db_config_information");

 $writer->startTag("db_user");
 $writer->dataElement("username", "mark");
 $writer->dataElement("password", "mark's password");
 $writer->endTag("db_user");

```

*continues*

Listing 5.3 **Continued**

```
22.   $writer->startTag("db_server", hostname=>"rocket", os=>"Linux");
23.   $writer->dataElement("server_ip", "192.168.1.10");
24.   $writer->dataElement("db_driver", "MySQL");
25.   $writer->dataElement("port", "3306");
26.   $writer->endTag("db_server");
27.
28.   $writer->startTag("db_server", hostname=>"scooter", os=>"Microsoft
Windows");
29.   $writer->dataElement("server_ip", "192.168.1.50");
30.   $writer->dataElement("db_driver", "ODBC");
31.   $writer->dataElement("port", "3379");
32.   $writer->endTag("db_server");
33.
34.   $writer->endTag("db_config_information");
35.
36.   # Destroy the XML::Writer object and close generated XML document.
37.   $writer->end();
38.   $output->close();
```

This example program is about the same size in terms of line count as the original example that generated the XML document by using only the Perl `print` function. However, as you can see, this program is much simpler and easier to maintain and modify. Let's examine this example a little more closely, and I'll explain exactly what happens in each section of the program.

### Example Discussion

**1–10** The first portion of the program contains the standard pragma (`use strict`) and two others that you haven't seen yet. First, note that to access the XML::Writer module, you'll need to include the `use XML::Writer` pragma to load the module. Second, you have the `use IO::File` pragma. The `use IO::File` statement loads the IO::File module that is part of the IO module family (Handle, Seekable, File, Pipe, Socket, Dir). In this example, you're using the IO::File module because it provides helper functions used for reading and writing files. So, you use the IO::File module to create a file handle and pass this file handle into the XML::Writer constructor. When you're finished, this file will contain the output XML data.

After creating the filehandle, you need create an XML::Writer object by using the `new` function call. As you can see, you're passing several arguments into the XML::Writer constructor. Note that all arguments are passed into the XML::Writer constructor as key=>value pairs. The first constructor argument (`$output`) is the handle to the output XML file that will be generated by the XML::Module. The `DATA_MODE=>1` argument tells the XML::Writer module to insert new lines around elements, while the `DATA_INDENT=>4` argument tells the

XML::Writer module the indent step size for elements in the output document. Note that both of these options are for human readability and aren't required. A large number of options are available for the XML::Writer module; however, the arguments that you employed here are some of the most commonly used. Now that you have a new XML::Writer object, you can start the process of actually generating the XML document.

```
1.  use strict;
2.  use XML::Writer;
3.  use IO::File;
4.
5.  # Open the output XML document.
6.  my $output = new IO::File(">ch5_dbi_config_writer.xml");
7.
8.  # Instantiate a new XML::Writer object.
9.  my $writer = new XML::Writer(OUTPUT => $output, DATA_MODE=>1,
10.                                DATA_INDENT=>4);
```

**Note**

For additional information on the IO family of modules, please see perldoc IO. If you're interested specifically in the IO::File module, please see perldoc IO::File.

**12–38** Next, we finally make our first XML::Writer calls with the `xmlDecl` and `startTag` methods. The `xmlDecl` method generates the XML declaration:

```
<?xml version="1.0" encoding="UTF-8"?>
```

Remember, this must be the first line of your generated XML document. Because the XML::Writer module generates XML data in the order called by the methods, you need to make sure that this is the first method called.

In this section of the program, you're basically using three XML::Writer methods, over and over again. The three primary calls are as follows:

- `startTag ($name, [attribute name=>attribute value])`—This method generates the start tag for a particular element. Two arguments for this method exist, one required and one optional. The required argument is the element name, and the optional argument is a hash of key-value pairs that correspond to attribute names and attribute values. You will usually need to use this method at the beginning of a block containing nested elements.
- `endTag`—This method generates the end tag for a particular element. It has one argument, the element name. If you don't provide an argument, the XML::Writer module will supply the name of the currently open element. Based on my experience, it is a good idea to provide the

element name as an argument. It helps with the readability of your source code, especially for more complex documents. As with the `startTag`, you will usually need to use this element at the end of a block containing nested elements.

- `dataElement`—This method combines some of the functionality of the `startTag` and `endTag` elements. It takes the same arguments as the `startTag` element—the element name and an optional hash containing attribute name and value pairs. However, this method generates both the start and end tags for a particular element. If you have a standalone element (that is, an element that doesn't contain any child elements), you will probably use this method. You'll see that you can't use this method at the beginning of a nested block because it generates both the start and end tags.

Now that you have an introduction to the methods that you'll be using, let's take a look at the code in the program that actually uses them.

The first thing you need to do (after printing the XML declaration statement) is create the opening tag for the root element. In the example, the root element is named `<db_config_information>`. As you can see in the code, we use the `<startTag>` method to create the opening tag.

Following the opening tag for the `<db_config_information>` element, we have a child element, `<db_user>`. The opening and closing tags for the `db_user` element surround its child elements (`<username>` and `<password>`). Note that because the `<username>` and `<password>` elements don't have any children, you can use the `dataElement` method rather than a combination of the `startTag` and `endTag` methods.

The same approach is followed to generate the contents of the `<db_server>` elements. One of the only differences between generating `<db_server>` elements and `<db_user>` elements is that each of the `<db_server>` elements has two attributes. Remember, the attributes are passed into the methods as hashes of key value pairs.

After generating all the required tags, you need to call the `end` method. This XML::Writer method verifies that all the start tags have corresponding end tags. If all the start tags don't have matching end tags, the XML::Writer module will generate a warning.

```
# Start generating the XML document.
$writer->xmlDecl("UTF-8");
$writer->doctype("db_config_information", "", "xml-simple.dtd");
$writer->startTag("db_config_information");

$writer->startTag("db_user");
```

```
$writer->dataElement("username", "mark");
$writer->dataElement("password", "mark's password");
$writer->endTag("db_user");

$writer->startTag("db_server", hostname=>"rocket", os=>"Linux");
$writer->dataElement("server_ip", "192.168.1.10");
$writer->dataElement("db_driver", "MySQL");
$writer->dataElement("port", "3306");
$writer->endTag("db_server");

$writer->startTag("db_server", hostname=>"scooter", os=>"Microsoft
➥Windows");
$writer->dataElement("server_ip", "192.168.1.50");
$writer->dataElement("db_driver", "ODBC");
$writer->dataElement("port", "3379");
$writer->endTag("db_server");

$writer->endTag("db_config_information");

# Destroy the XML::Writer object and close generated XML document.
$writer->end();
$output->close();
```

So, I've shown you your first example using the XML::Writer Perl module. Granted, it was a simple example, but the purpose was to show you that using the XML::Writer Perl module can reduce both the size and the complexity of your program, while still performing the same task (and not having to worry about all of the low-level details). In the next example, I'll show a more complex application.

## A More Advanced XML::Writer Perl Module Example

Let's take a look at another example that generates an XML file from the information contained in a simple Comma Separated Value (CSV) file. Several specialized Perl modules exist for working with CSV files (for example, XML::SAXDriver::CSV, Text::CSV_XS). However, you won't need any of those advanced capabilities because I'm using a simple example and want to focus on the XML generation aspect of the example. For this example, let's assume that you're employed by a bookstore, and they're upgrading their bar code reading system. The problem is that the store inventory in the old system can only be exported to a CSV file, while the new system requires the store inventory to be in a specifically structured XML document. So, basically your task is to convert a CSV file into an XML document that contains the same information.

How do you solve this problem? You need to make sure that you understand the formats of the input and output data. In this case, the CSV file is the input, and the XML file is the output. Let's first look at the structure of the input CSV file that contains the data related to each book. For the sake of simplicity, you will assume that the CSV file has six fields in the following format:

```
Title,Author,ISBN,Publisher,Price,Quantity
```

As you can see, the fields are ordered and separated by commas. This input information from the CSV file must then be mapped to the output XML document.

The first step in this mapping is to define a DTD or a schema (depending on what you're more comfortable working with). A DTD that defines the format of our XML document is shown in Listing 5.4.

Listing 5.4 **DTD that describes the book inventory XML document. (Filename: ch5_book_inventory.dtd)**

```
<?xml version="1.0" encoding="UTF-8"?>
<!ELEMENT book_inventory (book*)>
<!ELEMENT book (author,isbn,publisher,price,quantity)>
<!ATTLIST book title CDATA #REQUIRED>
<!ELEMENT author (#PCDATA)>
<!ELEMENT isbn (#PCDATA)>
<!ELEMENT publisher (#PCDATA)>
<!ELEMENT price (#PCDATA)>
<!ELEMENT quantity (#PCDATA)>
```

As you can see, the DTD is very straightforward and maps directly to the CSV input file. The `book_inventory` element is the root element, and it can have multiple `book` child elements. The `book` element also contains a `Title` attribute, which contains the title of the book. The other fields contained within the book node represent particular data about that book. Listing 5.5 shows an XML schema that corresponds to the required XML file format.

Listing 5.5 **XML schema that describes the book inventory XML document. (Filename: ch5_book_inventory.xsd)**

```
<?xml version="1.0" encoding="UTF-8"?>
<xs:schema xmlns:xs="http://www.w3.org/2001/XMLSchema"
elementFormDefault="qualified">
   <xs:element name="author" type="xs:string"/>
   <xs:element name="book">
      <xs:complexType>
         <xs:sequence>
            <xs:element ref="author"/>
            <xs:element ref="isbn"/>
```

```
            <xs:element ref="publisher"/>
            <xs:element ref="price"/>
            <xs:element ref="quantity"/>
         </xs:sequence>
         <xs:attribute name="title" type="xs:string" use="required"/>
      </xs:complexType>
   </xs:element>
   <xs:element name="book_inventory">
      <xs:complexType>
         <xs:sequence>
            <xs:element ref="book" minOccurs="0" maxOccurs="unbounded"/>
         </xs:sequence>
      </xs:complexType>
   </xs:element>
   <xs:element name="isbn" type="xs:positiveInteger"/>
   <xs:element name="price" type="xs:string"/>
   <xs:element name="publisher" type="xs:string"/>
   <xs:element name="quantity" type="xs:positiveInteger"/>+
</xs:schema>
```

Now that you are familiar with both the source and destination data formats, you can develop a Perl program to convert between the input (CSV) and output (XML) formats. The program shown in Listing 5.6 performs the conversion between the two formats.

Listing 5.6 **XML::Writer-based program used to convert from CSV to XML. (Filename: ch5_book_inventory_app.pl)**

```
use strict;
use XML::Writer;
use IO;

# Open the file provided in the command line argument.
my $input = new IO::File(shift);

# Open the output file.
my $output = new IO::File(">ch5_book_inventory_report.xml");

 # Instantiate an XML::Writer object.
 my $writer = XML::Writer->new(OUTPUT => $output, DATA_MODE => 1, DATA_INDENT
 ➥=> 2);

 # Start generating the XML document.
 $writer->xmlDecl("UTF-8");
 $writer->doctype("book_inventory", "", "ch5_book_inventory.dtd");
 $writer->comment("**** Book Inventory Database ****");
 $writer->startTag("book_inventory");

 # Create a list of names that match the input CSV column names.
 my @column_names = qw(Title Author ISBN Publisher Price Quantity);

```

*continues*

Listing 5.6 **Continued**

```
23.  # Loop the input file.
24.  while (   nput ) {
25.    chomp; # chomp the new line char from each line
26.
27.    # Remove leading and trailing whitespace, split on a ','.
28.    my @data = map {s/^\s+//; s/\s+$//; $_;} split /,/;
29.    $writer->startTag("book", "Title" => $data[0]);
30.
31.    # Loop through the data contained in this row.
32.    foreach my $index (1..$#column_names) {
33.      $writer->startTag($column_names[$index]);
34.      $writer->characters($data[$index]);
35.      $writer->endTag($column_names[$index]);
36.    }
37.    $writer->endTag("book");
38.  }
39.
40.  # Don't forget the end tag.
41.  $writer->endTag("book_inventory");
42.
43.  # Destroy the XML::Writer object and close the output file.
44.  $writer->end();
45.  $output->close();
```

## Example Discussion

**1–9** You first employ the *use* pragma to load the XML::Writer and IO modules. You then open two files using the IO module. The first file contains the input CSV data, and the filename will be provided through the command-line argument. The second file will be used for output and will contain the generated XML document. In this example, the output file is named ch5_book_inventory_report.xml.

```
1.  use strict;
2.  use XML::Writer;
3.  use IO;
4.
5.  # Open the file provided in the command line argument.
6.  my $input = new IO::File(shift);
7.
8.  # Open the output file.
9.  my $output = new IO::File(">ch5_book_inventory_report.xml");
```

**11–18** The new constructor method for the XML::Writer is called with `DATA_MODE` and `DATA_INDENT` attributes set to desirable values. As you recall from the previous example, the `DATA_MODE=>1` argument tells the XML::Writer module to insert new lines around elements, while the `DATA_INDENT=>4` argument tells the XML::Writer module the indent step size for elements in the output document. You can now start processing, transforming, and generating the XML data.

You start off by calling `xmlDecl()` to declare the XML, UTF-8 being the default encoding. You're using the XML::Writer `doctype` function to generate the DOCTYPE statement that will identify the external DTD. For others to be able to identify the content of the file and the date it was generated, you call the `comment()` function, which will print the string argument as a comment.

You call `startTag` with "books" as the argument to generate the root element.

```
11.  # Instantiate an XML::Writer object.
12.  my $writer = XML::Writer->new(OUTPUT => $output, DATA_MODE => 1,
     ➥DATA_INDENT => 2);
13.
14.  # Start generating the XML document.
15.  $writer->xmlDecl("UTF-8");
16.  $writer->doctype("book_inventory", "", "ch5_book_inventory.dtd");
17.  $writer->comment("**** Book Inventory Database ****");
18.  $writer->startTag("book_inventory");
```

**20–29** In this section of the application, you create an array named `@column_names` that contains literal column names.

```
my @column_names = qw(Title Author ISBN Publisher Price Quantity);
```

Note that these are the column names that appear in the CSV input file. The Perl `qw` function in this statement is equivalent to splitting the strings on whitespace. As you'll soon see, you'll use the column headings as your tag names when you generate the output XML file.

The next step reads through the file line by line and processes the data. You're using the Perl `chomp()` function to strip the new line ending from each line.

Because you didn't impose any spacing rules for your CSV file, you want to make sure that all the leading and trailing white spaces surrounding the data are removed, and you do that with the following line:

```
my @data = map {s/^\s+//; s/\s+$//; $_;} split /,/;
```

This is a busy expression, so let's take a moment to go through and explain it, so that you know what's happening here. What you're doing is basically combining three operations into one line of Perl code. Remember, this statement is inside the while (`<$input>`) loop, so each line of the input file is being processed, one at a time. Let's walk through this using a line of the input file as a sample. The first line of the input CSV file is shown in the following:

```
MySQL , Paul DuBois , 34-3485-2399, New Riders, 49.99, 4
```

The line is split using commas as the delimiters. So, for the first line, the `split` function has extracted the following strings:

- "`MySQL`"
- "`Paul DuBois`"
- "`34-3485-2399`"
- "`New Riders`"
- "`49.99`"
- "`4`"

The quotes are only included, so you can see that some of the records have spaces before and after the contents of the records. These five strings are passed to the map function that evaluates the substitution expressions for each element. The result is an array that contains the results of each substitution expression. The Perl statement `s/^\s+//` removes leading whitespace while the statement `s/\s+$//` removed trailing whitespace. After the evaluation, the array named `data` contains the following fields:

- `$data[0]` = "`MySQL`"
- `$data[1]` = "`Paul DuBois`"
- `$data[2]` = "`34-3485-2399`"
- `$data[3]` = "`49.99`"
- `$data[4]` = "`4`"

As you can see from the contents of the `@data` array, the leading and trailing whitespace has been removed from each element in the array. We now have clean input data to work with.

```
20.   # Create a list of names that match the input CSV column names.
21.   my @column_names = qw(Title Author ISBN Publisher Price Quantity);
22.
23.   # Loop the input file.
24.   while (<$input>) {
25.     chomp; # chomp the new line char from each line
26.
27.     # Remove leading and trailing whitespace, split on a ','.
28.     my @data = map {s/^\s+//; s/\s+$//; $_;} split /,/;
29.     $writer->startTag("book", "Title" => $data[0]);
```

**31–45** Now that you've cleaned up the input data, you're ready to start generating the XML document. The first step for each book element is to generate the `<book>` tag. Because each `<book>` tag contains the "`Title`" attribute, you generate the <book> tag by passing the key-value pair argument to the startTag function. The first argument to startTag is always the element name, and the following arguments consist of key/value pairs that denote the attribute name/value pairs. You use the first element of @data as the attribute value because the first field in the CSV file is the book Title. You then loop through the remaining elements in the array and generate the XML data for each book element.

Because the array @column_names subscripts match up with @data, you use $index to access the same subscript of both arrays, and therefore use @column_data as the element name and @data as the actual data.

> **Note**
>
> Remember that you are responsible for following the XML grammar and properly nesting the elements. Just follow the last in, first out procedure. If element 1 is opened and then element 2 is opened, element 2 must be closed before element 1.

After every tag is closed, you call the end method to finish the XML output (which verifies starting and ending tag pairs, among other things) and then close the output file. At this point, the script has generated a file named ch5_book_inventory_report.xml that contains the new book inventory in an XML format.

```
    # Loop through the data contained in this row.
    foreach my $index (1..$#column_names) {
      $writer->startTag($column_names[$index]);
      $writer->characters($data[$index]);
      $writer->endTag($column_names[$index]);
    }
    $writer->endTag("book");
  }

  # Don't forget the end tag.
  $writer->endTag("book_inventory");

  # Destroy the XML::Writer object and close the output file.
  $writer->end();
  $output->close();
```

Note that when you run this application from the command line, you must pass the input CSV filename as a command-line argument. The output of this program is shown in Listing 5.7.

Listing 5.7 **Generated XML book inventory. (Filename: ch5_book_inventory_report.xml)**

```
<?xml version="1.0" encoding="UTF-8"?>
<!DOCTYPE book_inventory SYSTEM "ch5_book_inventory.dtd">
<!— **** Book Inventory Database **** —>

<book_inventory>
  <book Title="MySQL">
    <Author>Paul DuBois</Author>
    <ISBN>34-3485-2399</ISBN>
    <Publisher>New Riders</Publisher>
    <Price>49.99</Price>
    <Quantity>4</Quantity>
  </book>
  <book Title="C++ XML">
    <Author>Fabio Arciniegas</Author>
    <ISBN>0-7357-1052-X</ISBN>
    <Publisher>New Riders</Publisher>
    <Price>39.99</Price>
    <Quantity>3</Quantity>
  </book>
  <book Title="Writing Compilers and Interpreters">
    <Author>Ronald Mak</Author>
    <ISBN>0-471-11353-0</ISBN>
    <Publisher>Wiley</Publisher>
    <Price>59.99</Price>
    <Quantity>7</Quantity>
  </book>
  <book Title="Object Oriented Perl">
    <Author>Damian Conway</Author>
    <ISBN>0-548-85785-0</ISBN>
    <Publisher>Manning</Publisher>
    <Price>34.99</Price>
    <Quantity>9</Quantity>
  </book>
</book_inventory>
```

The output shown in Listing 5.7 now contains all the inventory data that has been transformed from CSV to XML. As you will see in Chapter 7, "Transforming Miscellaneous Data Formats to XML (and Vice-Versa)," there is an easier way to convert directly from CSV to XML by using the XML::SAXDriver::CSV Perl module. However, in this chapter, we demonstrated the use of the XML::Writer Perl module combined with the standard Perl `split` function.

## Summary

As you've seen in this chapter, generating XML can be very straightforward and almost simple. I recommend that you use the XML::Writer to handle your XML writing needs. In some cases, you might find Perl's `print` function more suitable. However, those cases are probably few and far between.

## Exercise

1. Generate an XML file using a Perl data structure using the Perl `print` function and then again using the Perl XML::Writer module. The data structure consists of an array of hashes that holds email list information. Here is a sample data structure to use as input. Of course, you can change the data if you feel more comfortable using your personal information.

```
my @list = ({
              first => 'Ilya',
              last => 'Sterin',
              email => 'isterin@cpan.org'
           },
           {
              first => 'Mark',
              last => 'Riehl',
              email => 'mark_riehl@hotmail.com'
           });
```

The reason for using the data structure for an input data source is that it simulates XML generation as one part of a multistep process. For example, the XML document may get generated as a result of previous processing by the same application.

Which approach was easier? Can you see the benefit of the XML::Writer module in a long, complicated XML document?

The generated XML output file should conform to the following format:

```
<email_list>
  <name first="" last="" email=""/>
  <name first="" last="" email=""/>
...
...
</email_list>
```

Make sure you include a valid XML declaration with an encoding of your choice.

For suggested solutions to this exercise, be sure to check out the web site: `http://www.xmlproj.com/book/chapter05`.

# 6

# Generating XML Documents from Databases

## Chapter Roadmap

This chapter discusses how you can use Perl to produce XML documents using a database as your data source. As you will see, one of the largest uses of XML is as a data storage facility. Because XML is based on a hierarchical data format, it's suitable to store almost any information, and it has the capability to mimic some of the capabilities found in relational database management systems (RDBMSs). However, because XML is stored in a text format, data cannot be retrieved as quickly or stored as efficiently compared to the binary formats used by modern RDBMSs. So, XML probably won't be replacing databases anytime in the near future, although a number of people are working very hard to develop XML-based databases. Currently, XML-based databases aren't mature enough to replace our existing RDBMSs.

XML is often used to transfer data between disparate systems. A large number of systems are in use today that exchange data, although they were never designed to do so. An example of such a system could be an e-commerce business. Many times, orders are collected by one company and shipped by another company. In this situation, the companies could use XML to exchange order information. XML can also be used if a company is migrating to a new relational database system. It may not be a big issue moving between versions of a database from the same vendor; usually the new version of the software will support an older version. If the new database is from a different vendor, and chances are they are incompatible, XML can provide a common format.

These examples may initially seem to be complex, and you might think they would be difficult to implement. Thanks to some of the Perl modules currently available, I'll show you that these conversions are easily accomplished.

In this chapter, we'll focus on the XML::Generator::DBI and XML::DBMS Perl modules. Both of these Perl modules play a fundamental role in XML and DBMS integration.

You'll need to install the following Perl modules to test the code examples in this chapter:

- XML::Generator::DBI
- XML::DBMS
- DBI
- DBD::CSV
- DBD::MySQL

> **Note**
> If you have any questions about Perl modules (for example, where to get them, how to install them, and so forth), please refer to Appendix B, "Perl Essentials."

In addition to the modules, you're also going to be using a relational database. For the examples in this chapter, we're using MySQL, which is a very popular open source relational database server available for a number of platforms. Additional MySQL information and MySQL executables are available at `http://www.mysql.com`. Note that the XML::DBMS Perl module is not available on the normal CPAN web site; however, it can be found at `http://www.rpbourret.com/xmldbms/`.

## Why Store Data in XML?

Data storage facilities are very critical for today's business operations. Today's businesses continually accumulate data, whether it's customer information, production information, or any of thousands of other categories of information. This data needs to be stored some place, and better yet, it needs to be stored in a relational format for easy retrieval and integration with other data. RDBMS systems such Oracle, Microsoft SQL Server, MySQL, PostgreSQL, and many others are used to perform such tasks when security, speed, and efficiency pose concerns. RDBMS systems offer a great solution whenever internal or company-developed applications require access to the data.

The potential problem arises either when one application needs to access data of another application but does not have direct access to that application's database system, or when data need to be ported between different database systems (especially true if the systems are from different vendors). Most RDBMSs store their data in binary formats that are not directly accessible by other databases. Any external application wishing to interact with this data needs to utilize a database Application Programming Interface (API) provided by the RDBMS specifically for that product or a generalized interface, such as the Perl Database Interface (DBI). The Perl DBI provides a database independent API to a large number of databases. DBI's homepage is located at `http://dbi.perl.org`, where you can find a lot of information including the FAQ, documentation, mailing lists, and so forth.

## Introduction to the Perl Database Interface

Throughout the book, I've mentioned a number of reasons for the success of XML—platform independence, easy to read, easy to adapt, widespread acceptance, and a number of other reasons. Unfortunately, the same statements don't apply to the RDBMSs used today. All the major RDBMSs are based on proprietary code and usually include a proprietary programming interface. The problem with proprietary interfaces (in addition to the learning curve) is that they can tie your application to a particular RDBMS. The Perl DBI was developed by Tim Bunce to address these problems; it provides a consistent, platform-independent API to a large number of the most popular RDBMSs. In the next section, we'll take a look at the Perl DBI architecture.

## Perl Database Interface Architecture

The Perl DBI provides an API to a RDBMS by abstracting (and hiding) the differences between RDBMSs from different vendors. So, to you (and your application), the API remains the same, regardless of the database with which your Perl script is communicating. A high-level view of the Perl DBI is shown in Figure 6.1.

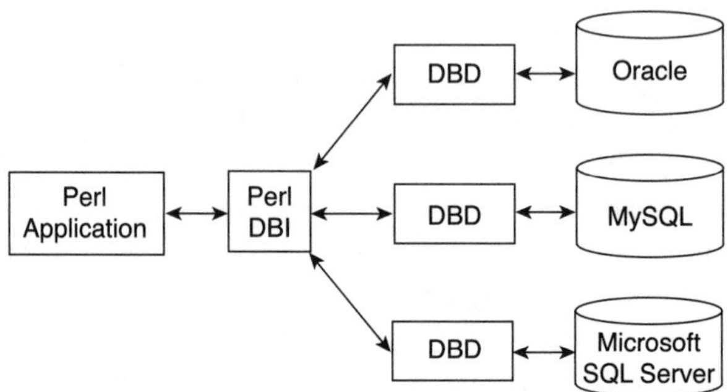


**Figure 6.1** Perl DBI architecture.

As you can see in the figure, the Perl DBI provides an API between your Perl application and the various RDBMSs. It is important to note that the API between your application and the Perl DBI remains consistent, regardless of the RDBMS. What does change, however, is a Database Dependent (DBD) driver that acts as the interface between the Perl DBI and the RDBMS. The DBD driver, as you can probably guess from the name, varies per database. It provides a translation between the RDBMS-independent DBI calls and the corresponding database-specific calls. As long as you load the appropriate DBD driver (which is just a Perl module) for your database, you only need to concern yourself with the API between your application and the Perl DBI—the underlying DBD drivers handle the rest.

## Perl Database Interface Example

Let's take a look at a short example showing a Perl DBI script. This example is using the MySQL open source database. Because we're demonstrating the Perl DBI, you can use any supported database. The only change that you will need to make to the example is to load and reference the appropriate driver for your database.

Back in Chapter 4, "Tree-Based Parser Modules," we discussed an example that used a short XML document containing contact information. The XML document from Chapter 4 is shown in the following as Listing 6.1.

Listing 6.1 **XML document containing contact information. (Filename: ch6_contacts.xml)**

```
<?xml version="1.0" encoding="UTF-8"?>
<contacts>
   <client>
      <name>Mark</name>
      <phone>111-222-3333</phone>
   </client>
   <client>
      <name>Joseph</name>
      <phone>222-333-4444</phone>
   </client>
</contacts>
```

Assume that this information is stored in a simple database table with two fields named name and phone. So, the database table would structure the contents as shown in Table 6.1.

Table 6.1 **Structure and contents of the contacts database table.**

| Name | Phone |
|---|---|
| Mark | 111-222-3333 |
| Joseph | 222-333-4444 |

The Perl program that demonstrates a simple database connection using the Perl DBI is shown in Listing 6.2. As you can see, it is a short program. However, it provides connectivity to a database and retrieves the data stored in a table named "contacts." Let's take a closer look at the example.

Listing 6.2 **Perl program that demonstrates the Perl DBI. (Filename: ch6_dbi_sample.pl)**

```
use strict;
use DBI;

# Initial required parameters.
my $database_name  = "example";
my $db_server      = "127.0.0.1";
my $db_port        = "3306";
my $db_user        = "mark";
my $db_password    = "mark's password";
my $databaseString = "DBI:mysql:$database_name:$db_server:$db_port";
```

*continues*

Listing 6.2 **Continued**

```
11.  my $array_ref;
12.
13.  # Connect to the RDBMS.
14.  my $dbh = DBI->connect($databaseString, $db_user, $db_password)
15.    or die "Can't connect to RDBMS: $DBI::errstr\n";
16.
17.  # This is the SQL statement we want to execute.
18.  my $sql_statement = "SELECT * FROM CONTACTS";
19.
20.  # Prepare and then execute the SQL statement.
21.  my $sth = $dbh->prepare($sql_statement);
22.  $sth->execute()
23.    or die "Can't execute SQL statement : $dbh->errstr";
24.
25.  # Loop through the array of results.
26.  while ( $array_ref = $sth->fetchrow_arrayref) {
27.    print "Name: $array_ref->[0]\nPhone: $array_ref->[1]\n\n";
28.  }
29.
30.  # Disconnect from the database.
31.  $dbh->disconnect;
```

**1–11** The opening section of the program includes the standard `use strict` pragma. Because this example uses the Perl DBI, we need to also have the `use DBI` pragma to load the Perl DBI module.

```
1.   use strict;
2.   use DBI;
3.
4.   # Initial required parameters.
5.   my $database_name  = "example";
6.   my $db_server      = "127.0.0.1";
7.   my $db_port        = "3306";
8.   my $db_user        = "mark";
9.   my $db_password    = "mark's password";
10.  my $databaseString = "DBI:mysql:$database_name:$db_server:$db_port";
11.  my $array_ref;
```

We'll need a few pieces of information to connect to the database. As you can see, we need to identify the following parameters:

- **Database name**—Name of the database.
- **Database server**—IP address or DNS resolvable hostname.
- **Database port**—Default port used by the database API.
- **Database user**—Username with appropriate permissions on the RDBMS.
- **Database password**—Password associated with the database username.

**13–23** After we've provided the appropriate information, we can go ahead and connect to the database. Note that if you're using a RDBMS other than MySQL, you'll need to insert the appropriate driver name.

After we're connected, we can start executing Structured Query Language (SQL) statements. In this example, because it is such a small table, we're going to execute the following SQL statement:

```
SELECT * FROM CONTACTS
```

This statement returns all the columns and rows in the `CONTACTS` table. We then use the `prepare` and `execute` methods to make the database query. The `prepare` statement sends the `query` statement to the database, which then verifies that it is properly formatted. After the statement has been prepared, we can execute the statement.

```
13. # Connect to the RDBMS.
14. my $dbh = DBI->connect($databaseString, $db_user, $db_password)
15.   or die "Can't connect to RDBMS: $DBI::errstr\n";
16.
17. # This is the SQL statement we want to execute.
18. my $sql_statement = "SELECT * FROM CONTACTS";
19.
20. # Prepare and then execute the SQL statement.
21. my $sth = $dbh->prepare($sql_statement);
22. $sth->execute()
23.   or die "Can't execute SQL statement : $dbh->errstr";
```

**25–31** After the SQL statement has been executed, we can retrieve a reference to the matching row(s) in the table. We then loop through all the matching rows and print out the results.

```
25. # Loop through the array of results.
26. while ( $array_ref = $sth->fetchrow_arrayref) {
27.   print "Name: $array_ref->[0]\nPhone: $array_ref->[1]\n\n";
28. }
29.
30. # Disconnect from the database.
31. $dbh->disconnect;
```

In our case, we had a very small table, and the SQL query yields the following results:

```
Name: Joseph
Phone: 222-333-4444

Name: Mark
Phone: 111-222-3333
```

After making the query, we call the `disconnect()` method to disconnect from the database.

Even though this was a simple example, you should be able to see that the Perl DBI is a very powerful tool, especially when combined with the XML modules that I'll discuss in the following sections. Let's start by looking at the XML::Generator::DBI module. It generates XML data based on the results of a SQL query.

## XML::Generator::DBI Perl Module

One of the most frequently performed tasks while integrating XML and RDBMS formats is transforming the query results returned by the database engine into XML data (either in memory, or written out in the form of an XML document). As I discussed earlier, the Perl DBI is a database-independent interface for accessing databases. It enables you to run SQL queries to extract data from a DBMS and returns this data in a Perl data structure. You can convert the results of a SQL query into XML by using the Perl XML::DBI::Generator module that was written by Matt Sergeant.

This module enables you to generate Simple API for XML (SAX) events that are created as the result of a SQL query to a RDBMS. Basically, this facilitates the transformation of the results of a SQL RDBMS query directly to XML.

The XML output can easily be customized by setting attributes when you instantiate an XML::DBI::Generator object. After the desired attributes are set, you can make the SQL query, and using a handler module (for example, XML::Handler::YAWriter), you can generate the SQL query results in XML. The module's wide range of supported attributes provides a number of different options. However, if this module still doesn't support something you need to do, you can easily write your own handler and customize the behavior. This demonstrates the power and flexibility of SAX-based XML parsing.

Let's now look at a scenario where XML::Generator::DBI can be put to work. We purposely avoided using a RDBMS in this first example; this scenario demonstrates the utility of the XML::Generator::DBI Perl module without requiring you to install a RDBMS. Depending on the RDBMS that you select, setup can range anywhere from trivial to challenging. I'll incorporate a RDBMS into a later example.

This first example uses a standard Comma Separated Value (CSV) file as our flat file database system. DBI has a driver for CSV that can manipulate the file as if it were a real RDBMS. This example only requires installation of the Perl DBI and DBD::CSV modules.

## XML::DBI::Generator Perl Module and CSV Example

In this example, we want to develop a Perl program that performs the following steps:

1. Create a table in the database.
2. Insert data into the table.
3. Query the database.
4. Convert the results of the query into XML.

Sounds like a real task requiring some code writing, right? In reality, this program is a lot shorter than you might think. This example requires less than one-half of a page of source code. This example demonstrates how quickly and easily you can create a real application by taking advantage of existing Perl modules. The Perl modules handle the low-level details, allowing you to focus on other aspects of the application.

### XML::DBI::Generator Perl Program

Now, let's take a closer look at the Perl program shown in Listing 6.3 that performs these tasks. In this example, we'll be using DBI and the DBD::CSV driver to create a database populated with some sample data that queries the data and generates a result set in XML format.

Listing 6.3 **Perl application using the XML::Generator::DBI module and DBI Perl modules. (Filename: ch6_dbi_csv_app.pl)**

```
use strict;
use XML::Generator::DBI;
use XML::Handler::YAWriter;
use DBI;

# Instantiate a new XML::Handler::YAWriter object.
my $ya = XML::Handler::YAWriter->new(AsFile => "-",
                  Pretty => {PrettyWhiteNewline => 1,
                   PrettyWhiteIndent => 1});

# Create a DBI connection.
my $dbh = DBI->connect("dbi:CSV:f_dir=./");
$dbh->{RaiseError} = 1;

# Create a database table with columns named id and name.
$dbh->do("CREATE TABLE USERS (ID INTEGER, NAME CHAR(10))");

# Insert data into the database table.
```

*continues*

Listing 6.3 **Continued**

```
19.  $dbh->do("INSERT INTO USERS (ID, NAME) VALUES (1, 'Larry Wall')");
20.  $dbh->do("INSERT INTO USERS (ID, NAME) VALUES (2, 'Tim Bunce')");
21.  $dbh->do("INSERT INTO USERS (ID, NAME) VALUES (3, 'Matt
     ➥Sergeant')");
22.  $dbh->do("INSERT INTO USERS (ID, NAME) VALUES (4, 'Ilya Sterin')");
23.  $dbh->do("INSERT INTO USERS (ID, NAME) VALUES (5, 'Robin Berjon')");
24.
25.  # Instantiate a new XML::Generator::DBI object.
26.  my $generator = XML::Generator::DBI->new(
27.                           Handler => $ya,
28.                           dbh => $dbh);
29.
30.  # Execute the enclosed SQL query.
31.  $generator->execute("SELECT ID, NAME FROM USERS");
32.
33.  # Remove the USERS table from the database.
34.  $dbh->do("DROP TABLE USERS");
35.
36.  # Disconnect from the CSV database.
37.  $dbh->disconnect();
```

**1–9** This program starts with the standard `use strict` pragma. Because we're using the XML::Generator::DBI, XML::Handler::YAWriter, and the DBI Perl modules, we need to include their respective `use` pragmas to load the modules. We're going to use the XML::Handler::YAWriter Perl module to serve as our event handler.

```
1.  use strict;
2.  use XML::Generator::DBI;
3.  use XML::Handler::YAWriter;
4.  use DBI;
5.
6.  # Instantiate a new XML::Handler::YAWriter object.
7.  my $ya = XML::Handler::YAWriter->new(AsFile => "-",
8.                               Pretty => {PrettyWhiteNewline => 1,
9.                                          PrettyWhiteIndent => 1});
```

**11–13** In this section, we call the DBI module's `connect()` function to connect a DBI object. The `RaiseError` attribute is then set to `true`; this will cause any DBI errors to terminate the program with an error message.

```
11.  # Create a DBI connection
12.  my $dbh = DBI->connect("dbi:CSV:f_dir=./");
13.  $dbh->{RaiseError} = 1;
```

**15–16** We call the DBI `do()` function, which allows us to immediately execute a query that does not require us to return a result set (for example, a `CREATE` or `INSERT SQL` statement). In this case, we execute the `CREATE TABLE` SQL statement that will create a new table named `USERS` with two fields, `ID` and `NAME`. Because we're using the DBD::CSV DBI driver case, this function will create a new file named `USERS`, which will act as our table.

```
15. # Create a database table with columns named id and name.
16. $dbh->do("CREATE TABLE USERS (ID INTEGER, NAME CHAR(10))");
```

**18–23** Now we insert some sample data into our newly created USERS table.

```
18. # Insert data into the database table.
19. $dbh->do("INSERT INTO USERS (ID, NAME) VALUES (1, 'Larry Wall')");
20. $dbh->do("INSERT INTO USERS (ID, NAME) VALUES (2, 'Tim Bunce')");
21. $dbh->do("INSERT INTO USERS (ID, NAME) VALUES (3, 'Matt Sergeant')");
22. $dbh->do("INSERT INTO USERS (ID, NAME) VALUES (4, 'Ilya Sterin')");
23. $dbh->do("INSERT INTO USERS (ID, NAME) VALUES (5, 'Robin Berjon')");
```

It just happens that I listed some of the major contributors in the Perl community. The contents of the database are show in Table 6.2.

Table 6.2 **Contents of the database table.**

| ID | Name |
|---|---|
| 1 | Larry Wall |
| 2 | Tim Bunce |
| 3 | Matt Sergeant |
| 4 | Ilya Sterin |
| 5 | Robin Berjon |

**25–28** Instantiate an XML::Generator::DBI object, setting its Handler and dbh attributes. Here we set XML::Handler::YAWriter as the SAX event handler that will receive events generated by the XML::Generator::DBI Perl module. In addition, we set the DBI database handle object ($dbh) to dbh. This is the database handle that the XML::Generator::DBI Perl module uses to execute database queries.

```
25. # Instantiate a new XML::Generator::DBI object.
26. my $generator = XML::Generator::DBI->new(
27.                           Handler => $ya,
28.                           dbh => $dbh);
```

**30–31** Here we call the XML::Generator::DBI execute() method, which actually executes our query and starts the transformation process from a result set to XML. Because XML::Handler::YAWriter's AsFile attribute was set to '-' in the XML::Handler::YAWriter constructor, the generated XML will be printed to STDOUT. If you need to generate an XML document instead of having it scroll by on STDOUT, supply an output filename to the XML::Handler::YAWriter constructor instead of the '-'.

```
30. # Execute the enclosed SQL query.
31. $generator->execute("SELECT ID, NAME FROM USERS");
```

**33–37** After making our queries and generating, we can now delete our `USERS` table and disconnect from the database. We execute the `DROP TABLE` function and then call the `disconnect()` function on the database handle.

```
33. # Remove the USERS table from the database.
34. $dbh->do("DROP TABLE USERS");
35.
36. # Disconnect from the CSV database
37. $dbh->disconnect();
```

The output of our XML::Generator::DBI Perl program is shown in Listing 6.4. As you can see, each `<row>` element in the XML document directly maps to a row from the database table. Note that the row elements and the root element in the generated XML document can be changed by using attributes from the XML::Generator::DBI module constructor.

Listing 6.4 **Output of the XML::Generator::DBI Perl program. (Filename: ch6_dbi_cvs_app_output.txt)**

```
<?xml version="1.0" encoding="UTF-8"?>
<database>
  <select
      query="SELECT ID, NAME FROM USERS">
    <row>
      <ID>1</ID>
      <NAME>Larry Wall</NAME>
    </row>
    <row>
      <ID>2</ID>
      <NAME>Tim Bunce</NAME>
    </row>
    <row>
      <ID>3</ID>
      <NAME>Matt Sergeant</NAME>
    </row>
    <row>
      <ID>4</ID>
      <NAME>Robin Berjon</NAME>
    </row>
    <row>
      <ID>5</ID>
      <NAME>Ilya Sterin</NAME>
    </row>
  </select>
</database>
```

This example was fairly simple and demonstrates an easy way to generate XML from a database result set where a more powerful approach is not needed. It allows a certain flexibility, but does not enable you to map database columns to XML element names or perform other types of customization. In the next section, we will look at another XML and RDBMS integration module that provides a more flexible approach.

## XML::DBMS Perl Module

The XML::DBMS Perl module is middleware for transferring data between XML and relational databases. Originally written by Ronald Bourret as a Java library, it was later ported to Perl by Nick Semenov. In this section, I'll be discussing version 1.1 of this library. Although it is a very powerful module, it is still lacking some important features. Most (if not all) of the missing features will be addressed in Version 2.0.

One of the missing features in the current version is type checking. The type-checking feature will allow users to transfer data between different database types. Using Version 1.1, you have to manually manage the different data types. As of this writing, Version 2.0 is still in alpha stages, so I won't discuss it here. As the development progresses, information becomes available on the official XML-DBMS web site, `http://www.rpbourret.com/xmldbms/`, as well as available on a number of mailing lists.

### XMl::DBMS Perl Module Example

Let's revisit the scenario discussed earlier of transferring data from one database to another. The XML::DBMS Perl module can be used to develop a middleware component using a mapping syntax to bind database column names to XML elements and vice versa.

In this example, we'll use XML as an intermediate storage facility during the translation. Why, you might ask, do I need an XML-based middleware component if I can just query one database and insert it into another? Well, if you have simultaneous access to both databases, you can easily develop a Perl DBI-based application to perform that task. However, the problem is a little more difficult if you have separate applications (one to read the source database and another to write to the source database), or if they don't have access to both databases at the same time. Let's say that your company is teaming with another company to compete for a contract and you both need to exchange some of your research and development work, and both databases reside behind firewalls. You'll need to use some type of a two-step process to transfer the data.

This example will consist of two databases, a source database named `from_db` and a destination database named `to_db`. The `from_db` database has a table named `membership`, and the `to_db` database has a table named `user_info`. For this example, we'll use a middleware XML component to transfer the contents of the `membership` table in the `from_db` database to the `user_info` table in the `to_db` database. The process is illustrated in Figure 6.2.

**Figure 6.2** Using XML middleware to translate between two databases.

Using XML as the intermediate data format has several benefits over a standard text file. For example, XML supports data type mapping and validation. In the next section, we'll take a look at the example based on the XML::DBMS Perl module.

### Create and Populate the Source Database Tables

To test the application, we'll need to first create two databases with tables and populate one table with sample seed data. The SQL statements must be entered at the `mysql` prompt or using the Perl DBI. To access the `mysql` prompt, type `mysql` at the command prompt on a Unix machine or from a DOS console. Another option is to download the MySQL GUI available for download at `http://www.mysql.com`.

> **Using a RDBMS for This Example**
>
> This example was developed using a MySQL database. MySQL is an open source database available for a number of platforms from `http://www.mysql.com`. You can follow along with any RDBMS as long as the Perl DBI supports your RDBMS (that is, a database driver is available for it). If you are using a RDBMS other than MySQL, you may need to modify the following SQL statements, but the majority of SQL standard-compliant databases process the SQL statements without any problems. An excellent MySQL book is *MySQL*, by Paul DuBois, available from New Riders.

Listing 6.5 **SQL statements to create and populate required databases and tables. (Filename: ch6_sql_statements.txt)**

```
create database from_db;
create database to_db;
use from_db;

create table if not exists membership (
user_id varchar(20),
first_name varchar(40),
last_name varchar(40));

insert into membership values ('isterin', 'Ilya', 'Sterin');
insert into membership values ('mriehl', 'Mark', 'Riehl');
insert into membership values ('pdubois', 'Paul', 'DuBois');
```

```
13.
14.  use to_db;
15.
16.  create table if not exists user_info (
17.  unique_user varchar(20),
18.  first_name varchar(40),
19.  last_name varchar(40));
```

Let's walk through the SQL statements shown in Listing 6.5. As I mentioned earlier, these are generic SQL statements that should work on any standards-compliant RDBMS.

**1–3** The first two lines create two databases named `from_db` and `to_db`. The `use from_db` statement selects the `from_db` as the current database. Until we select another database (by employing the use command again), all of our commands are directed at `from_db`.

```
1.  create database from_db;
2.  create database to_db;
3.  use from_db;
```

**5–12** This group of SQL commands creates a table named `membership` that has three columns: `user_id`, `first_name`, and `last_name`. All three columns are of the `varchar` data type. A `varchar` is a variable length character string, and the argument represents the maximum possible size. After creating the tables, we insert data. Note that the data is inserted in the same order that the columns were created (that is, `user_id`, `first_name`, and `last_name`). After these statements, we have a table named `membership`, and the contents are shown in Table 6.3.

```
5.  create table if not exists membership (
6.  user_id varchar(20),
7.  first_name varchar(40),
8.  last_name varchar(40));
9.
10. insert into membership values ('isterin', 'Ilya', 'Sterin');
11. insert into membership values ('mriehl', 'Mark', 'Riehl');
12. insert into membership values ('pdubois', 'Paul', 'DuBois');
```

Table 6.3 **Contents of the membership table.**

| user_id | first_name | last_name |
|---|---|---|
| Isterin | Ilya | Sterin |
| Mriehl | Mark | Riehl |
| Pdubois | Paul | DuBois |

**14–19** As I mentioned earlier, the use statement selects the current database. Now our commands are directed at the to_db database. We then create a table named user_info in the to_db database that has unique_user, first_name, and last_name columns defined. Note that the name of the first column has changed from user_id in the membership table to unique_user in the user_info table.

```
14. use to_db;
15.
16. create table if not exists user_info (
17. unique_user varchar(20),
18. first_name varchar(40),
19. last_name varchar(40));
```

### XML::DBMS Perl Application

The development of this application has three distinct steps. First, we create an XML document that holds the data pulled from the source database. Second, we generate an XML document that contains the mapping relationship between the source and destination databases. Finally, we develop the Perl program that actually performs the mapping. Let's take a look at the first step in the process.

#### *Develop the XML Storage Document*

We'll first need to create an XML::DBMS map file for the from_db database and specify the way it maps to the resulting XML file. The resulting XML file, as shown in Listing 6.6, is used as a temporary storage facility, which we'll then use to upload to the to_db database.

Listing 6.6 **XML document that will be used to store the contents of the source database. (Filename: ch6_from_db.xml)**

```
<?xml version="1.0" ?>
<!DOCTYPE XMLToDBMS SYSTEM "xmldbms.dtd">
<XMLToDBMS Version="1.0">
  <Options>
    <EmptyStringIsNull/>
  </Options>
  <Maps>
    <IgnoreRoot>
      <ElementType Name="users"/>
      <PseudoRoot>
        <ElementType Name="user"/>
        <CandidateKey Generate="No">
          <Column Name="user_id"/>
        </CandidateKey>
      </PseudoRoot>
```

```
16.       </IgnoreRoot>
17.       <ClassMap>
18.         <ElementType Name="user"/>
19.         <ToClassTable>
20.           <Table Name="membership"/>
21.         </ToClassTable>
22.         <PropertyMap>
23.           <ElementType Name="userid"/>
24.           <ToColumn>
25.             <Column Name="user_id"/>
26.           </ToColumn>
27.         </PropertyMap>
28.         <PropertyMap>
29.           <ElementType Name="firstname"/>
30.           <ToColumn>
31.             <Column Name="first_name"/>
32.           </ToColumn>
33.         </PropertyMap>
34.         <PropertyMap>
35.           <ElementType Name="lastname"/>
36.           <ToColumn>
37.             <Column Name="last_name"/>
38.           </ToColumn>
39.         </PropertyMap>
40.       </ClassMap>
41.     </Maps>
42.   </XMLToDBMS>
```

**1–3** Here we declare the XML document, specify an external DTD, and then declare the XMLToDBMS root tag, with which we specify the XML-DBMS version number.

```
1.  <?xml version="1.0" ?>
2.  <!DOCTYPE XMLToDBMS SYSTEM "xmldbms.dtd">
3.  <XMLToDBMS Version="1.0">
```

**4–6** The <Options> branch enables you to specify global options. In this example, the EmptyStringIsNull element indicates that we want to map empty values in the XML document to NULL columns in the database.

```
4.    <Options>
5.      <EmptyStringIsNull/>
6.    </Options>
```

**7–16** The IgnoreRoot element enables us to define the root element and the row element that will be used to wrap each individual row of data extracted from the database. Setting the ElementType's Name attribute to "users" indicates that we want the <users> element to be our root tag. The PseudoRoot element deals with the row element instances. We first define the element name we want to use for each row of data, so we set our ElementType's Name attribute to "user". Notice that we used the ElementType tag twice. We're allowed to do this because each use is in a different context because each case belongs to a different parent node. The `CandidateKey` construct enables us to specify the database column to use as our key. To define the key, we define a `Column` tag and set its `Name` attribute to `"user_id"`. As you can see, `"user_id"` is one of our columns names in the `from_db` database.

```
7.     <Maps>
8.       <IgnoreRoot>
9.         <ElementType Name="users"/>
10.        <PseudoRoot>
11.          <ElementType Name="user"/>
12.          <CandidateKey Generate="No">
13.            <Column Name="user_id"/>
14.          </CandidateKey>
15.        </PseudoRoot>
16.      </IgnoreRoot>
```

**17–42** We then proceed to define our `ClassMap` structure. The number of class maps should equal the number of tables from which the data is extracted. So, if data is extracted from two tables, we'll have to define two `ClassMap` structures, with each containing each table's map information. The `ElementType` tag appears again, and here it acts as a hint to map the rows from this particular `ClassMap` to the `<user>` element, which we already specified earlier to act as our row instance tag. The `ToClassTable` definition is used to specify the name of the table to which this `ClassMap` is mapping, therefore, we define the `Table` element and set its `Name` attribute to `"membership"`. Our last task is to define the `PropertyMap` construct(s) to map the column names to XML tag names. We must define one `PropertyMap` for each column name we want to map. The first instance of `PropertyMap` maps the `user_id` column within the membership table to `userid` tag in the resulting XML. The next two do the same for the `first_name` and `last_name` database columns.

```
17.      <ClassMap>
18.        <ElementType Name="user"/>
19.        <ToClassTable>
20.          <Table Name="membership"/>
21.        </ToClassTable>
22.        <PropertyMap>
23.          <ElementType Name="userid"/>
24.          <ToColumn>
25.            <Column Name="user_id"/>
26.          </ToColumn>
27.        </PropertyMap>
28.        <PropertyMap>
29.          <ElementType Name="firstname"/>
30.          <ToColumn>
31.            <Column Name="first_name"/>
```

```
        </ToColumn>
      </PropertyMap>
      <PropertyMap>
        <ElementType Name="lastname"/>
        <ToColumn>
          <Column Name="last_name"/>
        </ToColumn>
      </PropertyMap>
    </ClassMap>
  </Maps>
</XMLToDBMS>
```

### *Develop the XML Mapping Document*

You now have a pretty good idea of how to map a database to a resulting XML file. Now, let's look at the other half of the problem, mapping the resulting XML document to a different database. After that has been finished, you can easily transfer data from the source database to an XML file and back into the destination database. Listing 6.7 shows you how we can map the XML document that was built from the source database membership table to the destination database `user_info` table.

Listing 6.7 **XML document that defines the mapping from the old database to the new database. (Filename: ch6_to_db.xml)**

```
<?xml version="1.0" ?>
<!DOCTYPE XMLToDBMS SYSTEM "xmldbms.dtd">
<XMLToDBMS Version="1.0">
 <Options>
                <EmptyStringIsNull/>
  </Options>
  <Maps>
     <IgnoreRoot>
        <ElementType Name="users"/>
        <PseudoRoot>
           <ElementType Name="user"/>
           <CandidateKey Generate="No">
              <Column Name="unique_user"/>
           </CandidateKey>
        </PseudoRoot>
     </IgnoreRoot>
        <ClassMap>
        <ElementType Name="user"/>
        <ToClassTable>
           <Table Name="user_info"/>
        </ToClassTable>
        <PropertyMap>
           <ElementType Name="userid"/>
           <ToColumn>
```

*continues*

Listing 6.7 **Continued**

```
25.                 <Column Name="unique_user"/>
26.              </ToColumn>
27.           </PropertyMap>
28.           <PropertyMap>
29.              <ElementType Name="firstname"/>
30.              <ToColumn>
31.                 <Column Name="first_name"/>
32.              </ToColumn>
33.           </PropertyMap>
34.           <PropertyMap>
35.              <ElementType Name="lastname"/>
36.              <ToColumn>
37.                 <Column Name="last_name"/>
38.              </ToColumn>
39.           </PropertyMap>
40.        </ClassMap>
41.     </Maps>
42.  </XMLToDBMS>
```

**8–16** Starting with the `IgnoreRoot` element, we notice there is some similarity to Listing 6.6 (ch6_from_db.xml). The only change is that the `Name` attribute in the `<Column>` element is set to `"unique_user"` instead of `"user_id"`. This column is the key column in the `to_db` database. The root tags and the record tag remain the same as `users` and `user`, respectively.

```
8.        <IgnoreRoot>
9.           <ElementType Name="users"/>
10.          <PseudoRoot>
11.             <ElementType Name="user"/>
12.             <CandidateKey Generate="No">
13.                <Column Name="unique_user"/>
14.             </CandidateKey>
15.          </PseudoRoot>
16.       </IgnoreRoot>
```

**19–21** The `Table`'s `Name` attribute is also modified to contain the table name in the destination (`to_db`) database.

```
19.          <ToClassTable>
20.             <Table Name="user_info"/>
21.          </ToClassTable>
```

**22–42** The `PropertyMap` elements are used as they were in the previous map file to define the relationships between the tag names from the XML file containing the data and the database column's receiving the data.

```
22.          <PropertyMap>
23.             <ElementType Name="userid"/>
24.             <ToColumn>
25.                <Column Name="unique_user"/>
26.             </ToColumn>
```

```
            </PropertyMap>
            <PropertyMap>
               <ElementType Name="firstname"/>
               <ToColumn>
                  <Column Name="first_name"/>
               </ToColumn>
            </PropertyMap>
            <PropertyMap>
               <ElementType Name="lastname"/>
               <ToColumn>
                  <Column Name="last_name"/>
               </ToColumn>
            </PropertyMap>
         </ClassMap>
      </Maps>
   </XMLToDBMS>
```

After we define both map files—the first to map our `from_db` database to the XML file and the second to map the XML file's data to the `to_db` database—we can write a program to test our mappings and see if all is working as expected.

### *Developing the XML::XMLtoDBMS Perl Program*

Now that we've defined the XML document for data storage and data mapping, we can focus on the Perl program that actually does the transformation, as shown in Listing 6.8. Our program will first read the data from the source database (`from_db`), and then insert it into the destination database (`to_db`).

Keep in mind that in a real world application, this process might be divided into two steps. Remember, I mentioned the case where both databases might not be available due to a firewall or some other reason. In that case, we would retrieve the information and create the intermediate XML file using the XML document shown in Listing 6.6 (ch6_from_db.xml) then send it using the network connection to another location (possibly behind the destination RDBMS firewall). Then, we would use the XML document shown in Listing 6.7 (ch6_to_db.xml) to perform the mapping and to upload the contents into the destination database.

Listing 6.8 **Perl program that performs mapping between two databases. (Filename: ch6_xmltodbms_app.pl)**

```
use strict;
use DBI;
use XML::XMLtoDBMS;

# Instantiate a DBI connection to the source database.
my $dbh_from = DBI->connect(
```

*continues*

```
7.                      "dbi:mysql:database=from_db;host=localhost",
8.                      "username",
9.                      "password",
10.                     {RaiseError => 1, PrintError => 0});
11.
12. # Instantiate a new XMLtoDBMS object.
13. my $xmlToDbms = new XML::XMLtoDBMS($dbh_from);
14.
15. # Identify the first XML document required.
16. $xmlToDbms->setMap('ch6_from_db.xml');
17.
18. my $doc = $xmlToDbms->retrieveDocument('membership');
19.
20. # Open an intermediate output file.
21. open (XML, ">ch_6_middleware.xml") or
22.   die "could not open file for writing: $! \n";
23. print XML $doc->toString;
24. close XML or die "error closing file 'middleware.xml': $!";
25.
26. # Instantiate a DBI connection to the destination database.
27. my $dbh_to = DBI->connect(
28.                     "dbi:mysql:database=to_db;host=localhost",
29.                     "username",
30.                     "password",
31.                     {RaiseError => 1, PrintError => 0});
32.
33. # Perform the mapping.
34. $xmlToDbms->{DBh} = $dbh_to;
35. $xmlToDbms->setMap('ch6_to_db.xml');
36. $doc = $xmlToDbms->storeDocument( Source => {File =>
'middleware.xml'} );
37.
38. $xmlToDbms->destroy;
39.
40. # Disconnect from the source and destination databases.
41. $dbh_to->disconnect;
42. $dbh_from->disconnect;
```

**1–3** The opening section of the Perl program contains the standard `use strict` pragma. For this particular application, we need to load both the DBI and XML::XMLtoDBMS Perl modules.

```
1.  use strict;
2.  use DBI;
3.  use XML::XMLtoDBMS;
```

**5–10** We first make a database connection to the `from_db` database, from which we'll be retrieving our data. We also set the `RaiseError` attribute to `1` to turn on error checking, and the `PrintError` attribute is set to `0` to turn off printing errors to the console. Our program will now exit with an error message if anything goes wrong while communicating with the database. For more information on DBI methods and attributes (there are quite a few), see perldoc DBI.

```
5.   # Instantiate a DBI connection to the source database.
6.   my $dbh_from = DBI->connect(
7.                      "dbi:mysql:database=from_db;host=localhost",
8.                      "root",
9.                      "",
10.                     {RaiseError => 1, PrintError => 0});
```

**12–18** Now we create a new `XMLtoDBMS` object and pass it the database handle that we've just created, so that it will use this database connection handle to retrieve the data. Then we set the map using the `setMap()` function and pass it the path to the map that we are using for the `from_db` database. After we have provided the `XMLtoDBMS` object with a database handle and the XML mapping document (ch6_from_db.xml), we call the `retrieveDocument()` function and pass it the name of the table that contains the source data. Because we haven't specified any criteria to the SQL query (for example, select `user_id` from `membership`), all the contents of the table are retrieved by our query.

```
12.  # Instantiate a new XMLtoDBMS object.
13.  my $xmlToDbms = new XML::XMLtoDBMS($dbh_from);
14.
15.  # Identify the first XML document required.
16.  $xmlToDbms->setMap('ch6_from_db.xml');
17.
18.  my $doc = $xmlToDbms->retrieveDocument('membership');
```

**20–24** Here we write the resulting XML data to a file named ch6_middleware.xml. We first open a file for writing, then we call a `toString()` function on the object that was returned by the `retrieveDocument()` function. The `toString()` function returns XML data, which we then write to the file.

```
20.  # Open an intermediate output file.
21.  open (XML, ">ch_6_middleware.xml") or
22.    die "could not open file for writing: $! \n";
23.  print XML $doc->toString;
24.  close XML or die "error closing file 'middleware.xml': $!";
```

Listing 6.9 shows the contents of the intermediate XML document. This XML document stores the data retrieved from the source database (`from_db`) based on our custom XML mapping document (ch6_from_db.xml).

Listing 6.9 **Contents of the XML middleware document. (Filename: ch6_middleware.xml)**

```
<?xml version="1.0"?>
<users>
   <user>
      <firstname>Ilya</firstname>
      <userid>isterin</userid>
      <lastname>Sterin</lastname>
   </user>
   <user>
      <firstname>Mark</firstname>
      <userid>mriehl</userid>
      <lastname>Riehl</lastname>
   </user>
   <user>
      <firstname>Paul</firstname>
      <userid>pdubois</userid>
      <lastname>Dubois</lastname>
   </user>
</users>
```

**26–31** After we have generated our intermediate XML data storage file, we upload it to the destination database (`to_db`). Note that we need to create a new DBI connection because we're communicating with a different database. Using the Perl DBI, this connection could be to a different database (for example, Oracle) running on a different host.

```
26.  # Instantiate a DBI connection to the destination database.
27.  my $dbh_to = DBI->connect(
28.                   "dbi:mysql:database=to_db;host=localhost",
29.                   "username",
30.                   "password",
31.                   {RaiseError => 1, PrintError => 0});
```

**33–36** This section of the application is where we finalize our data upload process. We first assign our new database connection handle for the `to_db` database to the `DBh` attribute of the `$xmlToDbms` instance of the `XMLToDBMS` object. Notice, we don't need to create a new object instance, but rather we can dynamically change the `DBh` attribute and use it to perform operations on a different database. We also reset the map file using the `setMap()` function to ch6_to_db.xml, which is the XML map file that holds mapping information between our XML file and destination (`to_db`) database. After our new environment has been set up to upload the data, we call the `storeDocument()` function and pass it the ch6_middleware.xml file path through the `Source => {File => 'ch6_middleware.xml'}` hash of hashes data structure.

```
33. # Perform the mapping.
34. $xmlToDbms->{DBh} = $dbh_to;
35. $xmlToDbms->setMap('ch6_to_db.xml');
36. $doc = $xmlToDbms->storeDocument( Source => {File => 'ch6_middleware.xml'} );
```

**38–42** After all the processing has completed, we call the `destroy` function on the `XMLToDBMS` object instance, which deallocates and finalizes anything else it has outstanding and frees the resources. Finally, we disconnect from both of the databases.

```
38. $xmlToDbms->destroy;
39.
40. # Disconnect from the source and destination databases.
41. $dbh_to->disconnect;
42. $dbh_from->disconnect;
```

This was a fairly short example that performed a translation between two database tables. Granted, the tables were small, but you should be able to see how this process can easily be extended to larger tables, multiple tables, table filtering, and communication between multiple databases using the Perl DBI.

## Summary

As I've demonstrated in this chapter, XML can be easily integrated with database-driven applications and represent relational data. The inherent hierarchy of XML fits in very well with the relational database model. In addition, because XML is plain text, it can easily be transferred between two applications on different platforms (for example, Microsoft Windows and Linux) written in different languages (for example, Perl and Java). This chapter illustrates the power of XML—it is platform and language independent and can easily be used as the common middleware format when converting or working with two or more foreign data types.

## Exercises

1. What needs to be changed in the example in Listing 6.8 to support a two-step process (similar to what was discussed in the chapter)?
2. Assume that you need to develop a two-step application because the source database server and the destination database server are located in two different buildings. If you can't FTP between the machines, how would you transfer the XML middleware document? What would you need to change in the Perl DBI calls to connect to another database server on another host?

For suggested solutions to this exercise, be sure to check out the web site: `http://www.xmlproj.com/book/chapter6`.

## Relevant Links

Perl DBI Home Page: `http://dbi.perl.org`.
XML and Database Links: `http://www.rpbourret.com/xml/XMLDBLinks.htm`.
XML DBMS Middleware: `http://www.rpbourret.com/xmldbms/`.

# 7

# Transforming Miscellaneous Data Formats to XML (and Vice-Versa)

## Chapter Roadmap

This chapter discusses generating XML documents from various input data formats. The concept seems to be pretty simple; however, there is more to it than you might think. I'll also demonstrate the power of XML SAX technology when it is applied to other formats. You will see how the SAX interface can be implemented to process other data formats and how powerful this implementation can be. Although SAX stands for Simple API for XML, it's now becoming a lot more than that thanks to its well-defined standard and the generality of its implementation. SAX-like interfaces are now being implemented in other communities that deal with different data formats, so eventually the SAX acronym might stand for Simple API for X, with X being the unknown, and you fill in the blank.

Here is a quick summary of the topics discussed in this chapter.

- The section, "Why Convert Another Data Format to XML?" provides the answer to the question it poses.
- The section, "XML::SAXDriver::CSV Perl Module" covers XML generation based on the CSV (Comma Separated Value) input.

- The section, "XML::SAXDriver::Excel Perl Module" covers XML generation based on Microsoft Excel binary data.
- The section, "Developing a Custom Event Handler" goes over the concepts and contains an example of how to write a SAX driver for non-XML data.

To run the examples in this chapter, you will need to install the following Perl modules:

- XML::SAXDriver::CSV
- XML::SAXDriver::Excel

> **Note**
> If you have any questions about Perl modules (for example, where do you get them, how do you install them, and so forth), please refer to Appendix B, "Basic Perl Concepts."

## Why Convert Another Data Format to XML?

XML is everywhere. You see it online, read about it in publications, see it in the bookstore, and that's just the beginning. XML has quickly become the de facto way for applications to communicate. Although XML enjoys huge popularity, it is just now beginning to be widely implemented in applications; new standards are evolving almost weekly, and the technology still isn't even close to reaching its full potential.

Now, you might ask, how does that apply to this chapter? XML is powerful and there are numerous tools available to make it work. A majority of new applications are incorporating XML as the primary data interchange and data storage format. Given that, most applications that want to seamlessly integrate into the applications that utilize XML must adapt to the XML standard. Many legacy applications that are still deployed use either their native binary format or other widely adapted data formats to communicate. One of the most popular formats is CSV. Because CSV-formatted documents are just plain text, it is an easy format to adopt. One problem with CSV is that the data is not structured and can't be easily described, as it can with XML.

Another format that is commonly used and distributed among users on Microsoft Windows platforms is the binary Microsoft Excel format. Microsoft Excel is a spreadsheet application that supports data input, manipulation, and storage. This being the case, many applications enable their users to enter their data in Excel and then upload it into the system by accepting the binary Microsoft Excel files as input.

Because these types of problems exist, there are Perl modules designed to help you solve them. Remember, someone has probably already run into the problem you're having. SAXDriver modules are designed to facilitate converting other data formats into XML by giving you the flexibility of providing your own conversion rules and by being very efficient and light-weight (that is, small memory footprint). These are important qualities that would enable you to deploy these applications in a critical production environment and deal with large XML documents. Imagine the tasks that you could accomplish if you create an XML communication middleware application, and then effortlessly adapt any other format by converting it to XML without having to change the middleware business rules. Currently, two Perl modules enable you to easily accomplish this task: XML::SAXDriver::CSV and XML::SAXDriver::Excel. Let's take a closer look at these modules.

## XML::SAXDriver::CSV Perl Module

CSV format used to be the format of choice for small information interchange tasks between two applications. Just insert the data with each field separated by a comma and send. Here is a small sample of a CSV file that contains accounts receivable information:

```
Account Num,Name,Address,Balance
1,Mark Riehl,1600 Main Street,$39.95
2,Ilya Sterin,1299 Pine Street,$29.95
```

Note that each CSV record is on a separate line delimited by a newline. Usually (but not always), CSV files have a column title that appears on the first line of the file.

The receiving application just splits this data based on its delimiter, a comma, and proceeds to process this information. Several potential problems associated with using CSV files exist. First, the application must know the order of the fields in the file to make any sense out of this data. With XML, because every field is described by its tag name (and possibly attributes), the data does not necessarily have to be in any order, as long as both ends are communicating with data formatted using XML. Second, CSV files can be confusing if the data contains any embedded commas. The parsing application (whether it is Perl, C/C++, or Java) assumes that all commas separate fields (even if they should appear in the field). XML also has a facility for specifying data types (for example, text, float, integer, and so forth) by using XML schemas. Finally, CSV files don't have the notion of a data type, so applications that use CSV files treat all columns as plain text. Even with these disadvantages, CSV files are widely used and will continue to be for some time. So, we'll need to support them. Let's take a look at how easily we can develop a Perl program to convert a CSV file to XML.

## Converting a CSV File to XML

Let's assume that you've recently developed an application that processes XML data and updates the address book for the corporate mail server. It has been widely accepted throughout the company. Recently, your company merged with another company and you've been asked to consolidate the address book data from several of their legacy mail servers into one corporate database. The problem is that the legacy mail servers have been in place long before anyone heard of XML, so they can only export data in CSV format.

So, for this task, you will be given all the exported CSV address book data, but you need to convert all the CSV data to XML before your new application can process it. What's the best way to approach this problem? There are several ways to solve this problem. One solution is to use the XML::SAXDriver::CSV module, so let's take a closer look at how to do this.

### XML::SAXDriver::CSV Perl Module-Based Example

This example demonstrates the use of the XML::SAXDriver::CSV module that was written by Ilya Sterin (one of the authors) to covert our data from CSV to XML. This module supports fast stream-based conversions using a simple SAX-like interface. Because the XML::SAXDriver::CSV module is SAX2-compliant, the object properties resemble that of any SAX2 parser. That is one of the benefits of a SAX interface in the Perl modules—after you're familiar with the interface, you'll find that there are numerous applications for the interface. This module also provides options that can be utilized to customize the CSV to XML conversion. These module options are listed at the end of this section.

To solve this problem, we'll need to perform the following steps:

1. Identify the input data format (that is, fields in the CSV file).
2. Design the format of the output XML document.
3. Develop the Perl program to convert between the two defined formats.

Granted, these steps seem like common sense (and for the most part, they are), but you would be surprised how often people jump right into writing code. Things go a lot smoother when both the input and output formats are defined. Let's take a look at the format of the incoming CSV file.

### CSV Input Data Format

The CSV file exported from our legacy mail system contains customer address book information. Sometimes in an application such as this, you won't have the opportunity to design the content of the CSV file. It may come in only one format that may or may not support the format you're planning to use. So, you may need to perform some manipulation (for example, delete fields, reorder fields, and so forth). Listing 7.1 shows the input CSV file from the legacy mail server that contains two sample address book entries.

Listing 7.1 **Sample address book records in CSV format. (Filename: ch7_address_book.csv)**

```
First Name,Last Name,Nick,Title,Business Name,Address,City,State,Zip,
➥Phone Number 1,Phone Number 2
Ilya,Sterin,listerin,CTO,Unravelnet Software,3044 Perl Dr.,
➥Farmington Hills,MI,48334,247-555-1212,247-555-1213
Mark,Riehl,mark,Systems Developer,Software Company,4488 XML Street,
➥New Jersey,NJ,08736,255-545-8585,255-886-1432
```

The first row of the file contains the field names that identify the data in each column in the CSV file. As mentioned earlier, each row of the CSV column represents one record. Now that we know the format of the input data, our next step is to design the structure of the XML output file.

**CSV files and column headings**

Note that our example has column headings, however, this varies from application to application (that is, there aren't any rules that say they're required). So, don't count on always having column headings to define the fields; sometimes, the column heading titles are defined in separate files. I've included column headings to illustrate a particular feature of the Perl module.

### XML Output File Format

Our application that converts between CSV and XML uploads this data based on the field names that appear in the column names in the first row of the CSV file. These column names will be used as the names of our elements in the generated XML file. So, we need to verify that the column heading names are the element names that we'd like to use in the generated XML file. If not, we can either change the names of the column headings in the CSV file or perform a mapping in the conversion program.

We're almost at the point where we can start discussing the program that performs the conversion between CSV and XML. Before we do that, let's take a look at a sample record in XML, based on the format we just discussed. The sample XML file is shown in Listing 7.2. Note that the root element named `address_book` has one child `record` element. The `record` element has multiple children. Remember, this is considered a single record because the file contains only one `record` element.

Listing 7.2 **Sample XML file containing one record from the CSV file. (Filename: ch7_address_book.xml)**

```
<address_book>
   <record>
    <First_Name>Ilya</First_Name>
    <Last_Name>Sterin</Last_Name>
    <Nick>listerin</Nick>
    <Title>CTO</Title>
    <Business_Name>Unravelnet Software</Business_Name>
    <Address>3044 Perl Dr.</Address>
    <City>Farmington Hills</City>
    <State>MI</State>
    <Zip>48334</Zip>
    <Phone_Number_1>247-555-1212</Phone_Number_1>
    <Phone_Number_2>247-555-1213</Phone_Number_2>
  </record>
</address_book>
```

As you can see, all the column names in the CSV file have spaces, which are replaced with underscores (_) when using them as tag names. This is the default behavior of XML::SAXDriver::CSV—it replaces any illegal XML element name character with an underscore. The substitution character is user-defined (as you'll see in Listing 7.3).

### CSV to XML Conversion Using the XML::SAXDriver::CSV Perl Module

Let's now take a look at a simple Perl program that performs the CSV to XML conversion required of the address book data. The program is shown in Listing 7.3. Let's take a closer look at the program and walk through each of the major sections.

Listing 7.3 **CSV to XML conversion program. (Filename: ch7_csv_xml_app.pl)**

```
use strict;
use XML::SAXDriver::CSV;
```

```
3.   use XML::Handler::YAWriter;
4.   use IO::File;
5.
6.   my $input_file = shift;
7.
8.   my $csv = XML::SAXDriver::CSV->new();
9.
10.  my $writer = XML::Handler::YAWriter->new(
11.            Output => IO::File->new(">ch7_csv_to_xml.xml"),
12.                      Pretty => {PrettyWhiteIndent => 1,
13.                      PrettyWhiteNewline => 1});
14.
15.  $csv->parse(Source => {SystemId => $input_file},
16.              Handler => $writer,
17.              Declaration => {Version => '1.0'},
18.              Dynamic_Col_Headings => 1);
```

### *Initialization*

**1–6** The opening section of the program has the standard pragma statement (`use strict`). For this program, we need to use the following three modules:

- XML::SAXDriver::CSV
- XML::Handler::YAWriter
- IO::File

All three modules are required because they work together in this particular application. The XML::SAXDriver::CSV Perl module is a SAX driver, so it requires a SAX2 handler to process the SAX-generated events. The XML::Handler::YAWriter Perl module serves as that handler and is a writer module that will also format and output the XML data. You can also write your own custom handlers if this one does not serve your purpose. Finally, the IO::File module is used to create a file object that is provided as input to the XML::Handler::YAWriter module.

After all the modules are loaded, we use `shift()` to retrieve the name of the input file that will be provided as a command-line argument for this program.

```
1.   use strict;
2.   use XML::SAXDriver::CSV;
3.   use XML::Handler::YAWriter;
4.   use IO::File;
5.
6.   my $input_file = shift;
```

### *Creating the Required Objects*

**8–13** Now that we have the input file handle, we next need to create an XML::SAXDriver::CSV object calling the `new()` function. You can initialize the properties of the XML::SAXDriver::CSV by just simply passing them in a hash of typical key/value pairs. Any properties set at this time will be global for this object instance, and any method that is called using this instance of the XML::SAXDriver::CSV object will use those global values. Global values can be reset or changed by modifying the value that was assigned to the property.

```
8.   my $csv = XML::SAXDriver::CSV->new();
9.
10.   my $writer = XML::Handler::YAWriter->new(
11.            Output => IO::File->new(">ch7_csv_to_xml.xml"),
12.                      Pretty => {PrettyWhiteIndent => 1,
13.                      PrettyWhiteNewline => 1});
```

Also, you can override the global value with a call to another function that will localize the value until the end of that particular function. This relationship is illustrated in Figure 7.1.

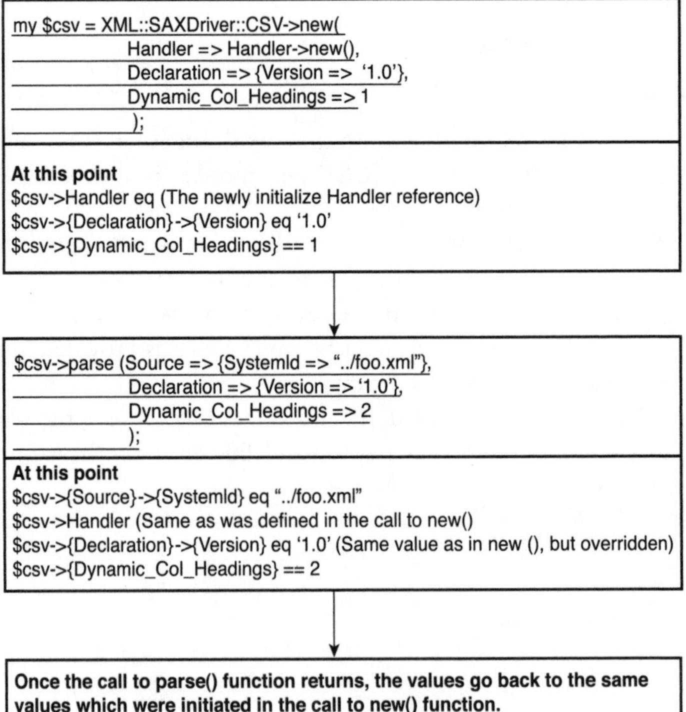


**Figure 7.1** The `Object` property's scope.

After we initialize our XML::SAXDriver::CSV object, the next step is to create and initialize an XML::Handler::YAWriter object, so that we can use it as a handler. The XML::Handler::YAWriter module's new method is where we do our customization to output the XML data in a particular format. For example, we can specify the output type (such as, file or scalar), custom escaping, and formatting.

The `Output` property is assigned the handle to a file, `out.xml`, which is used to output the generated XML data and is opened for writing. `Pretty` is an anonymous hash that contains information for pretty printing, and we set `PrettyWhiteIndent` and `PrettyWhiteNewline` to true (`1`), to place each element on its own line as well as indent it based on the depth level.

### *Converting from CSV to XML*

**15–18** Now, all the setup work has been finished and we're actually ready to call the XML::SAXDriver::CSV `parse` function to perform the conversion.

```
15.   $csv->parse(Source => {SystemId => $input_file},
16.               Handler => $writer,
17.               Declaration => {Version => '1.0'},
18.               Dynamic_Col_Headings => 1);
```

As I mentioned before, most properties resemble those of SAX2 parsers that were discussed in Chapter 3, "Event-Driven Parser Modules," although a few extra additional capabilities have been added to enable customization of the conversion process. One of the properties used in this example is `Dynamic_Col_Headings`. This property tells the conversion processor to use the values in the first row (that is, the column headings) as the XML element names. Remember, some CSV files may not have the column names in the first row, so verify this before using this property. If any of the column names contain an illegal character (for example, a space), it will be replaced with an underscore (_) by default. If, for some reason, you don't want to use an underscore as the replacement character, you can specify a different replacement character by setting the `SubChar` property.

### *CSV to XML Conversion Program Output*

When we run the CSV to XML conversion program, the file ch7_csv_to_xml.xml is created. The contents of the ch7_csv_to_xml.xml file are shown in Listing 7.4. Remember, the conversion program takes the name of the input CSV file as a command-line argument.

Listing 7.4 **Results of the conversion from CSV to XML. (Filename: ch7_csv_to_xml.xml)**

```
<?xml version="1.0" encoding="UTF-8"?>
<records>
  <record>
    <First_Name>Ilya</First_Name>
    <Last_Name>Sterin</Last_Name>
    <Nick>listerin</Nick>
    <Title>CTO</Title>
    <Business_Name>Unravelnet Software</Business_Name>
    <Address>3044 Perl Dr.</Address>
    <City>Farmington Hills</City>
    <State>MI</State>
    <Zip>48334</Zip>
    <Phone_Number_1>247-555-1212</Phone_Number_1>
    <Phone_Number_2>247-555-1213</Phone_Number_2>
  </record>
  <record>
    <First_Name>Mark</First_Name>
    <Last_Name>Riehl</Last_Name>
    <Nick>mark</Nick>
    <Title>System Developer</Title>
    <Business_Name>Software Company</Business_Name>
    <Address>4488 XML Street</Address>
    <City>New Jersey</City>
    <State>NJ</State>
    <Zip>08736</Zip>
    <Phone_Number_1>255-545-8585</Phone_Number_1>
    <Phone_Number_2>255-886-1432</Phone_Number_2>
  </record>
</records>
```

As you can see, with less than 10 lines of Perl source code, we converted a CSV file to an XML file. These drivers were designed to be this easy to use; however, they are also very flexible and can support more complex situations if required. For example, if the XML::SAXDriver::CSV's options don't satisfy your requirements, you can easily write your own customized handler class. This will be demonstrated later in this chapter.

# XML::SAXDriver::Excel Perl Module

I've demonstrated how to generate XML data from a CSV file. Now, we're going to look at another SAX-based Perl module, XML::SAXDriver::Excel. As you may have already guessed from the name, this Perl module facilitates the conversion between standard Microsoft Excel spreadsheet files and XML. Why not just save the Microsoft Excel spreadsheet file as CSV and use the Perl module that we discussed in the previous section? Well, you can do that. However, one situation when this module comes in handy is when you have a large number of Microsoft Excel spreadsheet files to convert to XML; this can save you the trouble of converting a large number of files to CSV format. Let's take a look at an example of how to use this module.

## Converting Microsoft Excel Spreadsheet Files to XML

Let's assume that your company has a financial application that tracks company expenses. This information is maintained for use by other applications within the company and is accessed by a reporting application that provides customized reports to users. As with any integration project, this data is best kept in XML format, so that any application (internal or even external to your company) that needs access to the data can easily retrieve it. The problem is that most accountants don't know XML, nor do they need to. One of their most widely used tools of choice is Microsoft Excel, which is used to store, manipulate, and save their data. However, they occasionally need to upload their data to a database server to share the data with those within the company, however, it may be physically located at different geographical sites. One of the tools that you've developed provides an upload capability; however, your application requires XML as input. So, you will need to convert the Microsoft Excel spreadsheet files to XML format.

What's the best way to do this? As I mentioned earlier, you can save each Microsoft Excel spreadsheet file as a CSV file and use the XML::SAXDriver::CSV module. However, for large-scale conversions (that is, a large number of Microsoft Excel spreadsheet files), this would be too time consuming. Imagine how long it would take to open 100 Microsoft Excel spreadsheet files and save them as CSV; this is not an option. A better choice in this situation is to use the XML::SAXDriver::Excel Perl module to facilitate the conversion directly from a Microsoft Excel spreadsheet file to XML. Let's take a look at how to do this conversion with an example.

## XML::SAXDriver::Excel Perl Module Example

The solution is actually pretty simple, especially after I just demonstrated the XML::SAXDriver::CSV Perl module. The XML::SAXDriver::Excel module has the same interface as the XML::SAXDriver::CSV module, thanks in part to SAX standard. The complexities of parsing the underlying Microsoft Excel spreadsheet file are hidden from the user.

The Microsoft Excel document that needs to be converted to XML is shown in Table 7.1. As you can see, it is a typical spreadsheet that contains expense or budgeting information. Note that the spreadsheet has column headings in the first row and several records of data.

Table 7.1 **Microsoft Excel file containing business expenses. (Filename: Ch7_excel_input.xls)**

| Employee ID | Expense | Amount | Description | Date | Dept | Manager |
|---|---|---|---|---|---|---|
| 32884 | Hotel | $120 | One night stay during training travel | 1/5/2002 | 38 | John Smith |
| 29833 | Restaurant | $50 | Client entertainment | 2/20/2002 | 11 | Jane Wilson |
| 10997 | Gas | $25 | Two day training travel expense | 2/17/2002 | 38 | John Smith |
| 27342 | Office Supplies | $45 | Misc. Office Supplies | 1/10/2002 | 94 | Jonathan Dawson |

To convert this Microsoft Excel file to XML, we exercise the XML::SAXDriver::Excel Perl module in the same way we used the XML::SAXDriver::CSV Perl module in the last example. The new program based on the XML::SAXDriver::Excel Perl module is shown in Listing 7.5. If you compare this listing to the XML::SAXDriver::CSV-based program shown back in Listing 7.3, you'll see that the programs are basically the same except for two changes. First, we need the following statement at the top of the file to load the XML::SAXDriver::Excel module instead of the XML::SAXDriver::CSV module:

```
2.   use XML::SAXDriver::Excel;
```

The second change between the programs occurs on line 7. In the previous example, we created a new XML::SAXDriver::CSV object; however, in this example, we need to create a new XML::SAXDriver::Excel object. So, we use the following line to accomplish this:

```
7.   my $csv = XML::SAXDriver::Excel->new();
```

Note that the two changed lines are both shown in bold text in Listing 7.5. Other than that, the programs are identical. This is very powerful if you think about it. We added support to our application for a different input data type with literally a two-line change.

Listing 7.5 **Program to convert a Microsoft Excel input file to XML. (Filename: Ch7_excel_xml_app.pl)**

```
use strict;
use XML::SAXDriver::Excel;
use XML::Handler::YAWriter;
use IO::File;

my $input_file = shift;
my $csv = XML::SAXDriver::Excel->new();
my $writer = XML::Handler::YAWriter->new(
            Output => IO::File->new(">ch7_excel_to_xml.xml"),
            Pretty => { PrettyWhiteIndent => 1,
                        PrettyWhiteNewline => 1
            }
);

$obj->parse(Source => {SystemId => $input_file},
      Handler => $writer,
      Declaration => {Version => '1.0'},
      Dynamic_Col_Headings => 1
);
```

We could easily merge the last two examples together to support both input files within the same program. One approach would be to create two subroutines—one to convert input CSV files and the other to convert input Microsoft Excel files. We could filter the input files based on the file name extension (that is, .csv or .xls) and then easily call the appropriate subroutine based on the input data type.

### Microsoft Excel File to XML Conversion Program Output

When we run our Microsoft Excel spreadsheet file to XML conversion program, the file out.xml is generated. Listing 7.6 shows the contents of out.xml. As you can see, this XML file contains the information that was originally stored in the Microsoft Excel spreadsheet. Note that the application takes a single command-line argument—the name of the input Microsoft Excel file.

Listing 7.6 **Output XML generated by the conversion from Microsoft Excel to XML. (Filename: ch7_excel_to_xml.xml)**

```
<?xml version="1.0" encoding="UTF-8"?>
<records>
  <record>
    <Employee_ID>32884</Employee_ID>
    <Expense>Hotel</Expense>
    <Amount>120</Amount>
    <Description>One night stay during training travel</Description>
    <Date>1-5-02</Date>
    <Department>38</Department>
    <Manager>John Smith</Manager>
  </record>
  <record>
    <Employee_ID>29833</Employee_ID>
    <Expense>Restaurant</Expense>
    <Amount>50</Amount>
    <Description>Client entertainment</Description>
    <Date>2-20-02</Date>
    <Department>11</Department>
    <Manager>Jane Wilson</Manager>
  </record>
  <record>
    <Employee_ID>10997</Employee_ID>
    <Expense>Gas</Expense>
    <Amount>25</Amount>
    <Description>Two day training travel expense</Description>
    <Date>2-17-02</Date>
    <Department>38</Department>
    <Manager>John Smith</Manager>
  </record>
  <record>
    <Employee_ID>27342</Employee_ID>
    <Expense>Office Supplies</Expense>
    <Amount>45</Amount>
    <Description>Misc. Office Supplies</Description>
    <Date>1-10-02</Date>
    <Department>94</Department>
    <Manager>Johnathan Dawson</Manager>
  </record>
</records>
```

Note that the root XML file element and its child element are named `<records>` and `<record>`, respectively. This is the default behavior of both the XML::SAXDriver::CSV and XML::SAXDriver::Excel modules. You can easily redefine these tags by setting the `File_Tag` and `Parent_Tag` properties as shown in the following, or by providing them as an argument to either the `new()` or the `parse()` functions.

```
$obj->{File_Tag} = "Expense_Report";
$obj->{Parent_Tag} = "Expense";
```

Doing so, we'll appropriately use these properties for the output XML file elements.

```
<Expense_Report>
  <Expense>
    ...
    ...
  </Expense>
</Expense_Report>
```

Note that the rest of the `<record>` element's children directly correspond to the first row headings in the Microsoft Excel spreadsheet file.

We've now seen how easily you can convert both CSV and Microsoft Excel files to XML. Both the XML::SAXDriver::CSV and XML::SAXDriver:: Excel modules provide a simple, flexible interface.

As flexible as these modules are, there are times where we may need to extend the functionality of one of these modules to accomplish a more complex task. If so, then you'll need to develop your own custom event handler. I'll demonstrate how to write your own custom event handler in the next section.

# Developing a Custom Event Handler

There may be situations when the standard event handler modules won't support what you need to do. For example, let's say that you want to combine standard event handling with regular expression matching, substitutions, or state management. These are tasks that aren't supported by the standard event handlers.

Depending on the requirements, the standard event handler may seem somewhat limited. So, to get around the limitations of the standard event handler, we can create our own SAX handler. This handler will use the SAX interface to manipulate and generate XML data. It's very simple as long as the standard method names are used for different events. Each method can be customized to fit our needs on a specific project. Let's take a look at an example.

## Custom Event Handler Package Example

In this example, we're going to create a customized event handler as a package. What is a package? A *package* is a block of Perl source code that is assigned its own namespace. Because the package is assigned to its own namespace, there can't be any conflicts with an application (for example, duplicate variable names).

Note that packages are not the same as files. Multiple packages can reside in one Perl file, however, you cannot spread a package across multiple files. Typically, there is one package per file. If you have one package in a file, you're required to name the file the same name as the package, and the extension to the file must be .pm, which identifies a Perl module.

Let's take a look at Listing 7.7 and see how to create your own customized event handler package. Each of the handlers in the package are discussed in the following.

Listing 7.7 **Customized event handler package. (Filename: ch7_custom_handler.pl)**

```
package Custom_Handler;

sub new {
  my $class= ref $_[0] || $_[0];
  return bless {}, $class;
}

# start_document handler
sub start_document {
  my $code_handler= shift;
  my $document= shift;
}

# end_document handler
sub end_document {
  my $code_handler= shift;
  my $document= shift;
}

# start_element handler
sub start_element {
  my $code_handler= shift;
  my $element= shift;
  my $name= $element->{Name};
  my $atts= $element->{Attributes};
  print "<$name";

  # Loop through all the attributes
  foreach my $att (sort keys %$atts) {
    print " $att='$atts->{$att}'";
  }
  print ">";
}

# characters handler
```

```
36.  sub characters {
37.    my $code_handler= shift;
38.    my $character= shift;
39.      print $character->{Data} if( defined $character->{Data});
40.  }
41.
42.  # end_element handler
43.  sub end_element {
44.    my $code_handler= shift;
45.    my $element= shift;
46.      my $name= $element->{Name};
47.    print "</$name>";
48.  }
```

**1–6** Our `Custom_Handler` package needs to contain the `new()` method to create a new instance of the object to later pass as the handler. This is a non-SAX2 standard method in our case, although it is pretty standard for the majority of Perl Object Oriented (OO) modules. The module is considered to be non-standard because it provides additional capabilities in addition to those defined in the standard. All other methods must be included, even if they don't contain any code. If we don't define one of the required methods, the interpreter will complain of a missing subroutine.

```
1.   package Custom_Handler;
2.
3.   sub new {
4.     my $class= ref $_[0] || $_[0];
5.     return bless {}, $class;
6.   }
```

**8–18** The `start_document()` and the `end_document()` methods create a new instance of XML data. In our case, we don't use it for any particular purpose, although we must still include the method because XML::SAXDriver::Excel and XML::SAXDriver::CSV modules will attempt to call it.

```
8.   # start_document handler
9.   sub start_document {
10.    my $code_handler= shift;
11.    my $document= shift;
12.  }
13.
14.  # end_document handler
15.  sub end_document {
16.    my $code_handler= shift;
17.    my $document= shift;
18.  }
```

**20–33** The `start_element()` method is called when the parser wants to output the opening XML tag. Two arguments are passed to this subroutine, the first being the `Handler` instance and the second being a reference to a hash containing the tag information needed to output a valid XML tag. Line 24 assigns the `$element->{NAME}` which contains the XML tag name. Line 25 refers to `$element->{Attributes}` which is another reference to a hash that holds the attributes names/data in the hash-like key/value format. As you can see from the code, you must output tag opening < and closing > characters yourself.

```
20.  # start_element handler
21.  sub start_element {
22.    my $code_handler= shift;
23.    my $element= shift;
24.    my $name= $element->{Name};
25.    my $atts= $element->{Attributes};
26.    print "<$name";
27.
28.    # Loop through all the attributes
29.    foreach my $att (sort keys %$atts) {
30.      print " $att='$atts->{$att}'";
31.    }
32.    print ">";
33.  }
```

**35–40** The `characters()` subroutine is called when the parser encounters the actual data to be written in between the opening and closing XML tags. The sub is passed the instance of the object as well as a reference to a hash with the data assigned to its `{Data}` key.

```
35.   # characters handler
36.  sub characters {
37.    my $code_handler= shift;
38.    my $character= shift;
39.      print $character->{Data} if( defined $character->{Data});
40.  }
```

**42–48** Now we define the `end_element()` subroutine, which is used to close the XML tag. It is passed the same arguments as the `start_element()` method, although you would not expect the reference `{Attributes}` to contain data because XML 1.0 specifications do not allow attributes for closing tags.

```
# end_element handler
sub end_element {
  my $code_handler= shift;
  my $element= shift;
    my $name= $element->{Name};
  print "</$name>";
}
```

Now that we've developed this custom handler, how do we use it? This handler can be used in the following manner:

```
my $handler= new Custom_Handler;
my $driver_obj = XML::SAXDriver::CSV->new(Source => {SystemId =>

"customer_signup.csv"},
                                          Handler => $code_handler,
                                          Dynamic_Col_Headings => 1,
                                          File_Tag   => 'code');
$driver_obj->parse();
```

As you can see, we easily developed a `Custom_Handler` object to use the handler with either XML::SAXDriver::Excel or XML::SAXDriver::CSV modules. This is by no means a complete version of the handler, but it can definitely be used as a template.

One important part that we would also need to implement is the escaping subroutine, which is used to escape/convert illegal characters in the XML tag names as well as XML data. We can do this by simply converting &, <, ", >, and ' to the equivalent of `&`, `<`, `"`, `>`, and `'`. This is the simplest implementation of the escaping subroutine, although there are some more encoding issues that might need to be taken into consideration, however this is a totally different issue that I will not cover in this section.

My recommendation is to first always try to use an existing handler modules, such as the XML::Handler::YAWriter Perl module. This module is well documented, stable, and widely used. Because XML::Handler::YAWriter is a popular Perl module, most (if not all) of the bugs have been encountered and eliminated. However, there may be times when the standard modules can't support your requirements. Now, with the option of a custom module, you should be able to handle just about any task.

## Summary

This chapter presented several methods of converting from various data formats to XML. The input data formats that I discussed were CSV and Microsoft Excel spreadsheet files. These are two popular formats for exchanging data. Other data formats (for example, text files using other delimiters, such as spaces, tabs, or pipes) can easily be converted to CSV, so the examples discussed in this chapter would still be applicable.

The next chapter, Chapter 8, "XML Transformation and Filtering," will also discuss the conversion between formats. However, the major difference is that in Chapter 9, "AxKit," we'll start with an XML file and convert it to different formats using XSLT. I'll provide several examples to illustrate the different Perl modules available for these tasks.

## Exercises

1. Given the CSV data shown in the following, create a file named **exer_1.csv**. Write a Perl program using the XML::SAXDriver::XML module that will convert the CSV file to XML.

   Name the root element `<exercise1>` and then use the first column names as the element names (hint: `Dynamic_Col_Headings`). Use the XML::Handler::YAWriter as the event handler. Generate a new file named **exer_1.xml** containing the results.

   ```
   Class,Teacher,Time,Room,Lab
   Biology,Mrs. Riehl,10:00 - 11:00,103,Y
   Marine Science,Mrs. Riehl,11:30 - 12:30, 103,N
   Algebra,Mr. McCarthy,1:00 - 2:00,114,N
   Computer Science,Mr. Burns,3:00 - 4:00,204,Y
   ```

2. Now modify the program and write your own handler to handle the CSV data. Don't forget to take out the XML::Handler::YAWriter dependency (that is, use XML::Handler::YAWriter as well as the Handler assignment).

For suggested solutions to all these exercises, be sure to check out the book's web site.

# IV
# Advanced XML and Perl

# 8

# XML Transformation and Filtering

## Chapter Roadmap

This chapter discusses XML transformation and filtering. XML transformation is the process of converting an XML document into one or more output documents. These output documents can be any one of a number of different formats. Some of the possible resulting document formats include the following: XML, XHTML, HTML, WML, RTF, and CSV.

Two types of XSL-based transformations exist—a formatting language and a transformation language. The formatting language, XML Formatting Objects (XSL-FO) is used to create text layouts for documents. As of this writing, no major browsers support XSL-FO, so most XSL-FO is converted into another format (for example, PDF or $T_EX$) for viewing.

In this chapter, we're going to focus on the XSL Transformation (XSLT) standard that defines the transformation language. This language is a tags-based scripting language that enables you to generate output from XML data in a wide variety of text formats. An XSLT processor applies these rules to an input XML document and generates the desired output. These rules are stored in an XSLT stylesheet.

Filtering describes the process of using XSLT to generate a new XML document that is a subset of the larger XML source document. In essence, you develop a set of rules that filter out the portion(s) of the source XML document that you require.

This chapter discusses the format of transformation rules and demonstrate how to apply them. As is usually the case with Perl, there are several Perl modules that can be used to perform the transformation. I will provide an example for each of the major Perl XSLT modules and discuss the differences between each of the modules. This will assist you in making the proper decision about which module you should use for a particular task.

To run the examples presented in this chapter, you'll need to install the following Perl modules:

- XML::LibXSLT
- XML::Sablotron
- XML::Xpath

> **Note**
>
> Remember, if you have any questions about Perl modules (for example, where do you get them, how to install them, and so forth) please refer to Appendix B, "Perl Essentials."

## XSLT Introduction

XSLT is a very powerful tool in the XML toolkit. It is an XML-based standard that facilitates the transformation of an XML document into another format. Depending on your requirements, the output document can be one of (but not limited to) the following formats:

- XML
- XHTML
- HTML
- WML
- RTF
- CSV
- Others

As you can see, the term XSLT processing describes any one of a number of tasks. Given an input XML document, a transformation could change an element name; the character data inside an element can be modified; an attribute can be changed; or elements and attributes can be filtered, so that they don't appear in the output XML document. XSLT is a powerful tool that enables us to easily change the contents of an XML document based on our requirements.

Figure 8.1 shows the components of an XSLT process. As you can see in the figure, there are three required components to any XSLT-based transformation:

- Input XML document
- XSLT processor
- XSLT stylesheet

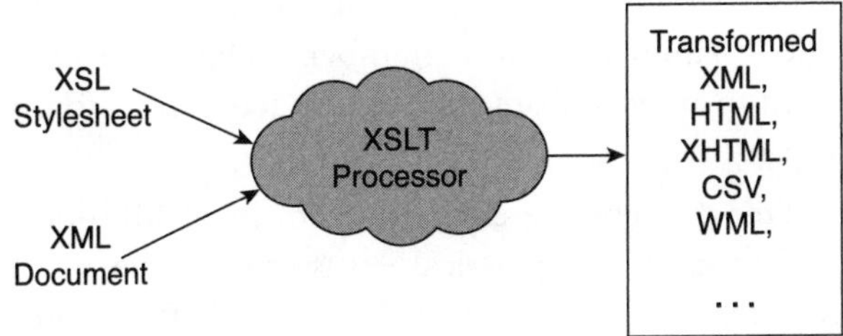


**Figure 8.1** XSLT transformation process.

An important concept to take away from Figure 8.1 is that the data only flows in one direction. The input is always XML to XSLT; processors don't generate XML, they only transform XML to other formats.

The input XML document is the source of the data that will be transformed. Note that this is the only data source available for this transformation (that is, all information in the transformed files is the entire contents or a subset of the input XML document). The fundamental components of the XSLT transformation process are XSLT stylesheets and the XSLT processor.

Why would we want to convert an XML document into another XML document? Several situations exist in which we would want to convert between XML and another format.

Probably the two most widely used transformations are converting XML documents to other XML documents and converting XML documents to HTML documents. Let's take a look at a few situations in which these two transformations would be used.

## Converting XML Documents to Other XML Documents

The ability to convert from one XML document to other XML document formats can be used in a number of situations and provides a great deal of flexibility. Let's take a look at a few everyday scenarios when this conversion could be used. This conversion can be used if you need to filter an XML document or convert it to support another DTD or XML schema format. We'll take a closer look at each of these cases in the following sections.

### XML Document Filtering

The subject of XML document filtering has a number of applications. For example, let's say that your company exchanges XML formatted documents with other companies. Assume that internal to your company, you use and distribute an XML document that is based on a corporate DTD or schema containing information about products and customers. However, this DTD or schema contains several elements that contain company-sensitive information (for example, client names and phone numbers). This is clearly information that you will need to remove from the XML document before you send it to another company.

One way to filter the sensitive elements from the XML document is to manually edit it. This isn't very practical—it is error prone and may be a nearly impossible task if the XML document is large. The better approach is to use an XML document filter to generate a new XML document. The first step is to generate a new external DTD or XML schema that doesn't contain the sensitive elements. Then, use XSLT to transform the original internal document into a version that conforms with the new DTD or XML schema that does not contain sensitive information. This approach also provides a better long-term solution because it can easily be reused.

### Transforming XML to Support a Different DTD or XML Schema

When companies exchange data using XML, the ideal situation is for all the companies involved to standardize on a common DTD or XML schema. However, that may not always happen for a number of reasons. For example, one of the companies may not be willing (or able) to change their internal applications to support a common DTD or XML schema.

One approach is to transform your XML document to another company's preferred format. This process isn't as smooth as it could be if both companies had agreed on a common DTD or XML schema. However, there are workarounds you can use to facilitate the transfer of data. In this case, you could follow an approach similar to the one discussed in the last section. Develop a DTD or XML schema that matches the preferred format of the other company. Then, develop an XSLT stylesheet to transform your XML document to comply with a different DTD or XML schema.

Another example of transforming to use a different format would be different companies using the Electronic Business using XML (ebXML) format to exchange data. ebXML is a group of related specifications designed to facilitate global exchange of business-related information. ebXML is a powerful suite of specifications; however, for internal corporate information interchange, it is probably more than you need. In cases such as this, a company can translate internal XML documents to ebXML documents to send data to a global partner. The same approach can be followed for incoming ebXML documents you may want to convert into a local, internal corporate format.

### Converting XML Documents to HTML Documents

Another widely used transformation is from XML to HTML/XHTML. As you can imagine, this is an important application of XSLT, especially on the web. For example, users can query a database using the Perl DBI, convert the results of the query to XML by using any number of modules (for example, XML::Writer) and dynamically generate HTML reports. One of the benefits of this conversion is that the format and content of the reports can be predefined by using an XSLT stylesheet. After the stylesheet has been defined, reports can be generated over and over again using the same stylesheet.

For example, let's say that you're responsible for generating a dynamic accounting report that tracks charges based on project number. The accounting for each project can change on a daily basis depending on travel, purchases, and so forth By using an XSLT stylesheet to convert from XML to HTML/XHTML, you can easily provide reports that will always be based on the latest available data. The next few sections go into more detail on how to perform these types of transformations.

If you remember, earlier in the book I mentioned that one of the major benefits of XML is that it separates the data from the presentation of the data. XSLT can be used to generate different versions (or views) of the same data depending on the client that requests the data. This can easily be accomplished by developing multiple XSLT stylesheets for each report. Each of the XSLT stylesheets can be used to generate the HTML for a particular device. For example, let's assume that you have a report that contains graphics (for example, charts or photographs), and some of the clients requesting the report aren't capable of displaying all the graphics (for example, mobile phone). A WAP-specific XSLT stylesheet can be used to filter out the graphics and just send the text of the report.

## XPath Introduction

XPath is a non-XML language that was developed to search and access portions of an XML document. In addition to the searching capability, XPath also provides a few basic functions for manipulating data. The name XPath comes from the fact that the standard uses path notation (similar to a URL) to work with the hierarchical structure of a document. We can compare the relationship between XPath and XML to the relationship between SQL and a database. Granted, they are not the same, but the relationship between XPath and XML can be compared to the relationship between SQL and a database.

XPath provides the capability to select the first occurrence of an element, the third occurrence of another element, or to retrieve the social security attribute of an employee element that has the firstname "Mark." It is a very powerful capability, and it is an important component of a number of XML-based standards, such as XPointer, XML Schemas, and XSLT. So, before discussing XSLT stylesheets, I thought it would be advantageous to provide an introductory discussion of the XPath standard.

> **Note**
>
> One advantage of using XPath in the other standards is commonality among the standards. After you're familiar with XPath, you'll be able to apply the knowledge in a number of areas. This is an example of when reuse of a technology is beneficial to you as the user.

Because we're concerned with XPath and XSLT in this chapter, what is their relationship? When using XSLT to transform an input XML document, we'll generally have an input XML document, an input XSLT stylesheet, and an output document (which could be in any number of formats). XSLT searches the input XML document using XPath by comparing the rules defined in the XSLT stylesheet (also called templates) to the input XML document. After a match has been found in the input XML document, the matching construct can be copied by the XSLT processor and then processed based on the rule in the XSLT stylesheet. This rule might call for the conversion to HTML, filtering of the XML document, or any of a number of possibilities.

We have an idea of what XPath does, but how does it work, and what is the format of the syntax? One important point to keep in mind is that XPath works on an XML document that has already been parsed and stored in a tree. So, similar to the DOM parsers (which were discussed in Chapter 4, "Tree-Based Parser Modules"), XPath views an XML document as a tree of nodes. The notation used to describe the tree structure is basically the same, so if you're familiar with the DOM trees, you shouldn't have a problem understanding the XPath notation.

It is easier to discuss XPath in the context of an XML document. Let's assume that your company employs a web-based timekeeping system, and that an application generates an XML document containing all the submitted timecard information. A sample of an XML document with timecard information is shown in Listing 8.1.

Listing 8.1 **Corporate timesheet information in XML. (Filename: ch8_xpath_timesheet.xml)**

```
<?xml version="1.0" encoding="UTF-8"?>
<!DOCTYPE timesheet SYSTEM "timesheet.dtd">
<timesheet week="5/31">
   <employee type="salary">
      <name>Joseph</name>
      <project>Book development</project>
      <hours>40</hours>
   </employee>
   <employee type="hourly">
      <name>Kayla</name>
      <project>Editing</project>
      <hours>45</hours>
   </employee>
      <employee type="hourly">
      <name>Marijo</name>
      <project>Artwork</project>
      <hours>45</hours>
   </employee>
   <employee type="salary">
      <!— Dan had a busy week, as usual !—>
      <name>Dan</name>
      <project>Indexing</project>
      <hours>70</hours>
   </employee>
</timesheet>
```

As far as XPath is concerned, there are seven types of possible nodes that might appear in the node tree. All the different types of XML objects (for example, elements, attributes, and so forth) are mapped to node types in the tree. The seven types are

- **Root node**—Appears only once in a tree because there is only one root element in an XML document. Note that the root node does not have a parent.
- **Element node**—Every element in the input XML document will have a corresponding element node in the node tree (for example, `<name>` in Listing 8.1). Note that an element has a parent and may have child nodes.
- **Attribute node**—Every attribute in the document appears as an attribute node in the tree (for example, the `type` attribute in Listing 8.1).
- **Text node**—Contains the text from an element (for example, "`Joseph`" from the first `<name>` element in Listing 8.1). Note that a text node has a parent but cannot have any children.
- **Comment node**—Contains the text from the comment nodes, minus the opening `<!–` and the closing `–>` (for example, "`Dan had a busy week!`"). Note that comment nodes have a parent but don't have any children.
- **Processing Instruction (PI) node**—Provided so that XML can pass additional information to a processor that may read the XML document. Remember, a PI node starts with "`<?`" and ends with "`?>`". The contents of the PI in the node tree does not include the "`<?`" and "`?>`" that surround the instruction. In Listing 8.1, the PI is `xml version="1.0" encoding="UTF-8"`.
- **Namespace node**—Represents the namespace on an element or node. Each namespace node has a parent element but isn't considered to be a child of that parent (that is, the parent doesn't consider the namespace node to be a child).

An XPath expression contains the information required to match an XML object, such as an element or an attribute. The format of the expressions are similar to the paths used in a Unix filesystem, where the "/" represents the root element, and other directories can be specified by using their path. For example, on a Unix machine, the path `/home/mark/xml` would point to the xml directory in the mark directory, which is part of the home directory.

Let's try and look at a few simple XPath expressions that are based on the XML document shown in Listing 8.1. A majority of your XPath expressions refer to the root node, element nodes, or attribute nodes. Let's take a look at the XPath expressions required to access each of these node types.

**Retrieving the Root Node**

The simplest XPath expression is "/", which would match on the root node. Because this XPath expression would match on the entire document, the result returned by this XPath expression would be the entire XML document except for the PIs at the top of the XML document.

**Retrieving Element Nodes**

XPath expressions can be used to match groups of element nodes, or an individual element node. For example, the XPath expression `/timesheet/employee` would match on all the employee nodes of the current context node. At this point, the context node is timesheet, so we'll retrieve all the employee elements and their children. In our case, that would be the following:

```
<employee type="salary">
   <name>Joseph</name>
   <project>Book development</project>
   <hours>40</hours>
</employee>
<employee type="hourly">
   <name>Kayla</name>
   <project>Editing</project>
   <hours>45</hours>
</employee>— NODE —
<employee type="hourly">
   <name>Marijo</name>
   <project>Artwork</project>
   <hours>45</hours>
</employee>— NODE —
<employee type="salary">
   <!— Dan had a busy week, as usual !—>
   <name>Dan</name>
   <project>Indexing</project>
   <hours>70</hours>
</employee>
```

If we want to go one layer deeper into the XML document and retrieve all the name nodes in the tree, we could use nearly the same XPath expression as the previous example; however, we'd add one additional branch onto the tree.

For example, the XPath expression `/timesheet/employee/name` would return all the name nodes from the node tree. In our case, the following elements would be returned:

```
<name>Joseph</name>
<name>Kayla</name>
<name>Marijo</name>
<name>Dan</name>
```

We can retrieve a particular element node based on the node location in the tree. If we wanted to find the name of the second employee in the node tree, we would use the following XPath expression: `/timesheet/employee[2]/name`. As you can see, we have an index on the employee node that tells XPath which employee node we're interested in. Note that the index of the first occurrence starts at 1 rather than 0 (for those of you who are used to arrays starting at 0). Using this XPath expression, the result would be

```
<name>Kayla</name>
```

### Retrieving Attribute Nodes

Attributes can also be retrieved using XPath by specifying the attribute name using the at symbol "@". For example, let's say that we want to retrieve the `week` attribute of root `timesheet` node. We can use the XPath expression `/timesheet/@week`, and the result would be

```
week="5/31"
```

Attributes can also be retrieved from a particular element node. For example, let's say that we want to retrieve the salary type of the second employee in the node tree. We can use the XPath expression `/timesheet/employee[2]/@type`, and the result will be

```
type="hourly"
```

Unfortunately, we can't cover all the possible examples of XPath expressions. However, we've given you a few examples of the most widely used types of XPath expressions. For additional XPath information, take a look at the XPath standard available online at `http://www.w3.org/TR/xpath`.

## XSLT Stylesheets

XSLT stylesheets are XML files that define the rules for the transformation between XML and other text formats. The XSLT stylesheets contain all the information regarding output content (that is, which elements and attributes you want to have appear in the output document) and format (for example, colors, font, and so forth).

**Note**

This is a very involved topic that can easily fill a book all by itself (and there are already several available). Unfortunately, I don't have the luxury of time (and paper) to go into great detail about XSLT stylesheets. However, I will present enough material to get you started and introduce the topic of XSLT stylesheets. This, combined with the XSLT stylesheets used in the examples throughout this chapter, should provide you with a good understanding of the topic. A great book that you should add to your library is *Inside XSLT*, by Steven Holzner from New Riders.

Let's take a look at a sample XSLT stylesheet that converts an XML document to an HTML document containing a bulleted list. However, I'll start at the beginning of the process, so that you can see all the steps involved in developing a stylesheet.

First, Listing 8.2 shows a DTD for a very simple XML document that will contain a listing of XML-related book titles. Because this DTD defines an XML document that is about as simple as you can build, this is probably the equivalent of our "Hello World" example. As you can see, this XML document has a root element named `<xml_library>` and has one or more child elements named `<book>`. Listing 8.3 shows the XML schema that describes the same document.

Listing 8.2 **DTD for the XML library document. (Filename: ch8_xml_library.dtd)**

```
<?xml version="1.0" encoding="UTF-8"?>
<!ELEMENT xml_library (book+)>
<!ELEMENT book (#PCDATA)>
```

Listing 8.3 **XML schema for the XML library document. (Filename: ch8_xml_library.xsd)**

```
<?xml version="1.0" encoding="UTF-8"?>
<xs:schema xmlns:xs="http://www.w3.org/2001/XMLSchema"
elementFormDefault="qualified">
   <xs:element name="book" type="xs:string"/>
   <xs:element name="xml_library">
      <xs:complexType>
         <xs:sequence>
            <xs:element ref="book" maxOccurs="unbounded"/>
         </xs:sequence>
      </xs:complexType>
   </xs:element>
</xs:schema>
```

Listing 8.4 shows the XML document that was built using the DTD shown in Listing 8.2. As you can see, it contains a short list of some of the XML-related books currently available from New Riders Publishing. This XML document is the input XML file for the transformation to HTML.

Listing 8.4 **Simple XML document for XML to HTML conversion. (Filename: ch8_xml_library.xml)**

```
<?xml version="1.0" encoding="UTF-8"?>
<!DOCTYPE xml_library SYSTEM "ch8_xml_library.dtd">
<xml_library>
   <book>
      XML and PHP
   </book>
   <book>
      XML and ASP.NET
   </book>
   <book>
      XML, HTML, XHTML Magic
   </book>
   <book>
      Inside XML
   </book>
   <book>
      Designing SVG Web Graphics
   </book>
   <book>
      XML and Perl
   </book>
</xml_library>
```

Remember, our goal here is to convert this XML file to an HTML file that will display all the books in a bulleted list. Listing 8.5 shows the XSLT file that contains the rules used by the XSLT processor to transform the input file to HTML. Let's take a closer look at the XSLT file.

Listing 8.5 **XSLT stylesheet to convert from XML to HTML. (Filename: ch8_xml_library.xslt)**

```
<?xml version="1.0"?>
<xsl:stylesheet version="1.0"
➥xmlns:xsl="http://www.w3.org/1999/XSL/Transform">

<xsl:template match="/">
<html>
   <head>
      <title>My XML Library</title>
   </head>
   <body>
   <h2>Library Report</h2>
      <ul>
         <xsl:for-each select="xml_library/book">
            <li><xsl:value-of select="."/></li>
         </xsl:for-each>
      </ul>
   </body>
```

```
17. </html>
18. </xsl:template>
19.
20. </xsl:stylesheet>
```

**1–2** The first important property of XSLT stylesheets that you should be aware of is on line 1. An XSLT stylesheet is an XML document. This is important for a few reasons. First, it is important because an XML parser can read the XSLT stylesheet—that is, it is in an already understood and well-defined format. Second, because the XSLT stylesheet is an XML document, it must follow all the rules related to format and content as any other XML document does. Because you're now familiar with the format of an XML document (that is, elements, attributes, and so forth), you'll understand the format of an XSLT stylesheet and what the stylesheet is trying to do.

```
1.  <?xml version="1.0"?>
2.  <xsl:stylesheet version="1.0"
    ➥xmlns:xsl="http://www.w3.org/1999/XSL/Transform">
```

All XSLT elements are in the `http://www.w3.org/1999/XSL/Transform` namespace. Typically, most users represent this namespace by using an xsl prefix. As you can see, the xsl prefix is used throughout our stylesheet.

**Note**

The root element of this XSLT stylesheet is named `stylesheet`; however, `transform` can also be used. These two terms have the same meaning to an XSLT processor.

**4–10** All the elements that we want to appear in the output document must be identified by a `xsl:template` element. This element has an attribute named `match` that contains the element we want to extract from the source XML document. In our case, we're matching the "`/`" element, which is the root of our document. So, starting at the root of the document (that is, the entire XML document), this stylesheet is enclosing our XML document with HTML `<html>` and `<body>` body tags. The `<html>` tag is the outermost tag and identifies the document as an HTML document, and the `<head>` tag contains the `<title>` tag, which contains the string that will show up in the title bar of the browser window.

```
4.  <xsl:template match="/">
5.  <html>
6.     <head>
7.        <title>My XML Library</title>
8.     </head>
9.     <body>
10.    <h2>Library Report</h2>
```

**11–20** This section contains the definition for the unordered list. The `<ul>` tags display an unordered bulleted list, and the `<li>` tag indicates an itemized element preceded by a bullet. As you can see, we're using the `<xsl:for-each>` element to iterate through all the elements that match the XPath expression `xml_library/book`. In our case, we'll match on all the `<book>` elements. After we find a matching element, we retrieve the contents of the current or context element by using the `select="."` attribute.

```
11.       <ul>
12.          <xsl:for-each select="xml_library/book">
13.             <li><xsl:value-of select="."/></li>
14.          </xsl:for-each>
15.       </ul>
16.    </body>
17. </html>
18. </xsl:template>
19.
20. </xsl:stylesheet>
```

At this point, I have defined all the inputs required for an XSLT processor (that is, a well-formed XML document and an XSLT stylesheet). I've purposely skipped showing the code for the XSLT processor—that is covered in the next section. The purpose here was to focus on the input files that are required. At this point, think of an XSLT processor as the cloud or black box that takes an XML document and an XSLT stylesheet as input and performs some type of translation. In this example, the XSLT processor would now take these input files and generate an HTML document. The generated HTML document is shown in Listing 8.6. As you can see, it is a simple HTML document that has the contents of our title element and the contents of the input XML document formatted in an unordered bulleted list.

Listing 8.6 **HTML generated from the XSLT transformation. (Filename: ch8_xml_library.html)**

```
<html>
   <head>
      <meta content="text/html; charset=UTF-8" http-equiv="Content-Type">
      <title>Library Report</title>
   </head>
   <body>
   <h2>My XML Library </h2>
     <ul>
       <li>
          XML and PHP
       </li>
       <li>
```

```
            XML and ASP.NET
         </li>
         <li>
            XML, HTML, XHTML Magic
         </li>
         <li>
            Inside XML
         </li>
         <li>
            Designing SVG Web Graphics
         </li>
         <li>
            XML and Perl
         </li>
      </ul>
     </body>
  </html>
```

Viewed from within a browser, the HTML file shown in Listing 8.6 would produce the output shown in Figure 8.2.

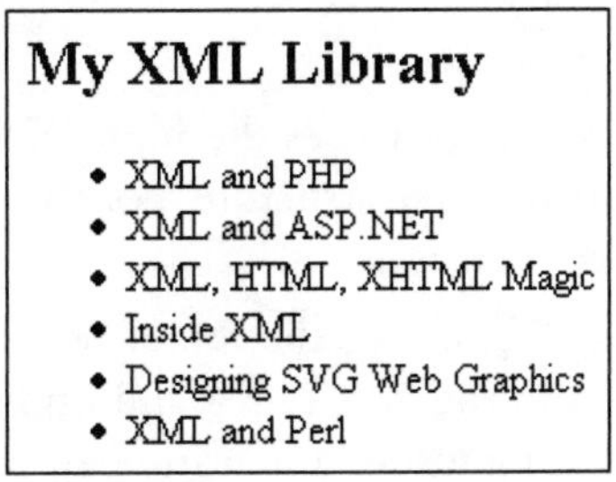

**My XML Library**

- XML and PHP
- XML and ASP.NET
- XML, HTML, XHTML Magic
- Inside XML
- Designing SVG Web Graphics
- XML and Perl

**Figure 8.2** Browser view of the XML library HTML file.

Granted, this was a very simple example, but I just wanted to present a simple example how a stylesheet works and the process involved in using a stylesheet. A lot of options exist that can be used with stylesheets. Unfortunately, I can't cover them all; however, I'll have several examples and use different stylesheet options.

Now that we've taken a look at XSLT stylesheets, let's talk about the XSLT processor.

## What Is an XSLT Processor?

Because XSLT is an XML-based standard, XSLT processors are available for all the major programming languages (for example, C/C++, Java, and of course, Perl). Several Perl modules exist (for example, XML::LibXSLT and XML::Sablotron) that perform XSLT processing, and I'll present examples of the most popular modules a little bit later in this chapter.

Looking back at Figure 8.1, recall that the XSLT processor accepts an XML document or a DOM-like tree and an XSLT stylesheet as input and then generates output based on the rules in the XSLT stylesheet. All XSLT processors follow several basic steps.

1. First, the XSLT processor requires that the input XML is converted (by parsing) into a DOM-like tree structure. Some XSLT processors perform the parsing themselves, while others expect the tree structure as input. Either way, the XSLT processor then parses the stylesheet and stores the contents in another tree structure. For our discussion, let's call this the XSLT tree. If you remember, tree-based parsing was discussed back in Chapter 4.
2. Second, the XSLT processor parses the input XML document and stores the contents in a separate tree structure. For this discussion, let's call this the XML input document tree.
3. Finally, the XSLT processor uses the template specified by the `<xsl:template>` element(s) in the XSLT tree and finds the corresponding elements in the XML input document tree. In our simple example, we only had one `<xsl:template>` element and it was `<xsl:template match="/">`, so we basically matched the entire XML input document tree. In a more advanced stylesheet, the XSLT processor would walk through the XSLT tree and for each new `<xsl:template>` it encountered, it would recursively search the XML input document tree for matching elements.

We've had a chance to walk through the mechanics of a generic XSLT processor, but haven't mentioned anything about Perl. So, let's take a look at a few examples using the different Perl XSLT modules that are currently available.

# XML::XPath Perl Module

The XML::XPath module was written by Matt Sergeant and provides access to the contents of an XML document using the XPath standard. XML::XPath was developed to strictly comply with the XPath standard. The strict compliance to the standard is important because after you're familiar with the standard, it is very easy to use this module. However, the design of the module is open enough so that users can expand the base functionality of the module by adding additional functions. Let's take a look at an example.

## XML::XPath Perl Module Example

Let's say that you're part of the Information Technology (IT) staff and you've been given the task of analyzing the traffic on your network. Your company recently purchased a sniffer software package that records all the network traffic and stores the recorded traffic in an XML document. Your specific task is to generate a report that shows a breakdown of the traffic on your network. In addition, you want to identify the hosts that generate the most network traffic and separate the traffic by protocol (for example, HyperText Transfer Protocol (HTTP), Simple Mail Transfer Protocol (SMTP), File Transfer Protocol (FTP), and so forth).

The recently purchased sniffer software package works as expected; however, it doesn't generate the reports you've been asked to generate. So, you need to process the XML document and produce a report that summarizes the contents. To generate this report, you've decided to use the XML::XPath module. The XML::XPath module enables you to quickly search the XML document and generate the required statistics.

### Input XML Log File Format

As with all our examples, the first step is to look at the format of the input XML document. The DTD for the input XML document is shown in Listing 8.7, and the corresponding XML schema is shown in Listing 8.8.

Listing 8.7 **DTD for the network sniffer XML log file. (Filename: ch8_xpath_network_traffic.dtd)**

```
<?xml version="1.0" encoding="UTF-8"?>
<!ELEMENT network_traffic (packet)>
<!ELEMENT packet (src, dst, protocol) >
<!ELEMENT src (#PCDATA) >
<!ELEMENT dst (#PCDATA) >
<!ELEMENT protocol (#PCDATA) >
```

Listing 8.8 **XML schema for the network sniffer XML log file. (Filename: ch8_xpath_network_traffic.xsd)**

```
<?xml version="1.0" encoding="UTF-8"?>
<xs:schema xmlns:xs="http://www.w3.org/2001/XMLSchema"
elementFormDefault="qualified">
   <xs:element name="dst" type="xs:string"/>
   <xs:element name="network_traffic">
      <xs:complexType>
         <xs:sequence>
            <xs:element ref="packet"/>
         </xs:sequence>
      </xs:complexType>
   </xs:element>
   <xs:element name="packet">
      <xs:complexType>
         <xs:sequence>
            <xs:element ref="src"/>
            <xs:element ref="dst"/>
            <xs:element ref="protocol"/>
         </xs:sequence>
      </xs:complexType>
   </xs:element>
   <xs:element name="protocol" type="xs:string"/>
   <xs:element name="src" type="xs:string"/>
</xs:schema>
```

### XML Network Traffic Log File

The format of our XML log file is very simple—a real log would contain many more fields; however, this will suffice for our purposes. For a busy network, it is advantageous to make each packet element as small as possible, so that the log file remains at a reasonable size. As you can see, the XML document is comprised of multiple packet elements. Each packet element contains the source and destination hostnames, transmission time, and protocol. Now that we have looked at the format of the XML document, let's look at the log containing the network traffic that is shown in Listing 8.9.

Listing 8.9 **Network traffic log stored in XML. (Filename: ch8_network_traffic.xml)**

```
<?xml version="1.0" encoding="UTF-8"?>
<!DOCTYPE network_traffic SYSTEM "ch8_xpath_network_traffic.dtd">
<network_traffic>
   <packet>
      <src>bugs</src>
      <dst>daffy</dst>
      <protocol>SMTP</protocol>
   </packet>
```

```
    <packet>
       <src>bugs</src>
       <dst>daffy</dst>
       <protocol>SMTP</protocol>
    </packet>
    <packet>
       <src>foghorn</src>
       <dst>wiley</dst>
       <protocol>HTTP</protocol>
    </packet>
    <packet>
       <src>daffy</src>
       <dst>wiley</dst>
       <protocol>HTTP</protocol>
    </packet>
    <packet>
       <src>bugs</src>
       <dst>daffy</dst>
       <protocol>SMTP</protocol>
    </packet>
    <packet>
       <src>daffy</src>
       <dst>wiley</dst>
       <protocol>FTP</protocol>
    </packet>
 </network_traffic>
```

The network traffic log in Listing 8.9 shows the network traffic that was collected as part of our network analysis. As you can see, the network traffic is sent from three different hosts (`bugs`, `daffy`, `foghorn`) while there were two destination hosts (`daffy`, `wiley`).

### XML::XPath Perl Program

This program can be written a number of other ways using other modules. For example, we could have written a program using either an event-based XML parser (as discussed in Chapter 3, "Event-Driven Parser Modules") or a tree-based parser (as discussed in Chapter 4) to perform this task. However, as is usually the case with Perl, there is always more than one way to do it. When you see how short and simple this Perl program actually is, I think that you'll agree that the XML::XPath module was the proper choice for this particular situation.

The XML::XPath program searches through the XML network sniffer log file and counts the number of occurrences of several elements. First, it counts the number of occurrences of each supported protocol. In our case, the only protocols that appear in the XML log file are FTP, HTTP, and SMTP.

Second, it searches for the number of transmitted packets to and from each host. Our network has four hosts: `bugs`, `daffy`, `foghorn`, and `wiley`. The results are calculated and presented in the form of small tables. Let's take a look at Listing 8.10 to see how the program actually operates.

Listing 8.10 **XML::XPath module-based program to summarize network traffic. (Filename: ch8_xpath_app.pl)**

```
use strict;
use XML::XPath;
use XML::XPath::XMLParser;

my ($nodeset, $protocol, %srcHash, %dstHash, %protocolHash);
my ($thisHost, $key);
my @protocolArray = ("HTTP", "FTP", "SMTP");
my @hostArray = ("bugs", "daffy", "foghorn", "wiley");

# Open the XML document.
my $xp = XML::XPath->new(filename => 'ch8_xpath_network_traffic.xml');

# Loop through our protocol array and try to find a packet
# with the matching protocol type.  If we find a match,
# store it in %protocolHash.
foreach $protocol (@protocolArray) {
  $nodeset = $xp->find("/network_traffic/packet[protocol=\"$protocol\"]");
  $protocolHash{$protocol} = $nodeset->size();
}

# Loop through our host array track find all of the packets
# sent and received by this host.  Store the results in
# %srcHash and %dstHash.
foreach $thisHost (@hostArray) {
  $nodeset = $xp->find("/network_traffic/packet[src=\"$thisHost\"]");
  $srcHash{$thisHost} = $nodeset->size();

  $nodeset = $xp->find("/network_traffic/packet[dst=\"$thisHost\"]");
  $dstHash{$thisHost} = $nodeset->size();
}

# Print the protocol results.
print "Protocol count\n";
print "-------------\n";
foreach $key (sort keys %protocolHash) {
  print "$key, count = $protocolHash{$key}\n";
}

# Print the source host results.
print "\nSource\n";
```

```
41.  print "------\n";
42.  foreach $key (sort keys %srcHash) {
43.    print "$key, count = $srcHash{$key}\n";
44.  }
45.
46.  # Print the dest host results.
47.  print "\nDestination\n";
48.  print "-----------\n";
49.  foreach $key (sort keys %dstHash) {
50.    print "$key, count = $dstHash{$key}\n";
51.  }
```

**1–11** The first section of the program has the standard pragma `use strict`. Because we're using the XML::XPath module, we need the use XML::XPath pragma. Also, XML::XPath requires the use XML::XPath::XMLParser pragma. The XML::XPath::XMLParser module is the XML parser used by the XML::XPath module to build the node tree. Remember, the node tree was discussed earlier in the XPath section.

We're declaring scalars and hashes in this section that will be used a little later in the program. The two arrays `@protocolArray` and `@hostArray` contain the protocols and hostnames that we'll be searching for in the XML document. We'll look through these arrays and use an XPath expression to search for each member of the array.

After declaring all the required variables, we instantiate an XML::XPath object. Note that the only argument that we're using is the name of the input XML file (`network_traffic.xml`). Other parameters can be used; however, the input XML file is all that is required for examples such as ours.

```
1.   use strict;
2.   use XML::XPath;
3.   use XML::XPath::XMLParser;
4.
5.   my ($nodeset, $protocol, %srcHash, %dstHash, %protocolHash);
6.   my ($thisHost, $key);
7.   my @protocolArray = ("HTTP", "FTP", "SMTP");
8.   my @hostArray = ("bugs", "daffy", "foghorn", "wiley");
9.
10.  # Open the XML document.
11.  my $xp = XML::XPath->new(filename => 'ch8_network_traffic.xml');
```

**13–19** This block is the first time we're actually using an XML::XPath function. First, we're looping through the array that contains the protocol names—FTP, HTTP, and SMTP. Then, we build the following XPath expression:

```
/network_traffic/packet[protocol=\"$protocol\"]
```

This expression selects the packet node children that have protocol children nodes with a string-value equal to `$protocol`. In our case, the value of `$protocol` changes as we loop through the array. If a match is found, the XML::XPath find function returns an XML::XPath::NodeSet object. Then, by utilizing the XML::XPath::NodeSet function `size()`, we can determine the number of nodes in this nodeset (that is, the number of packet nodes that matched our XPath query). The result is stored in a hash named `$protocolHash` in the normal key=>value format, where the key is the protocol name, and the value is the number of packets that were sent using the protocol.

```
# Loop through our protocol array and try to find a packet
# with the matching protocol type.  If we find a match,
# store it in %protocolHash.
foreach $protocol (@protocolArray) {
  $nodeset = $xp->find("/network_traffic/packet[protocol=\"$protocol\"]");
  $protocolHash{$protocol} = $nodeset->size();
}
```

**21–30** This block performs basically the same function as the previous block, only this time we're looking for the source and destination hosts. We have an outer `foreach()` loop that loops through all the hosts from the `@hostArray` and assigns the current host to the scalar named `$thisHost`. We then search the node tree with the following XPath expressions:

```
/network_traffic/packet[src=\"$thisHost\"]
```

and

```
/network_traffic/packet[dst=\"$thisHost\"]
```

As in the previous block, the results of each XPath search are returned as an XML::XPath::NodeSet object, and we can use the `size()` function to retrieve the number of packets sourced and received by each host, respectively. After the number of packets have been retrieved, we stored the results in the corresponding hash using the standard key=>value format. In these hashes, the keys are the hostnames, and the values are the number of packets transmitted (`%srcHash`) or received (`%dstHash`).

```
21.  # Loop through our host array track find all of the packets
22.  # sent and received by this host.  Store the results in
23.  # %srcHash and %dstHash.
24.  foreach $thisHost (@hostArray) {
25.    $nodeset = $xp->find("/network_traffic/packet[src=\"$thisHost\"]");
26.    $srcHash{$thisHost} = $nodeset->size();
27.
28.    $nodeset = $xp->find("/network_traffic/packet[dst=\"$thisHost\"]");
29.    $dstHash{$thisHost} = $nodeset->size();
30.  }
```

**32–51** The last section of the program just prints the contents of the hashes that contain the traffic counts by protocol, the number of packets sourced by each host, and the number of packets received by each host.

```
32. # Print the protocol results.
33. print "Protocol count\n";
34. print "--------------\n";
35. foreach $key (sort keys %protocolHash) {
36.   print "$key, count = $protocolHash{$key}\n";
37. }
38.
39. # Print the source host results.
40. print "\nSource\n";
41. print "------\n";
42. foreach $key (sort keys %srcHash) {
43.   print "$key, count = $srcHash{$key}\n";
44. }
45.
46. # Print the dest host results.
47. print "\nDestination\n";
48. print "-----------\n";
49. foreach $key (sort keys %dstHash) {
50.   print "$key, count = $dstHash{$key}\n";
51. }
```

As you can see, the XML::XPath module provides a simple, easy-to-use XPath-based API to our XML document. When you install the XML::XPath module, you also get a command-line utility that enables you to build and test XPath expressions from the command line.

## XPath Perl Command-Line Utility

The XML::XPath module installation also installs a command-line utility named `xpath`. This utility provides a command-line XPath API to an XML document that can be a valuable tool. For example, let's say that you're modifying a web-based application to add an XPath capability. Instead of running the entire web-based application, you can use the command-line `xpath` utility to test your XPath expressions. The command-line arguments for the `xpath` utility are

```
xpath <input XML document> <XPath expression>
```

For example, using the network XML traffic log file shown in Listing 8.9 as input, we can use the `xpath` utility to test the following XPath expression:

```
xpath ch8_xpath_network_traffic.xml /network_traffic/packet[1]/src
```

Returns the following:

```
Found 1 node:
-- NODE --
<src>bugs</src>
```

As we mentioned earlier, the `xpath` utility is a very useful tool that you will use often if your work involves developing XPath expressions.

> **Additional XPath information**
> For additional XPath information, please see perldoc XML::XPath. Several functions are available that I didn't cover that might be more applicable to your requirements. The XPath standard can be found at `http://www.w3.org/TR/xpath`.

# XML::LibXSLT Perl Module

The XML::LibXSLT Perl module was written by Matt Sergeant and is based on the GNOME Project's libxslt C library. The libxslt C library is a fast, stable, and portable XSLT processor library. Another important feature is that it strictly follows the XSLT standard. Let's take a look at an example that uses the XML::LibXSLT Perl module.

## XML::LibXSLT Perl Module Example

This example will demonstrate how to use a Perl XSLT processor to convert an XML document into an HTML document. Depending on your requirements, this process can be performed offline, or it can reside on a web server to produce HTML documents based on dynamically generated XML documents.

### Input XML Document Format

For this example, let's assume that we have an XML document stored as a file and want to transform the XML document to an HTML document. The XML document to be transformed is shown in Listing 8.11. This XML document is similar to the XML document that was used for an example back in Chapter 4. Our task for this example is to convert the XML document to HTML and display the contents of the file in a table. We won't be doing any filtering in this example so all the elements (and any corresponding attributes) from the input XML document will appear in the output HTML document.

As you can see in Listing 8.11, each customer element has one attribute (`account_number`) and three elements (`name`, `balance`, and `due_date`). Based on the structure of our input XML document, we'd like to have one row in the output table per customer. Because we've seen the input data, let's next take a look at the XSLT stylesheet that will support our requirements.

Listing 8.11 **Input XML document for XSLT transformation. (Filename: ch8_libxslt_customers.xml)**

```
<?xml version="1.0" encoding="UTF-8"?>
<!DOCTYPE customer_data SYSTEM "customers.dtd">
<customer_data>
   <customer account_number="cid_1">
      <name>Joseph Burns</name>
      <balance>19.95</balance>
      <due_date>May 5</due_date>
   </customer>
   <customer account_number="cid_2">
      <name>Kayla Burns</name>
      <balance>29.95</balance>
      <due_date>May 12</due_date>
   </customer>
   <customer account_number="cid_3">
      <name>Roger Smith</name>
      <balance>100.25</balance>
      <due_date>May 19</due_date>
   </customer>
   <customer account_number="cid_4">
      <name>James Kennedy</name>
      <balance>0.00</balance>
      <due_date>N/A</due_date>
   </customer>
   <customer account_number="cid_5">
      <name>Margaret Pelligrino</name>
      <balance>0.00</balance>
      <due_date>N/A</due_date>
   </customer>
   <customer account_number="cid_6">
      <name>Michael Harwell</name>
      <balance>1000.00</balance>
      <due_date>May 22</due_date>
   </customer>
   <customer account_number="cid_7">
      <name>Riley Corgi</name>
      <balance>100.00</balance>
      <due_date>June 1</due_date>
   </customer>
</customer_data>
```

### XSLT Stylesheet to Convert XML to HTML

The XSLT stylesheet that will generate an HTML table based on our requirements is shown in Listing 8.12. Listing 8.12 may seem like a long stylesheet (and it is), however, you'll see when we walk through it that there are several repeated sections. It's not as intimidating as it may first appear.

Listing 8.12 **XSLT stylesheet to perform our XML to HTML transformation. (Filename: ch8_libxslt_customers.xslt)**

```
1.    <?xml version="1.0"?>
2.    <xsl:stylesheet version="1.0"
      ➥xmlns:xsl="http://www.w3.org/1999/XSL/Transform">
3.
4.    <xsl:template match="/">
5.    <html>
6.       <head>
7.          <title>Customer Report</title>
8.       </head>
9.       <body>
10.      <h2>Customer Report</h2>
11.         <table border="2">
12.            <tr align="center">
13.               <th>Account Number</th>
14.               <th>Name</th>
15.               <th>Balance</th>
16.               <th>Due Date</th>
17.            </tr>
18.
19.            <xsl:for-each select="customer_data/customer">
20.               <tr align="center">
21.                  <td><xsl:value-of select="@account_number" /></td>
22.                  <td><xsl:value-of select="name" /></td>
23.                  <td><xsl:value-of select="balance" /></td>
24.                  <td><xsl:value-of select="due_date" /></td>
25.               </tr>
26.            </xsl:for-each>
27.
28.         </table>
29.      </body>
30.   </html>
31.   </xsl:template>
32.
33.   </xsl:stylesheet>
```

**1–2** The first two lines of the XSLT stylesheet identify it as an XML document and also as an XSLT stylesheet.

```
1.    <?xml version="1.0"?>
2.    <xsl:stylesheet version="1.0"
      ➥xmlns:xsl="http://www.w3.org/1999/XSL/Transform">
```

**4–17** This section of the stylesheet starts off with an `<xsl:template>` element and the `match="/"` attribute to indicate that this template applies to the root element of the XML document. This portion contains the opening `<html>`, `<head>`, and `<body>` tags that will appear in the output HTML document. Basically, our entire XML document will be wrapped by the `<html>` and `<body>` elements. In this section, we're also defining the table column titles.

```
4.  <xsl:template match="/">
5.  <html>
6.     <head>
7.        <title>Customer Report</title>
8.     </head>
9.     <body>
10.    <h2>Customer Report</h2>
11.       <table border="2">
12.          <tr align="center">
13.             <th>Account Number</th>
14.             <th>Name</th>
15.             <th>Balance</th>
16.             <th>Due Date</th>
17.          </tr>
```

**19–26** This section contains a `<xsl:for-each>` element. This element acts as an iterator, basically looping through a list of matched elements. In this case, the `select` attribute is set to match all the elements based on the XPath expression `customer_data/customer`. The `<xsl:for-each>` element will match once for each of our `<customer>` elements. After the `<xsl:for-each>` element matches a `<customer>` element (which in our case, this will be all the `customer` elements), we extract the information contained in the `customer` element. As you can see, we retrieve the value of the `account_number` attribute (using the '`@`' symbol to indicate an attribute), and the `<name>`, `<balance>`, and `<due_date>` elements. Each `<customer>` element will occupy one row in the generated table. Note that each matching customer element is wrapped by a `<tr>` tag, and each column value is wrapped by a `<td>` tag.

```
19.          <xsl:for-each select="customer_data/customer">
20.             <tr align="center">
21.                <td><xsl:value-of select="@account_number" /></td>
22.                <td><xsl:value-of select="name" /></td>
23.                <td><xsl:value-of select="balance" /></td>
24.                <td><xsl:value-of select="due_date" /></td>
25.             </tr>
26.          </xsl:for-each>
```

**28–33** The last section of the XSLT stylesheet contains all the required closing tags. Note that each opening tag has a corresponding closing tag.

```
28.         </table>
29.     </body>
30. </html>
31. </xsl:template>
32.
33. </xsl:stylesheet>
```

Now that I've shown you the XSLT stylesheet, let's take a look at the Perl program that actually performs the transformation from XML to HTML. As you will see, most of the hard work has been done using the Perl XML::LibXSLT module; the transformation is actually the easy part of the process.

### XML::LibXSLT-Based Perl Program

The Perl program that performs the transformation for us is shown in Listing 8.13. As you can see, it is probably one of the shorter Perl programs I've discussed so far. Most of the work in a task such as this is spent in designing the XSLT stylesheet, and writing the Perl program is usually the easy part. Let's walk through this program and explain the steps required to perform the transformation.

Listing 8.13 **XML::LibXSLT-based Perl program to generate the output HTML file. (Filename: ch8_libxslt_app.pl)**

```
use strict;
use XML::LibXML;
use XML::LibXSLT;

# Instantiate parser and xslt objects.
my $parserObject = XML::LibXML->new();
my $xsltObject = XML::LibXSLT->new();

# Open the XML document and the XSLT stylesheet.
my $inputXmlObject = $parserObject->parse_file("ch_libxslt_customers.xml");
my $inputStylesheetObject = $parserObject->parse_file
➥("ch_libxslt_customers.xslt");

# Parse the stylesheet, transform the input XML document,
# and output the result to the $htmlFile scalar.
my $xsltObject = $xsltObject->parse_stylesheet($inputStylesheetObject);
```

```
16.  my $resultsObject = $xsltObject->transform($inputXmlObject);
17.  my $htmlFile = $xsltObject->output_string($resultsObject);
18.
19.  # Write the results to an output file.
20.  open (HTML_REPORT, "> ch8_libxslt_customer_report.html")
21.    or die "Can't open ch8_libxslt_customer_report.html $!\n";
22.
23.  print HTML_REPORT $htmlFile;
24.
25.  close (HTML_REPORT);
```

**1–3** The opening section of the Perl program has the standard `use strict` pragma. In addition, you need to include the `use XML::LibXML` and `use XML::LibXSLT` pragmas. The XML::LibXSLT has a dependence on the XML::LibXML module because it expects XML::LibXML::Document objects as inputs.

```
1.  use strict;
2.  use XML::LibXML;
3.  use XML::LibXSLT;
```

**5–11** In this section of the program, we're creating all the objects required for the transformation. First, we create a new XML::LibXML parser object and a new XML::LibXSLT object. After we've created these new objects we parse the input XML document and the XSLT stylesheet document and create XML::LibXML::Document objects. These are the trees that we discussed during the high-level discussion about XSLT processors.

```
5.  # Instantiate parser and xslt objects.
6.  my $parserObject = XML::LibXML->new();
7.  my $xsltObject = XML::LibXSLT->new();
8.
9.  # Open the XML document and the XSLT stylesheet.
10. my $inputXmlObject = $parserObject->parse_file("ch_libxslt_customers.xml");
11. my $inputStylesheetObject = $parserObject-
    ➥>parse_file("ch_libxslt_customers.xslt");
```

**13–25** This is the portion of the program that does all the difficult work, and note that it is only a few lines long. Now that we've built the tree objects containing the contents of both the input XML document and the XSLT stylesheet, we can perform the transformation. The first step is to call the `parse_stylesheet()` function which returns an XML::LibXSLT::Stylesheet object. After we have the XML::LibXSLT::Stylesheet object, we can call the `transform` method. Note that the arguments to both of the previous methods were XML::LibXML::Document objects.

At this point, the input XML document has been transformed to HTML, and the only remaining task is to call the output_string() method that returns a scalar containing the resulting output file. After calling the output string method, the HTML document is stored in the $htmlFile scalar. Because our task was to generate an HTML file for this example, we simply write it to an output file.

```
# Parse the stylesheet, transform the input XML document,
# and output the result to the $htmlFile scalar.
my $xsltObject = $xsltObject->parse_stylesheet($inputStylesheetObject);
my $resultsObject = $xsltObject->transform($inputXmlObject);
my $htmlFile = $xsltObject->output_string($resultsObject);

# Write the results to an output file.
open (HTML_REPORT, "> ch8_libxslt_customer_report.html")
  or die "Can't open ch8_libxslt_customer_report.html $!\n";

print HTML_REPORT $htmlFile;

close (HTML_REPORT);
```

**Working with Dynamically Generated Files**

If the XML document and XSLT stylesheets were dynamically generated (for example, because of a user's selection on a web page), the basic procedures are the same, with only subtle differences. For this example, we would only need to make minor changes (for example, parse_file() changes to parse_string() or parse_fh(), depending on the situation).

### Generated HTML Output File

Listing 8.14 shows the HTML file that was generated by our Perl program.

Listing 8.14 **HTML file generated by XSLT transformation. (Filename: ch8_libxslt_customer_report.html)**

```
<html>
    <head>
  <meta content="text/html; charset=UTF-8" http-equiv="Content-Type">
    </head>
    <body>
      <span style="font-weight:bold">Customer Report</span><br><br>
     <table border="1"><thead>
         <tr>
      <td align="center"><span style="font-weight:bold">Account Number</span></td>
      <td align="center"><span style="font-weight:bold">Name</span></td>
      <td align="center"><span style="font-weight:bold">Balance</span></td>
```

```
      <td align="center"><span style="font-weight:bold">Due Date</span></td>
         </tr></thead><tbody>
         <tr>
      <td align="center">cid_1</td>
      <td align="center">Joseph Burns</td>
      <td align="center">19.95</td>
      <td align="center">May 5</td>
         </tr>
         <tr>
      <td align="center">cid_2</td>
      <td align="center">Kayla Burns</td>
      <td align="center">29.95</td>
      <td align="center">May 12</td>
         </tr>
         <tr>
      <td align="center">cid_3</td>
      <td align="center">Roger Smith</td>
      <td align="center">100.25</td>
      <td align="center">May 19</td>
         </tr>
         <tr>
      <td align="center">cid_4</td>
      <td align="center">James Kennedy</td>
      <td align="center">0.00</td>
      <td align="center">N/A</td>
         </tr>
         <tr>
      <td align="center">cid_5</td>
      <td align="center">Margaret Pelligrino</td>
      <td align="center">0.00</td>
      <td align="center">N/A</td>
         </tr>
         <tr>
      <td align="center">cid_6</td>
      <td align="center">Michael Harwell</td>
      <td align="center">1000.00</td>
      <td align="center">May 22</td>
         </tr>
         <tr>
      <td align="center">cid_7</td>
      <td align="center">Riley Corgi</td>
      <td align="center">100.00</td>
      <td align="center">June 1</td>
         </tr>
       </tbody>
     </table>
    </body>
</html>
```

### Output Report Viewed in a Browser

Figure 8.3 shows the output customer report as it appears in a web browser. As you can see, it has all the columns and is formatted as I described when I discussed the XSLT stylesheet.

**Customer Report**

| Account Number | Name | Balance | Due Date |
|---|---|---|---|
| cid_1 | Joseph Burns | 19.95 | May 5 |
| cid_2 | Kayla Burns | 29.95 | May 12 |
| cid_3 | Roger Smith | 100.25 | May 19 |
| cid_4 | James Kennedy | 0.00 | N/A |
| cid_5 | Margaret Pelligrino | 0.00 | N/A |
| cid_6 | Michael Harwell | 1000.00 | May 22 |
| cid_7 | Riley Corgi | 100.00 | June 1 |

**Figure 8.3** Output customer report as viewed in a browser.

This was a fairly straightforward example that demonstrated the power of transforming XML documents to HTML documents. As I mentioned, the most difficult part of the entire process is developing the XSLT stylesheet—the Perl XSLT module handles all the remaining details.

In the next example, we'll take a look at another Perl XSLT module; however, our output result will be a filtered XML document rather than an HTML document.

> **Note**
>
> For additional information on the XML::LibXSLT Perl module, please see perldoc XML::LibXSLT.

# XML::Sablotron Perl Module

This example demonstrates how to use the XML::Sablotron Perl module. Sablotron is an open source multi-platform XML toolkit that was developed in C++ by the Ginger Alliance Open Resource Center (`http://www.gingerall.com`).

The Sablotron toolkit implements an XSLT processor, a DOM parser, and the XPath standard. This toolkit provides extensions and APIs for several programming languages, and this toolkit is the basis for the XML::Sablotron Perl module that was developed by Pavel Hlavnicka.

## XML::Sablotron Perl Module Example

Let's take a look at a Perl program that utilizes the XML::Sablotron module. In this example, we will filter an XML document by removing particular elements and generate another XML document as the output product of the transformation process. This type of transformation could be used between two companies who have agreed to exchange data in XML, but maybe have not agreed on a common DTD or XML schema. Another possible situation is illustrated by our example when the output XML document needs to have several elements (or attributes) changed or filtered in the output version of the XML document.

### Input XML Document

For this example, let's assume that you work for a major accounting firm and that you're responsible for collecting and storing information for the annual corporate report. To provide maximum flexibility (and because you're a forward-thinking individual), the information is stored in an XML document. However, some of the information in the XML document is considered to be proprietary because you've signed non-disclosure agreements with your customers, promising not to publicly disclose certain information. So, several of the elements in your input XML document must be removed before sending the XML document to the production staff.

Before we look at the XML document containing the annual report information, let's look at the DTD. The DTD for the annual report XML document is shown in Listing 8.15.

Listing 8.15 **DTD for the XML annual report. (Filename: ch8_sab_annual_report.dtd)**

```
<?xml version="1.0" encoding="UTF-8"?>
<!ELEMENT annual_report (customer*)>
<!ELEMENT customer (name, poc, years, revenue, telephone_num)>
<!ATTLIST customer account_number CDATA #REQUIRED>
<!ELEMENT name (#PCDATA)>
<!ELEMENT poc (#PCDATA)>
<!ELEMENT years (#PCDATA)>
<!ELEMENT revenue (#PCDATA)>
<!ELEMENT telephone_num (#PCDATA)>
```

As you can see, the XML document contains an `<annual_report>` root element that is comprised of multiple `<customer>` elements. Each customer element contains the customer account number, customer name, Point of Contact (POC) (that is, who you deal with directly at the company), how long you've had the company as a client, how much revenue your company has generated from the customer, and the telephone number of your POC at the company.

The XML schema for the annual report XML document is shown in Listing 8.16.

Listing 8.16 **XML schema for the annual report. (Filename: ch8_sab_annual_report.xsd)**

```
<?xml version="1.0" encoding="UTF-8"?>
<xs:schema xmlns:xs="http://www.w3.org/2001/XMLSchema"
elementFormDefault="qualified">
   <xs:element name="annual_report">
      <xs:complexType>
         <xs:sequence>
            <xs:element ref="customer" minOccurs="0" maxOccurs="unbounded"/>
         </xs:sequence>
      </xs:complexType>
   </xs:element>
   <xs:element name="customer">
      <xs:complexType>
         <xs:sequence>
            <xs:element ref="name"/>
            <xs:element ref="poc"/>
            <xs:element ref="years"/>
            <xs:element ref="revenue"/>
            <xs:element ref="telephone_num"/>
         </xs:sequence>
         <xs:attribute name="account_number" type="xs:string" use="required"/>
      </xs:complexType>
   </xs:element>
   <xs:element name="name" type="xs:string"/>
```

```
    <xs:element name="poc" type="xs:string"/>
    <xs:element name="revenue" type="xs:string"/>
    <xs:element name="telephone_num" type="xs:string"/>
    <xs:element name="years" type="xs:integer"/>
</xs:schema>
```

This isn't a difficult task if the XML document contains information for only a few customers. If the file was small, you could just edit it by hand, right? Fortunately, your employer is one of the major accounting firms, and unfortunately, the XML document contains information on tens of thousands of past and present customers. So, editing the XML document by hand is not an option. Luckily for us, we can use an XSLT stylesheet and filter the XML document. Let's take a look at the input XML document shown in Listing 8.17, so that we're familiar with the format. After we understand what needs to be changed in the XML document, we'll move on to the stylesheet generation.

Listing 8.17 **Input annual report XML document. (Filename: ch8_sab_annual_report.xml)**

```
<?xml version="1.0" encoding="UTF-8"?>
<!DOCTYPE annual_report SYSTEM "annual_report.dtd">
<annual_report>
    <customer account_number="id_1">
        <name>Microsoft Corporation</name>
        <poc>Bill Gates</poc>
        <years>10</years>
        <revenue>1,000.00</revenue>
        <telephone_num>111-222-3333</telephone_num>
    </customer>
    <customer account_number="id_2">
        <name>Oracle Corporation</name>
        <poc>Larry Ellison</poc>
        <years>12</years>
        <revenue>1,700.00</revenue>
        <telephone_num>222-333-4444</telephone_num>
    </customer>
    <customer account_number="id_3">
        <name>Cisco Systems</name>
        <poc>John Chambers</poc>
        <years>5</years>
        <revenue>2000.00</revenue>
        <telephone_num>333-444-5555</telephone_num>
    </customer>
    <customer account_number="id_4">
        <name>Dell Computer Corporation</name>
        <poc>Michael Dell</poc>
        <years>6</years>
        <revenue>3000.00</revenue>
        <telephone_num>444-555-6666</telephone_num>
    </customer>
</annual_report>
```

In the final generated annual report, we'd like to remove the <revenue> and <telephone_num> elements. While we want to promote the fact that we have these high profile companies as clients, we don't want to show our revenues, or release the private telephone numbers of their Chief Executive Officers (CEOs).

This is a fairly easy task if we use an XSLT stylesheet to filter the input XML document. Let's take a look at the XSLT stylesheet that performs this filtering for us.

### XSLT Stylesheet

Now that we understand the format of the input XML document and understand which elements have to be removed, let's take a look at the XSLT stylesheet that performs our transformation. The XSLT stylesheet is shown in Listing 8.18. Let's step through the stylesheet and make sure that we understand how it works.

Listing 8.18 **XSLT stylesheet to filter proprietary elements from the input XML document. (Filename: ch8_sab_annual_report.xslt)**

```
<?xml version="1.0" encoding="utf-8"?>
<xsl:stylesheet version="1.0"
➥xmlns:xsl="http://www.w3.org/1999/XSL/Transform">
<xsl:output method="xml" doctype-system="ch8_sab_annual_report.dtd"/>

   <xsl:template match="/">
      <annual_report>
         <xsl:apply-templates/>
      </annual_report>
   </xsl:template>

   <xsl:template match="annual_report">
      <xsl:for-each select="customer">
         <xsl:text>&#10;</xsl:text>
         <customer>
            <xsl:attribute name="account_number" >
               <xsl:value-of select="@account_number"/>
            </xsl:attribute>

            <xsl:text>&#10;</xsl:text>
            <xsl:element name="name">
               <xsl:value-of select="name"/>
            </xsl:element>

            <xsl:text>&#10;</xsl:text>
            <xsl:element name="poc">
               <xsl:value-of select="poc"/>
```

```
27.             </xsl:element>
28.
29.             <xsl:text>&#10;</xsl:text>
30.             <xsl:element name="years">
31.                <xsl:value-of select="years"/>
32.             </xsl:element>
33.             <xsl:text>&#10;</xsl:text>
34.          </customer>
35.       </xsl:for-each>
36.    </xsl:template>
37. </xsl:stylesheet>
```

**1–3** The opening portion of the XSLT stylesheet contains the standard XML stylesheet declarations that we discussed a little earlier in this chapter. The `<xsl:output>` element specifies some of the characteristics that will appear in the transformed document. In our case, we're only using the `method` attribute to specify that the output document will be XML and the `doctype-system` attribute to specify the value of the `SYSTEM` attribute of the `DOCTYPE` declaration.

```
1.  <?xml version="1.0" encoding="utf-8"?>
2.  <xsl:stylesheet version="1.0"
    ➥xmlns:xsl="http://www.w3.org/1999/XSL/Transform">
3.  <xsl:output method="xml" doctype-system="annual_report.dtd"/>
```

**5–9** The `<xsl:template>` element defines the output template that processes the root element, that is, all elements in this XML document. The `<xsl:apply-templates>` element commands the XSLT processor to apply templates to a node set. In our case, the node set is the root element, and as you can see, the results are wrapped by the start and end tags for the root element `<annual_report>`.

```
5.     <xsl:template match="/">
6.        <annual_report>
7.           <xsl:apply-templates/>
8.        </annual_report>
9.     </xsl:template>
```

**11–37** This section of the XSLT stylesheet performs the majority of the work in this transformation. First, we define a template that matches on the `<annual_report>` element. Starting at the `<annual_report>` element (our root), we're going to iterate through all the customer elements. The `<xsl:text>` tag with the `
` will insert new lines into the output XML document. Note that these new lines are not required (in fact, they're ignored by an XML parser) but we've added them for readability. Otherwise, your XML document would be printed on one long line.

```
11.    <xsl:template match="annual_report">
12.       <xsl:for-each select="customer">
13.          <xsl:text>&#10;</xsl:text>
14.          <customer>
```

*continues*

```
                <xsl:attribute name="account_number" >
                   <xsl:value-of select="@account_number"/>
                </xsl:attribute>

                <xsl:text>&#10;</xsl:text>
                <xsl:element name="name">
                   <xsl:value-of select="name"/>
                </xsl:element>

                <xsl:text>&#10;</xsl:text>
                <xsl:element name="poc">
                   <xsl:value-of select="poc"/>
                </xsl:element>

                <xsl:text>&#10;</xsl:text>
                <xsl:element name="years">
                   <xsl:value-of select="years"/>
                </xsl:element>
                <xsl:text>&#10;</xsl:text>
             </customer>
          </xsl:for-each>
       </xsl:template>
    </xsl:stylesheet>
```

Between the opening and closing tags for the `<customer>` element is where our filtering takes place. Remember, each customer element has an `<account_number>` attribute and `<name>`, `<poc>`, `<years>`, `<revenue>`, and `<telephone_num>` elements. At this point in the stylesheet, we'll have access to all the child elements of each `<customer>` element. So, all we need to do to perform our filtering is create the elements we want to keep (`<account_number>`, `<name>`, `<poc>`, and `<years>`), and skip over those that we don't want (`<revenue>` and `<telephone_num>`).

As you can see, first we create an attribute in the output document by using `<xsl:attribute>`. We use the same name and retrieve the current value of the attribute. Note that to retrieve the current value, we need an `@` symbol in front of the attribute name.

We then create a new element using `<xsl:element>`, using the same name as the original element, and then retrieving the values of each respective element. Note that we could have easily mapped the incoming element name to a new name in the output document. Also, we could have replaced the character data in the proprietary elements (`revenue` and `telephone_num`) with a string such as "`PROPRIETARY`."

Now that we've discussed the XSLT stylesheet, let's take a look at the Perl program that actually does the work for us.

### XML::Sablotron-Based Perl Filtering Program

Because we've looked at the input XML document and the XSLT stylesheet, we know what the output of the transformation process should be. But, how do we do it? Let's take a look at the XML::Sablotron–based Perl program shown in Listing 8.19.

Listing 8.19 **XML::Sablotron Perl program that filters an input XML document. (Filename: ch8_sab_app.pl)**

```
use strict;
use XML::Sablotron;

# Open the XSLT stylesheet.
open (XSLT, "ch8_sab_annual_report.xslt");
undef $/;
my $xslt = <XSLT>;
close XSLT;

# Open the input XML document.
open (INPUT_XML, "ch8_sab_annual_report.xml");
undef $/;
my $inputXML = <INPUT_XML>;
close INPUT_XML;

# Call the performTransform() subroutine, store the
# results in $transformedDoc.
my $transformedDoc = performTransform ($xslt, $inputXML);

# Write the results to an output file.
open (XML_REPORT, "> ch8_sab_filtered_report.xml")
  or die "Can't open ch8_sab_filtered_report.xml $!\n";
print XML_REPORT $transformedDoc;

close (XML_REPORT);

###################################
sub performTransform {
  my ($xsltDoc, $xmlDoc) = @_;

  # Instantiate the new Sablotron objects.
  my $sabObject = new XML::Sablotron;
  my $sitObject = new XML::Sablotron::Situation;

  # Pass the required arguments to the Sablotron objects.
  $sabObject->addArg($sitObject, 'xslt', $xsltDoc);
  $sabObject->addArg($sitObject, 'xml', $xmlDoc);

  # Perform the transformation.
  $sabObject->process($sitObject, 'arg:/xslt', 'arg:/xml', 'arg:/output');
```

*continues*

```
41.
42.    # Retrieve the results.
43.    my $result = $sabObject->getResultArg('arg:/output');
44.
45.    return ($result);
46. }
```

**1–12** The opening section of the program contains the usual `use strict` pragma, as well as the `use XML::Sablotron` pragma that is required to load the XML::Sablotron module.

This example is a little longer than it actually needs to be because we're going to do a few things differently in this example. In our previous examples, we read in the XML and XSLT stylesheet files directly (that is, we used the `parse_file` method in the XML::LibXSLT example). Here, we're going to utilize a subroutine that performs the parsing—it accepts the input XML document and XSLT stylesheet as arguments and returns the transformed XML document.

As you can see, we open and read the XSLT stylesheet and the input XML document and store the contents in the `$xslt` and `$inputXML` scalars, respectively. Pay particular attention to the `undef` function in this example. The `$/` symbol is the input record separator, which is by default a newline. The construct `undef $/` undefines the input record separator, so the entire file is read into the scalar. Typically, by default, the construct `<FILE>` would read only one line at a time.

```
1.  use strict;
2.  use XML::Sablotron;
3.
4.  # Open the XSLT stylesheet.
5.  open (XSLT, "ch8_sab_annual_report.xslt");
6.  undef $/;
7.  my $xslt = <XSLT>;
8.  close XSLT;
9.
10. # Open the input XML document.
11. open (INPUT_XML, "ch8_sab_annual_report.xml");
12. undef $/;
13. my $inputXML = <INPUT_XML>;
14. close INPUT_XML;
```

**16–25** Now we have the XSLT stylesheet and the XML input document in scalars. We call the locally defined `performTransform` subroutine and pass in the XSLT stylesheet and XML input document scalars, and the transformed document is returned. Note that if the XSLT stylesheet or XML input document was large, you would probably want to use references to the scalars.

```
16. # Call the performTransform() subroutine, store the
17. # results in $transformedDoc.
18. my $transformedDoc = performTransform ($xslt, $inputXML);
19.
20. # Write the results to an output file.
21. open (XML_REPORT, "> ch8_sab_filtered_report.xml")
22.   or die "Can't open ch8_sab_filtered_report.xml $!\n";
23. print XML_REPORT $transformedDoc;
24.
25. close (XML_REPORT);
```

**Note**

For additional information about Perl references, see perldoc perlref.

**28–46** This subroutine is what performs all the work for us in this program. After assigning the input scalars to local variables, we need to instantiate new `XML::Sablotron` and `XML::Sablotron::Situation` objects. The `XML::Sablotron` object is our XSLT processor, while the `XML::Sablotron::Situation` object is more of a helper object for the processor. The `XML::Sablotron::Situation` object provides several methods that are useful for debugging particular situations.

```
28. sub performTransform {
29.   my ($xsltDoc, $xmlDoc) = @_;
30.
31.   # Instantiate the new Sablotron objects.
32.   my $sabObject = new XML::Sablotron;
33.   my $sitObject = new XML::Sablotron::Situation;
34.
35.   # Pass the required arguments to the Sablotron objects.
36.   $sabObject->addArg($sitObject, 'xslt', $xsltDoc);
37.   $sabObject->addArg($sitObject, 'xml', $xmlDoc);
38.
39.   # Perform the transformation.
40.   $sabObject->process($sitObject, 'arg:/xslt', 'arg:/xml', 'arg:/output');
41.
42.   # Retrieve the results.
43.   my $result = $sabObject->getResultArg('arg:/output');
44.
45.   return ($result);
46. }
```

After instantiating the objects, we call the method `addArg()` to pass in arguments to the XSLT processor. The arguments to the `addArg()` method are situation object, buffer name, and XML data. In our case, the situation object is named `$sitObject`, the buffer names are specified in the `arg:/name` scheme, and the XML data is passed in as a scalar. After all the arguments are provided, we can call the XML::Sablotron method `process()` to actually perform the transformation. Finally, the result is retrieved from the XSLT processor by calling the `getResultArg()` method and the result is returned and then written to an output file. The output file contains the transformed XML document and is discussed in the next section.

> **Note**
> The Sablotron module has dependencies on two additional packages. To use the Sablotron module, you also need to install the Sablotron and Expat XML parser libraries. For additional information and links to download these libraries, see perldoc XML::Sablotron.

### Generated XML Output Document

The Perl program generates the filtered XML document that is shown in Listing 8.20. As you can see, the `<revenue>` and `<telephone_num>` elements have been removed from each occurrence of a `<customer>` element.

Listing 8.20 **Output filtered XML document. (Filename: ch8_sab_filtered_report.xml)**

```
<?xml version="1.0"?>
<!DOCTYPE annual_report SYSTEM "ch8_sab_annual_report.dtd">
<annual_report>
   <customer account_number="id_1">
      <name>Microsoft Corporation</name>
      <poc>Bill Gates</poc>
      <years>10</years>
   </customer>
   <customer account_number="id_2">
      <name>Oracle Corporation</name>
      <poc>Larry Ellison</poc>
      <years>12</years>
   </customer>
   <customer account_number="id_3">
      <name>Cisco Systems</name>
      <poc>John Chambers</poc>
      <years>5</years>
   </customer>
   <customer account_number="id_4">
      <name>Dell Computer Corporation</name>
      <poc>Michael Dell</poc>
      <years>6</years>
</customer></annual_report>
```

## Summary

This chapter demonstrated transforming XML documents by using several XSLT Perl modules. As you can see, these modules provide you with powerful tools for converting XML documents into other formats. It may take some practice to become comfortable with XSLT stylesheets, but as you have seen, they enable you to easily filter and transform XML documents into a number of output formats.

## Exercises

1. Modify the XSLT stylesheet used in the XML::LibXSLT example shown in Listing 8.8 to filter one of the fields from the output HTML table. Hint: look at the XSLT stylesheet that was used to perform the filtering in the example shown in Listing 8.12.
2. Modify the XML::Sablotron example in Listing 8.12, so that instead of removing the proprietary elements, the character data inside the proprietary elements is replaced with the string "PROPRIETARY." So, the customer elements in the output document would look like this:

```
<customer account_number="id_1">
   <name>Microsoft Corporation</name>
   <poc>Bill Gates</poc>
   <years>10</years>
   <revenue>PROPRIETARY</revenue>
   <telephone_num>PROPRIETARY</telephone_num>
</customer>
```

## Relevant Links

XSLT Standard Version 1.0: http://www.w3.org/TR/xslt

Sablotron: http://www.gingerall.com/charlie/ga/xml/x_sabperl.xml

XML Path Language (XPath): http://www.w3.org/TR/xpath

XSLT C Library for Gnome: http://xmlsoft.org/XSLT/

# 9 AxKit

## Chapter Roadmap

In this chapter we discuss installation, configuration, and use of the AxKit XML application and document server. AxKit is an application and document server that uses XML processing to generate content for delivery to several different types of clients (for example, web browsers or other applications).

To run the example discussed in this chapter, you need to install the following components:

- Apache web server
- AxKit
- mod_perl
- LibXML2
- LibXSLT2
- XML::LibXML Perl module
- XML::LibXSLT Perl module

If you have any questions about Perl modules (for example, where to get them, how to install them, and so forth), please refer to Appendix B, "Perl Essentials."

Later in this chapter, I'll show you how to install and configure the Apache web server, mod_perl, AxKit, and LibXSLT. Finally, I'll provide an application that demonstrates the benefits and functionality of AxKit.

## Serving Web Content with AxKit

First, let me say that AxKit is an outstanding piece of work—it has become the de facto standard for XML content delivery and publishing. AxKit was originally developed by Matt Sergeant and is now maintained and developed by a number of developers.

Before I discuss installing and configuring all the components required for AxKit, let's take a little time and discuss how AxKit actually works. AxKit uses XML processing to generate and process that allows XML content delivery in a variety of formats. Although AxKit can be used to deliver non-XML formats, most of the time it is used to deliver XML formatted documents. You already know that XML is great for content storage and retrieval, especially in web-based systems, but there are a number of advantages to using XML for server-side processing. Let's take a look at a few of these advantages.

XML can be easily transformed to a number of formats. For example, an XML document can be transformed to another XML document, WML, HTML, CSV, PDF, or a number of other formats. Even if you have control over the clients, it may make more sense to perform all transformation at a single location (that is, at a server).

Source data can be transformed to a number of different formats (or versions of the same format) to support clients with different capabilities. For example, let's assume you need to generate HTML documents to support two clients: a standard PC and a PDA. The HTML document for the PDA might present the source information a little differently from the HTML document used on a standard PC.

XML supports different character encodings, so the same source data can be viewed using a different character encoding (depending on client browser support).

XML is rapidly increasing in popularity. So, it makes sense to move toward this as a standard for document processing. In addition, because XML is an open standard, it is becoming easier and easier to find new employees who are fluent in XML.

So, how does AxKit tie all these things together? A high-level view of the data transaction data flow with AxKit is shown in Figure 9.1.

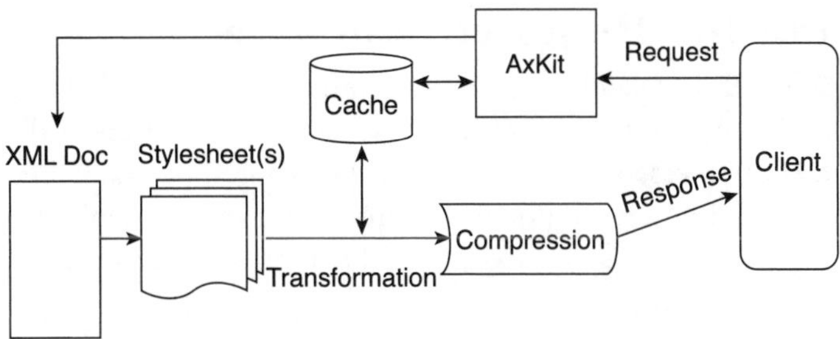


**Figure 9.1** AxKit process.

Starting on the right side of Figure 9.1, a client initiates a request to an Apache web server (that has AxKit installed) for a particular web page. Note that the client can be a browser or any other network application. AxKit then checks to see if the requested document is already cached. If the requested document has been cached (that is, requested once already and stored again for future use), then the cached version of the requested document is returned to the client. The benefit of using a cached copy is that it saves transformation time.

It is important to note that AxKit isn't limited to XML source documents. Non-XML documents and data sources can be converted to XML whenever required. Valid source data for AxKit includes a text file, the results of a database query, a Perl subroutine, or any number of other sources.

When AxKit receives a new request (that is, not cached), it retrieves and processes the requested page as needed. AxKit applies any required XSLT stylesheets to the source data to generate the required documents. AxKit then caches the results and checks to see if the requesting client supports compressed data. If so, then AxKit compresses the results and sends them back to the client. If the client doesn't support compressed data, AxKit returns the uncompressed results. AxKit has a number of complex features, but in our example, I'll demonstrate the most common basic XML content delivery.

For more information on AxKit, please visit `http://www.axkit.org`. Now that you've had a brief overview of AxKit, let's install, configure, and then run our example.

# Installing the Required Software

Our first task is to install all the software required to run the AxKit document server. Although Appendix B discusses Perl module installations, I think this is a unique enough case to cover it within the chapter, especially because you need to install other components. Here is a list of the required components,which can also be seen at the beginning of this chapter:

- Apache web server
- AxKit
- mod_perl
- LibXML2
- LibXSLT2
- XML::LibXML Perl module
- XML::LibXSLT Perl module

In this section, we'll discuss the installation instructions for each of the required components.

## Apache Web Server and mod_perl Installation

To publish web pages (either with or without AxKit), an HTTP server such as Apache needs to be installed, properly configured, and running. The Apache web server is the most powerful and popular web server in the world, and AxKit was specially designed to integrate tightly with Apache.

For our installation, we'll be using a version of the Apache web server that supports mod_perl. mod_perl is an Apache plug-in Perl interpreter that integrates with the Apache web server. It provides many benefits over CGI scripting, including increased performance, efficiency, and a persistent environment.

### Installing on Unix Systems

Binaries are available for some Unix systems, but sometimes it is just as easy to recompile locally. This usually assures that you're installing the latest version of the software. To compile a mod_perl-enabled Apache web server, you'll first need to download the source code for both packages.

The Apache web server source code is available from:

`http://www.apache.org/dist/httpd/`

The mod_perl source code is available from:

`http://perl.apache.org/dist/`

After you download the tar files to a location on the local machine, you'll need to start a command-line terminal and change directories (that is, the cd command) to the directory where both files now reside.

You can then untar and unzip the files with the following commands:

```
$ tar xvzf apache_1.3.24.tar.gz
$ tar xvzf mod_perl-1.26.tar.gz
```

The preceding commands uncompress the files into their own directories, apache_1.3.24 and mod_perl-1.26. If you use other decompression tools, use their decompression commands to untar and unzip the files.

You'll now need to cd into the mod_perl directory. As part of the mod_perl compilation, you specify the location of the Apache web server source code. The Apache web server is compiled along with the mod_perl during the compilation process. Once inside the mod_perl directory, issue the following commands:

```
$ perl Makefile.PL \
>   APACHE_SRC=/home/isterin/apache_1.3.24/src/ \
>   DO_HTTPD=1 \
>   USE_APACI=1 \
>   EVERYTHING=1

$ make
$ make test
$ su -
$ make install
```

**Note**

We'll assume that the Apache web server uncompressed source code files reside in /home/isterin/apache_1.3.24.tar and mod_perl source code files are in /home/isterin/mod_perl-1.26.tar.

The preceding commands compile, install, and configure Apache and mod_perl on standard Unix systems (for example, Linux and Solaris). Notice the su - command; it switches the current user to the root user before actually installing the software. This is required because you'll need root privileges to install the software in the default location. As with any other software, you can install Apache and mod_perl in a non-standard directory such as your home directory (this might be a good idea or your only option if you don't have root privileges on the machine). If you'd like to install it in a non-standard directory, set the APACHE_PREFIX and PREFIX flags when running perl Makefile.PL. The APACHE_PREFIX identifies the directory where you'd like the Apache binaries installed and PREFIX specifies the location where you'd like mod_perl installed. That's about it for a Unix installation of the Apache web server and mod_perl. Now let's take a look at a Microsoft Windows installation.

### Installing on Microsoft Windows

If you want to install the Apache web server and mod_perl on Windows, you either have to repeat the previous steps with Microsoft Visual C++ and the `nmake` utility, or you can download and install the Apache binary from `http://www.apache.org/dist/httpd/binaries/win32/`.

If you are running the ActiveState version of Perl under Microsoft Windows, you can use the `ppm` utility to install the mod_perl binary by running this command in the command line:

```
ppm install http://theoryx5.uwinnipeg.ca/ppmpackages/mod_perl.ppd
```

> **Note**
> If you have any questions about installing Perl modules using PPM, instructions can be found in Appendix B.

### Apache Web Server Configuration

After the Apache web server, mod_perl, and all required libraries and modules have been installed, you need to configure Apache to utilize AxKit for processing. You'll need to edit our Apache configuration file, httpd.conf.

> **Note**
> For our example, we're assuming that the Apache web server is accessed in the local machine using the default port 80.

Because we don't want to modify the server's configuration if it is already running, we'll create a new directory named `axkit-stuff` and configure Apache to serve from that directory using AxKit:

```
** Make sure you are executing this command as the root user
$ cd /usr/local/apache
$ mkdir axkit-stuff
```

> **Note**
> The following commands assume Apache is installed in the standard /usr/local/apache directory on Unix/Linux system. Microsoft Windows users have to modify the following commands a bit to accommodate the Microsoft Windows file structure as well as equivalent commands. Note also that starting and stopping the Apache web server can be accomplished by using the proper commands on the Start menu. Microsoft Windows users can check their httpd.conf files by using a tool found on the Start menu.

Now you'll configure Apache by adding these directives to the bottom of the httpd.conf file and saving it:

```
Alias /axkit-stuff "/usr/local/apache/axkit-stuff"

<Directory "/usr/local/apache/axkit-stuff">
    PerlModule AxKit
    AddHandler axkit .xml
    AxDebugLevel 10
    AxAddStyleMap  text/xsl  Apache::AxKit::Language::LibXSLT

    Options -All +Indexes +FollowSymLinks

    DirectoryIndex index.xml
</Directory>
```

You will now start your Apache web server:

```
$ /usr/local/apache/bin/apachectl start
```

Or if you already had the Apache web server up and running, you'll need to restart it:

```
$ /usr/local/apache/bin/apachectl restart
```

If everything went well, you shouldn't see any error messages. If you do happen to get errors, it most likely means you have an error in the httpd.conf file. You should then go back to the previous section, where we discussed the httpd.conf, and make sure you entered everything as shown. Make any corrections that are required and restart the Apache web server.

## Installing LibXML2 and LibXSLT2 Libraries

You'll also need to install the latest LibXML2 and LibXSLT2 libraries. You can find the latest rpm or source code versions from `ftp://xmlsoft.org/`.

If you want to recompile the source code versions locally, use the following commands to build each package. Just replace the `package.tar.gz` with the correct package name.

```
$ tar xvzf package.tar.gz
$ cd package
$ ./configure
$ make
$ make test
$ su -
$ make install
```

The latest Microsoft Windows versions of the libraries (already compiled) can be found at `http://www.fh-frankfurt.de/~igor/projects/libxml/index.html`.

If you are installing Microsoft Windows binaries, refer to the included installation instructions.

## Perl Modules

Several Perl modules need to be installed to use AxKit. Some modules are required and others are optional depending on the functionality required. The installation of the Perl modules varies depending on the operating system and distribution of Perl that you're using. I have provided instructions for installing Perl modules in Appendix B.

Some Perl modules are required and others are optional. The required modules are

- XML::LibXML
- XML::LibXSLT
- Digest::MD5 2.09 or higher
- Compress::Zlib
- Error 0.13 or higher
- Apache::Request 0.32 or higher
- HTTP::GHTTP 1.0 or higher

A number of Perl modules are optional depending on which AxKit options you use in your particular situation. The following Perl modules are optional (that is, not required for our example):

- XML::Parser 2.27 (not required in all cases, but nice to have for particular cases)
- XML::XPath 1.00 or higher is required for XPathScript
- XML::Sablotron 0.40

Although I list the required versions for most modules, as time passes, later module versions might be required. As with all the modules in the book, I recommend you use the latest stable version available.

## AxKit Perl Module Installation

Several methods exist for installing the AxKit Perl module. The first method is the manual Perl module installation. This method requires you to download the Perl module as well as all the dependencies from CPAN (or a mirror site) and install all the modules in the proper order. This method is fairly standard and works on both Unix and Microsoft Windows operating systems. Remember, a compiler is required, and it must be the same compiler that was used to build Perl for your system. For additional information, please see the detailed Perl module installation instructions in Appendix B.

The second method of installing the AxKit Perl module is to use the CPAN.pm Perl module. This method installs AxKit as well as any required dependencies all at once. If you don't already have this module installed, you can download it from CPAN (`http://www.cpan.org`) and install it. After the CPAN module is installed and configured, the following commands install AxKit.

```
$ su -
$ perl -MCPAN -e shell
cpan>install AxKit
```

This installs AxKit and all the required dependencies. After it is finished installing, you can exit the CPAN.pm prompt by typing **`quit`**.

The third method of installing the AxKit Perl module is to use the `PPM` utility. The `PPM` utility is included with ActiveState Perl distributions. To install the AxKit module using PPM, you use the following statement:

```
ppm install AxKit
```

Additional information on the `PPM` utility can be found in Appendix B.

# Making the Content for Delivery

So now that you have AxKit and all the associated components properly configured, you are ready to create some content for delivery. For this example, let's say you work for an online company that hosts resumés for job seekers. Your company is very forward-thinking, and all the resumés are stored in XML. Your task is to use Axkit, so that the original resumés in XML can be displayed in a web browser (that is, in HTML) upon request. To do this, you must transform the original XML data to HTML using XSLT. First, let's take a look at the format of the XML document that your application will be serving. A DTD for the resumé is shown in Listing 9.1.

Listing 9.1 **DTD that describes a resumé. (Filename: ch9_resume.dtd)**

```
<?xml version="1.0" encoding="UTF-8"?>
<!ELEMENT resume (name, contact, education, experience)>
<!ELEMENT name EMPTY>
<!ATTLIST name
   first CDATA #REQUIRED
   middle CDATA #REQUIRED
   last CDATA #REQUIRED>
<!ELEMENT contact (address, phone_number)>
<!ELEMENT address (street,city,state,zip)>
<!ELEMENT street (#PCDATA)>
<!ELEMENT city (#PCDATA)>
<!ELEMENT state (#PCDATA)>
```

*continues*

Listing 9.1 **Continued**

```
<!ELEMENT phone_number (#PCDATA)>
<!ELEMENT education (school, degree)>
<!ELEMENT school (#PCDATA)>
<!ELEMENT degree (#PCDATA)>
<!ELEMENT experience (work+)>
<!ELEMENT work (company, job)>
<!ELEMENT company (#PCDATA)>
<!ELEMENT job (#PCDATA)>
```

As you can see from the DTD, it describes the contents of a basic resumé. The root element is the `<resume>` element. Each `<resume>` element contains a `<name>`, `<contact>`, `<education>`, and `<experience>` element. The corresponding XML schema for an XML resumé document is shown in Listing 9.2.

Listing 9.2 **XML schema that defines the XML resumé. (Filename: ch9_resume.xsd)**

```
<?xml version="1.0" encoding="UTF-8"?>
<xs:schema xmlns:xs="http://www.w3.org/2001/XMLSchema"
elementFormDefault="qualified">
   <xs:element name="address">
      <xs:complexType>
         <xs:sequence>
            <xs:element ref="street"/>
            <xs:element ref="city"/>
            <xs:element ref="state"/>
            <xs:element ref="zip"/>
         </xs:sequence>
      </xs:complexType>
   </xs:element>
   <xs:element name="city" type="xs:string"/>
   <xs:element name="company" type="xs:string"/>
   <xs:element name="contact">
      <xs:complexType>
         <xs:sequence>
            <xs:element ref="address"/>
            <xs:element ref="phone_number"/>
         </xs:sequence>
      </xs:complexType>
   </xs:element>
   <xs:element name="degree" type="xs:string"/>
   <xs:element name="education">
      <xs:complexType>
         <xs:sequence>
```

```
            <xs:element ref="school"/>
            <xs:element ref="degree"/>
         </xs:sequence>
      </xs:complexType>
   </xs:element>
   <xs:element name="experience">
      <xs:complexType>
         <xs:sequence>
            <xs:element ref="work" maxOccurs="unbounded"/>
         </xs:sequence>
      </xs:complexType>
   </xs:element>
   <xs:element name="job" type="xs:string"/>
   <xs:element name="name">
      <xs:complexType>
         <xs:attribute name="first" type="xs:string" use="required"/>
         <xs:attribute name="middle" type="xs:string" use="required"/>
         <xs:attribute name="last" type="xs:string" use="required"/>
      </xs:complexType>
   </xs:element>
   <xs:element name="phone_number" type="xs:string"/>
   <xs:element name="resume">
      <xs:complexType>
         <xs:sequence>
            <xs:element ref="name"/>
            <xs:element ref="contact"/>
            <xs:element ref="education"/>
            <xs:element ref="experience"/>
         </xs:sequence>
      </xs:complexType>
   </xs:element>
   <xs:element name="school" type="xs:string"/>
   <xs:element name="state" type="xs:string"/>
   <xs:element name="street" type="xs:string"/>
   <xs:element name="work">
      <xs:complexType>
         <xs:sequence>
            <xs:element ref="company"/>
            <xs:element ref="job"/>
         </xs:sequence>
      </xs:complexType>
   </xs:element>
   <xs:element name="zip" type="xs:string"/>
</xs:schema>
```

The XML resumé document that we want to serve is shown in Listing 9.3 (ch9_resume.xml). Note that this is a simple example for demonstrating web delivery using AxKit.

Listing 9.3 **XML resumé that contains source data for web delivery. (Filename:ch9_resume.xml)**

```
<?xml version="1.0"?>
<?xml-stylesheet href="ch9_resume.xslt" type="text/xsl"?>
<resume>
   <name first="John" middle="R" last="Smith"/>
   <contact>
      <address>
         <street>2524 Samson Street</street>
         <city>Southfield</city>
         <state>MI</state>
         <zip>48076</zip>
      </address>
      <phone_number>248-555-8587</phone_number>
   </contact>
   <education>
      <school>Wayne State University (1992-1996)</school>
      <degree>Bachelors of Science in Computer Science</degree>
   </education>
   <experience>
   <work>
      <company>Unravelnet Software (1996-1998)</company>
       <job>Designed and developed networking applications using Perl, Java,
       ➥and XML.
       </job>
    </work>
    <work>
       <company>Ford Motor Company (1998-Present)</company>
       <job>Designed and developed web based applications using Perl, DBI, XML,
       ➥Oracle, and Apache
       </job>
    </work>
   </experience>
</resume>
```

The first step is to create an XSLT stylesheet to transform this content to HTML when the client browser requests it. The XSLT stylesheet used to perform the transformation is shown in Listing 9.4.

Listing 9.4 **XSLT stylesheet used to transform the XML resumé to HTML. (ch9_resume.xslt)**

```
<?xml version="1.0" encoding="UTF-8"?>
<xsl:stylesheet version="1.0" xmlns:xsl="http://www.w3.org/1999/XSL/Transform">
   <xsl:template match="resume">
      <html>
         <body>
            <center>
               <h2>
                  <xsl:value-of select="name/@first"/> 
                  <xsl:value-of select="name/@middle"/> 
                  <xsl:value-of select="name/@last"/></h2>
                  <xsl:value-of select="contact/address/street"/>
                  <br/>
                  <xsl:value-of select="contact/address/city"/> 
                  <xsl:value-of select="contact/address/state"/> 
                  <xsl:value-of select="contact/address/zip"/>
                  <br/>
                  <xsl:value-of select="contact/phone_number"/>
            </center>
            <br/>
            <b>
               <u>Education</u>
            </b>
            <br/>
            <xsl:value-of select="education/school"/>
            <br/>
            <xsl:value-of select="education/degree"/>
            <br/>
            <br/>
            <b>
               <u>Experience</u>
            </b>
            <br/>
            <xsl:apply-templates select="experience"/>
         </body>
      </html>
   </xsl:template>
   <xsl:template match="experience">
      <xsl:for-each select="work">
         <b>
            <xsl:value-of select="company"/></b>
         <br/>
         <xsl:value-of select="job"/>
         <br/>
         <br/>
      </xsl:for-each>
   </xsl:template>
</xsl:stylesheet>
```

You will now place both of the ch9_resume.xml and ch9_resume.xsl files into the axkit-stuff directory. At this point, everything has been configured and all the required files should be in place. How do we get AxKit to perform the XML transformation for us? Just request the ch9_resume.xml file through the browser with the URL `http://localhost/axkit-stuff/ch9_resume.xml`. The server identifies this file as needing to be processed with AxKit and proceeds with the transformation. It uses ch9_resume.xslt, specified in ch9_resume.xml, as the stylesheet. After the XML file is processed (transformed), the resulting HTML is sent to the browser. The generated HTML document is shown in Listing 9.5.

Listing 9.5 **HTML resumé document generated by AxKit. (Filename: ch9_resume.html)**

```
<html>
   <body>
      <center>
         <h2>John R Smith</h2>
           2524 Samson Street
           <br>
           Southfield MI 48076
           <br>
           248-555-8587
      </center>
      <br>
      <b><u>Education</u></b>
      <br>
      Wayne State University (1992-1996)
      <br>
      Bachelors of Science in Computer Science
      <br><br>
      <b><u>Experience</u></b>
      <br>
      <b>Unravelnet Software (1996-1998)</b>
      <br>
      Designed and developed networking applications using Perl, Java, and XML.
      <br><br>
      <b>Ford Motor Company (1998-Present)</b>
      <br>
      Designed and developed web based applications using Perl, DBI, XML, Oracle,
      ➥and Apache
   <br>
   <br>
   </body>
</html>
```

The HTML document generated by AxKit (and shown in Listing 9.5) is displayed in a browser as shown in Figure 9.2.

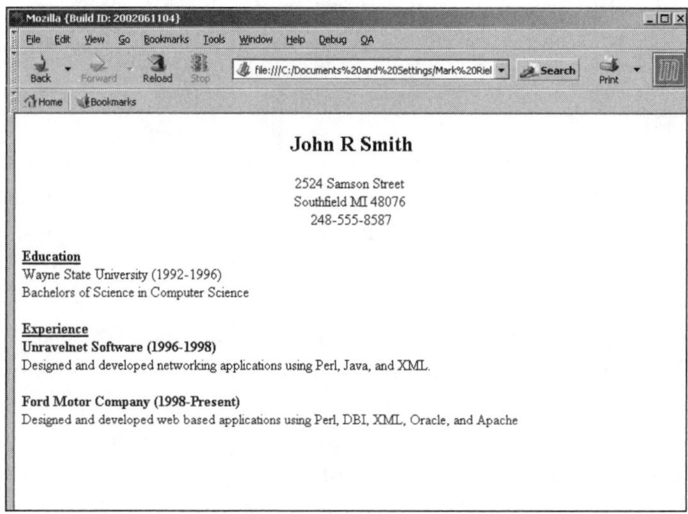


**Figure 9.2** The HTML formatted resumé generated by AxKit.

As you can see, the XML resumé was transformed to HTML and sent to the browser, nicely formatted for display. AxKit also enables you to specify multiple stylesheets, which process the document in a SAX pipeline. This enables you to apply a transformation on the result of a previous transformation.

As I have just demonstrated, AxKit can easily automate the delivery of XML content by performing on-the-fly transformations. In addition, AxKit can also support caching and compression for more efficient delivery of the generated documents.

## Additional AxKit Tools

AxKit includes a large number of tools. Unfortunately, I can't discuss all the features in detail (that would require another book); however, in the next section, I discuss the most widely used options.

### XPathScript

XPathScript is a stylesheet language for transformations that can act as a replacement for XSLT that was written by Matt Sergeant. The advantage of XPathScript over XSLT is that it enables you to embed Perl and XPath expressions within XML documents. This combines the power of XSLT with a programming language for dynamic content document creation comparable to Active Server Pages (ASP), JavaServer Pages (JSP), and PHP.

XPathScript is used the same way you use an XSLT stylesheet. The XPathScript stylesheet is specified using the `<?xml-stylesheet...?>` construct in the XML document. Let's modify the XML document used in the previous example to use XPathScript and demonstrate how it works. To demonstrate the dynamic capability of XPathScript, we'll add today's local time to the bottom of the output.

We'll first modify the ch9_resume.xml file to include the new stylesheet path. Let's replace this line in the XML document containing the resume:

```
<?xml-stylesheet href="ch9_resume.xslt" type="text/xsl"?>
```

with the following:

```
<?xml-stylesheet href="ch9_resume.xps" type="application/x-xpathscript"
title="default" alternate="no"?>
```

We now need to write XPathScript to transform the resume.xml (shown in Listing 9.6) and render proper output similar to our previous one (shown in Listing 9.7).

Listing 9.6 **XPathScript used to transform the XML document containing a resumé. (Filename: ch9_resume.xps)**

```
<html>
   <body>
      <center>
         <h2>
            <%= join(' ', findvalue('/resume/name/@first'),
                               findvalue('/resume/name/@middle'),
                               findvalue('/resume/name/@last'));
```

```
            %>
          </h2>
          <%= findvalue('resume/contact/address/street/text()') %>
          <br/>
          <%= join(' ', findvalue('/resume/contact/address/city/text()'),
                        findvalue('/resume/contact/address/state/text()'),
                        findvalue('/resume/contact/address/zip/text()'));
          %>
          <br/>
          <%= findvalue('/resume/contact/phone_number/text()') %></center>
          <br/>
          <b><u>Education</u></b>
          <br/>
          <%= findvalue('/resume/education/school/text()') %>
          <br/>
          <%= findvalue('/resume/education/degree/text()') %>
          <br/><br/>
          <b><u>Experience</u></b>
          <br/>
          <% my @nodes = findnodes('/resume/experience/work');
             foreach my $node (@nodes) {
               print "<b>".findvalue('./company/text()', $node)."</b>";
               print "<br/>";
               print findvalue('./job/text()', $node);
               print "<br/><br/>";
             }
          %>
          <br/>
          <br/>
          <% print "<b>Generated on: </b>";
             my $date = localtime();
             print $date;
          %>
      </body>
  </html>
```

As you can see, this is very similar to the XSLT stylesheet that we used earlier; however, there are a few important differences. For example, you can see following delimiters `<%` and `%>`. XPathScript follows the basic ASP approach of inserting code into a script. Note that we have inserted standard Perl code in between the `<%` and `>%` delimiters, and all the code is in bold typeface.

The XPathScript needs to be stored in the same directory as the ch9_resume.xml document. Because we modified the `<?xml-stylesheet...?>` directive in the XML document, we get the HTML output shown in Listing 9.7 by calling `http://localhost/axkit-stuff/ch9_resume_xps.xml` from the browser.

Listing 9.7 **Generated HTML document that includes the local time. (Filename: ch9_resume_xps.html)**

```
<html>
   <body>
      <center>
      <h2>John R Smith</h2>
      2524 Samson Street
      <br/>
      Southfield MI 48076
      <br/>
      248-555-8587</center>
      <br/>
      <b><u>Education</u></b>
      <br/>
      Wayne State University (1992-1996)
      <br/>
      Bachelors of Science in Computer Science
      <br/><br/>
      <b><u>Experience</u></b>
      <br/>
      <b>Unravelnet Software (1996-1998)</b><br/>
      Designed and developed networking applications using Perl, Java, and
      XML.<br/>
      <br/>
      <b>Ford Motor Company (1998-Present)</b><br/>
      Designed and developed web based applications using Perl, DBI, XML,
      Oracle, and Apache<br/><br/>
      <br/>
      <br/>
      <b>Generated on: </b>Mon Jun  3 19:10:51 2002
   </body>
</html>
```

The output is similar to the output generated with the ch9_resume.xslt file using XSLT. The main difference is that we utilized the power of Perl and added the current `localtime()` to the output. As you can see in Figure 9.3, I added a footer, `Generated on:`, that displays the current date and time and is dynamically generated every time you reload the page.

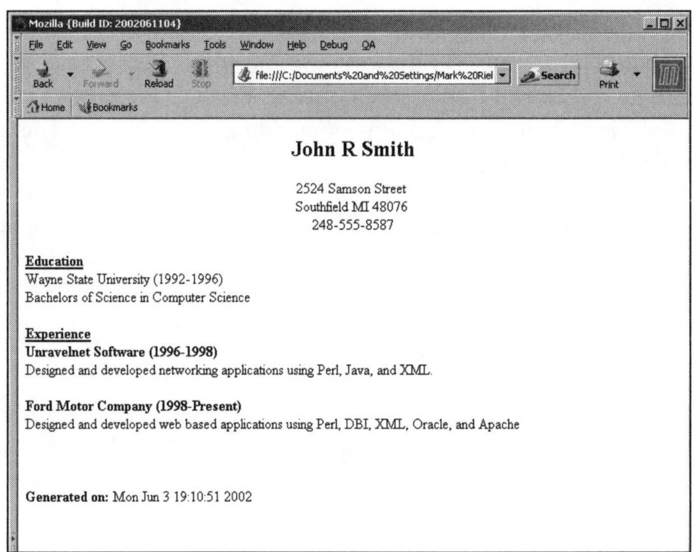


**Figure 9.3** Output resumé viewed in a browser XPathScript generated local time.

## eXtensible Server Pages

Another related technology supported by AxKit is eXtensible Server Pages (XSP). XSP is an XML-based technology that supports embedded code on a web server. So, XSP enables you to define and embed custom tags within the XML documents. These custom tags are executed each time the page is requested. XSP works similarly to Macromedia ColdFusion, for those who are familiar with that technology.

A small example of an XSP page, shown in Listing 9.8, demonstrates just how useful this utility can be. We'll use a small comma-delimited file of names, parse them, and output them from within our XSP-based application.

Listing 9.8 **Input source data for an XSP-based application. (Filename: ch9_names.csv)**

```
Ilya,Sterin
Mark,Riehl
Jennifer,Eberhardt
Elise,Walter
```

In this case, our input file is a simple CSV file that we can easily parse using Perl's `split()` function. Our task here is to use a simple application to parse the contents of a CSV file and display the contents in an HTML file. Listing 9.9 shows an XSP document that contains embedded Perl code that is executed whenever the document is accessed.

Listing 9.9 **XSP file used to parse and print the contents of a CSV input file. (Filename: ch9_names.xsp)**

```
<?xml version="1.0"?>
<xsp:page xmlns:xsp="http://www.apache.org/1999/XSP/Core"
              xmlns="uri://axkit.org/NS/MyHomePage"
              language="Perl">
<html>
  <body>
    <h1>XML and Perl Book</h1>
    <b><u>Authors and Staff</u></b>
    <br/>
      <xsp:logic><![CDATA[
        open FILE, "names.csv";
        my @lines = <FILE>;
        foreach (@lines) {
          print join(" ", split("," @lines))."\n<br/>";
        }
      ]]></xsp:logic>
  </body>
</html>
</xsp:page>
```

When called from the browser, as `http://localhost/axkit-stuff/names.xsp`, the HTML output appears as shown in Listing 9.10.

Listing 9.10 **XSP-generated HTML document. (Filename: ch9_names_xsp.html)**

```
<?xml version="1.0" encoding="UTF-8"?>
<html>
  <body>
    <h1>XML and Perl Book</h1>
    <b><u>Authors and Staff</u></b>
    <br/>
      Ilya Sterin
      <br/>Mark Riehl
      <br/>Jennifer Eberhardt
      <br/>Elise Walter
  </body>
</html>
```

Viewed from within a browser, the output from Listing 9.10 appears as shown in Figure 9.4.

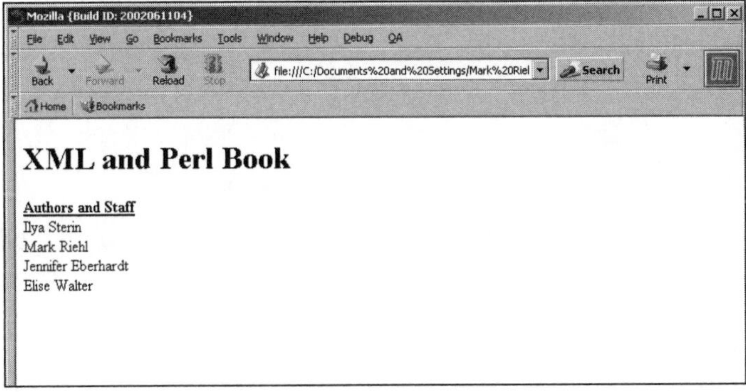


**Figure 9.4** HTML document generated using XSP.

# Summary

This chapter demonstrated the power of the AxKit Perl module. Even though the examples were simple for demonstration purposes, I believe they showed the capabilities offered by this module. AxKit opens the door for a number of potential applications. By taking advantage of XPathScript or the XSP capabilities of XML, you can quickly and easily build web pages with dynamic content. For example, in our last example, you can easily replace the opening and loading of the CSV file with results of a database query made using the Perl DBI.

# Exercise

1. Modify the example shown in Listing 9.9 to replace the CSV input data, so it displays the results of a database query using the Perl DBI.

For suggested solutions to this exercise, be sure to check out the web site: `http://www.xmlproj.com/book/chapter9`.

# Relevant Links

AxKit: `http://www.axkit.org`
XPathScript: `http://www.axkit.org/docs/xpathscript/guide.dkb?style=print`
XSP Documentation: `http://axkit.org/docs/xsp/index.xml`

# 10

# Perl and XML Web Services

## Chapter Roadmap

This chapter discusses web services and some of the Perl facilities that support them. First, I'll discuss web services in general and how they are transforming the World Wide Web and all its applications. Then, I'll briefly touch on several of the web service protocols available. Finally, I'll discuss the two most important and widely used web-related protocols, the Simple Object Access Protocol (SOAP) and XML-Remote Procedure Protocol (XML-RPC).

The SOAP discussion includes examples built with the SOAP::Lite module, which is the SOAP implementation module that includes some additional functionality. Examples include a SOAP daemon and client, as well as a section on using SOAP::Lite with web service applications that utilize the Web Services Description Language (WSDL).

XML-RPC is another protocol for web services, and it will be discussed using examples that utilize the Frontier::RPC Perl module. I'll discuss the advantages and disadvantages of both SOAP and XML-RPC and give you a good background that will allow you to choose the right approach for your implementation.

# What Are Web Services?

The term "web services" means different things to different people. From a technical point of view, web services describe a suite of protocols built upon XML and HyperText Transfer Protocol (HTTP). HTTP is widely available all across the Internet and it is very well supported. Why use XML and HTTP? Well, we all know the benefits of XML when it comes to exchanging data. When combined with HTTP, XML can be used to describe both simple and sophisticated transactions between clients and services across the Internet. But before we actually discuss web services, let's take a look back and see how and why they were developed.

Throughout the short history of web programming, developers have created unique ways of allowing applications to communicate with one another. Most of the time, the developers of both systems would get together, define their interface, and then modify their applications to adapt to the new protocol. In many cases, that worked fine, but the web is enormous and you can only imagine the complexity required if an application required a unique protocol to exchange information with a large number of other applications—you would need hundreds (if not thousands) of APIs to support this. The next section discusses the application of a simple web service.

## Example of a Web Service

Imagine that you are responsible for a web portal for a vacation resort. The web page includes resort-specific information, such as contact information, travel directions, and so forth. Now, as a convenient feature for potential customers, you'd like to display the current temperature in your city. There are several approaches to providing this information.

- You can get a thermometer and update the temperature frequently (not very practical).
- You can check `http://www.weather.com` and possibly have a link to their web site.
- The third, and most practical, approach would be to provide live temperature information from another organization such as `http://www.weather.com` that provides weather information as a web service.

Well, we're in luck because `http://www.weather.com` does provide temperature information as a web service. Now you can easily add an interface to your application that will access their web service and retrieve the current temperature for your resort. This way, whenever a customer looks at your web site, they'll see the current temperature. Because `http://www.weather.com` provides the temperature service without any restrictions (that is, anyone can use it), you need to provide the service with some type of geographic information (that is, where you live), so it can provide the proper temperature reading. Whenever you make a temperature query, all you need to do is provide a zip or postal code; this way, the service provider can look up the current weather in your area.

### Exchanging Data on the Web

One of the first approaches to exchanging data on the web was Electronic Data Exchange (EDI). EDI defined messages and protocols, but it didn't define any network requirements. Unfortunately, the end result was a series of proprietary networks with limited memberships that were difficult to interconnect.

Another approach to distributing information across the web attempted to build a distributed object infrastructure and distribute objects containing data. There were actually three similar implementations that built upon the idea of distributing objects. The three approaches were Common Object Request Broker Architecture (CORBA), Remote Method Invocation (RMI), and Distributed Component Object Model (DCOM). The problem with these approaches is that each implementation selected a different protocol to transport objects. For example, the CORBA developers decided to use Internet Inter-ORB Protocol (IIOP), the DCOM developers decided to use Object Remote Procedure Call (ORPC), and the RMI developers decided to use Java Remote Method Protocol (JRMP). The major problem with these approaches was the lack of interoperability. Following this schema, CORBA could only communicate to CORBA, RMI could only communicate to RMI, and DCOM could only communicate to DCOM. Also, none of the approaches could easily communicate directly to the web—each required an extra protocol layer that provided a special socket interface.

As you can see, the early approaches to exchanging data on the web all had their own problems. To address most (if not all) of these problems, new XML-based protocols for web services were developed. The most important of these protocols is discussed in the next section.

## Web Service Protocols

Web services use XML messaging as a means of communication. Because they use XML, web services and the language used to implement them are transparent to the platform on which they reside. This way, any application running on any platform and written in almost any programming language can communicate with an XML-based web service.

The three major protocols involved with web services are Simple Object Access Protocol (SOAP); Universal Description, Discovery, and Integration Protocol (UDDI); and Web Services Description Language (WSDL). In this section, I'll briefly discuss each of these protocols.

### Simple Object Access Protocol

Microsoft, Develop-Mentor, and Dave Winer developed a new protocol named SOAP to address the shortcomings of the previous approaches to distributing services. Version 1.0 of the SOAP specification was released in 1998. The W3C took over development of the standard and released version 1.2 in July 2001.

SOAP is an XML-based messaging protocol that was designed to facilitate exchanging structure information using the web or a web-like environment (that is, decentralized). SOAP messages are XML documents that are transported back and forth between servers and clients. SOAP can use a variety of network protocols to connect to web services, including HTTP, POP3, FTP, and SMTP. SOAP can also be used in a variety of applications that require XML messaging. I'll only discuss the most popular usage of SOAP, which is its facility for remote method invocation over HTTP. SOAP is cross-platform, as long as the programming language you use has the SOAP facilities. Even if your favorite programming language doesn't have the SOAP API, you can contribute to the open source community by writing your version of the SOAP API. SOAP specifications are open source and available at `http://www.w3.org` for anyone to implement.

What is so great about SOAP? It combines the best of both worlds by using the capabilities of XML with the transport capability of HTTP. By taking advantage of both of these open standards, SOAP eliminates the data transport problems associated with EDI and the interoperability problems associated with CORBA, RMI, and DCOM. Just as XML separates data from the presentation of the data, SOAP separates the data from the underlying transport protocol. In the next section, we'll take a look at the format of a SOAP message.

#### *Format of a SOAP Message*

A SOAP message is an XML document that follows a particular format. The SOAP message format has the following sections:

- **Envelope (required)**—The SOAP message envelope is actually the mandatory root element named `<Envelope>` of the SOAP message.
- **Header (optional)**—The SOAP message `<Header>` element is an optional component of a SOAP message. The `<Header>` element is used to instruct SOAP servers to perform some specialized processing before sending the SOAP message out to the next destination. An example of a `<Header>` element instruction would be to instruct a SOAP server to add some security-related information for authentication.
- **Body (required)**—The `<Body>` element of a SOAP message contains the transported XML document.

### Universal Description, Discovery, and Integration Protocol

The Universal Description, Discovery, and Integration (UDDI) protocol is used to describe the components of web services. After a web service has been described using UDDI, it can be registered with an Internet directory that advertises the web service. The Internet directories enable businesses to advertise their web services and find other web services. The major benefit of UDDI is that it provides a global and platform-independent method of describing and discovering web services.

### Web Services Description Language

The Web Services Description Language (WSDL) standard is an XML-based standard used to describe web services. WSDL defines XML grammar that describes both the interface and implementation details of web services. It is important to note that WSDL supports describing web services regardless of the message format or protocol that is used.

### Relationship Between Web Services Protocols

Now that I've introduced you to the web services protocols, let's take a look at how they work together to support web services. Figure 10.1 shows the interaction between web services protocols.

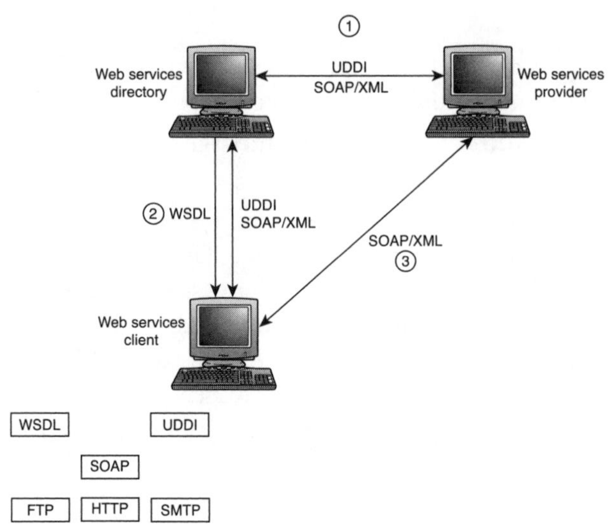


**Figure 10.1** Web services protocols interaction.

As you can see in Figure 10.1, we have a web services provider, a web services directory, and a web services client. The first step shown in Figure 10.1 is labeled with the number "1" and shows the exchange using UDDI between a web services provider and a web services directory. A web services provider registers a web service using UDDI with a web services directory, so that web clients can locate the web service. After the service has been registered with the web services directory, a web services client can locate the web service by searching the web services directory. This is labeled as step "2" in Figure 10.1. The web services client receives a WSDL XML document that provides all the required connection information. After the web services client has the XML WSDL document, it can connect to the web services provider. Later in this chapter, I'll show examples of web services clients connecting to web service providers.

As you can see, the web services directory has a function similar to a Domain Name Server (DNS). Usually, if your PC or workstation tries to ping a host on the Internet (let's say `www.newriders.com`), your PC or workstation first queries a DNS server and asks for the equivalent IP address. That's because PCs, workstations, and routers use IP addresses rather than hostnames. In the case of web services, we're asking the web services directory which web services provider offers a particular service and what information do I need to connect to it.

I think that you can now see the potential and usefulness of web services. The rest of the chapter concentrates on several examples that demonstrate how to access web services as well as how to develop your own web service.

## Web Service SOAP Client Examples

The SOAP::Lite Perl module provides a Perl API to SOAP and handles most of the low-level details for you. A SOAP server and a SOAP client are two applications that are usually (but aren't required to be) running on different machines. A SOAP client sends a request to a SOAP server, the server processes the request, and returns the result to the SOAP client. In the case of Remote Procedure Calls (RPCs), the request sent by the SOAP client is actually a request to execute a function on the SOAP server. When the SOAP server receives the requests, it executes the requested function, packages up the results in a SOAP message, and returns the results to the calling SOAP client.

Earlier, I discussed a web service provider that would return the current temperature for a particular postal zip code. In the next section, I'm going to show you how to build a Perl client that accesses a web service that provides temperature information.

### SOAP Client

In this section, we'll build several SOAP clients using the SOAP::Lite Perl module. Don't be misled by the name—the SOAP::Lite Perl module is a full and advanced implementation of SOAP. The word Lite in the module title applies to the Perl module's ease of use rather than its functionality.

The first step in building a SOAP client is to determine the web service that we want to use. Where are publicly available SOAP servers, and what services do they offer? Due to the popularity of SOAP, a number of web service repositories have been created that contain information about available web services. These repositories contain information about available web services (for example, where they are located) and provide the API documentation necessary to use them. One such web service repository that was particularly useful during the development of the book is `http://www.xmethods.net`. This web site provides a variety of web services itself and also provides information about web services available on other servers. Looking through the site, we found a web service provided by XMethods named Weather-Temperature. As you may have already guessed from the name, the Weather-Temperature service provides the current temperature based on a zip code.

Associated with each web service is an RPC profile. An RPC contains all the information that is required to manually configure SOAP RPC calls. The RPC profile for the Weather-Temperature web service is shown in Table 10.1.

Table 10.1 **RPC profile for the Weather-Temperature web service.**

| **Method Name** | **GetTemp** |
|---|---|
| Endpoint URL | `http://services.xmethods.net:80/soap/servlet/rpcrouter` |
| SOAPAction | |
| Method Namespace URI | `urn:xmethods-Temperature` |
| Input Parameters | Zip code string |
| Output Parameters | Return float |

Looking at the RPC profile in the preceding table, we can see that there is only one method available. The method is named `getTemp`. As you can see from Table 10.1, the method has one input parameter and one output parameter. The input parameter is the zip code from the area of interest, and the output method contains the current temperature. Note that the method is contained in the `urn:xmethods-Temperature` namespace and that the service URL is: `http://services.xmethods.net:80/soap/servlet/rpcrouter`

Now that we have the information that we need (that is, the contents of the RPC profile), we can create a SOAP::Lite client and use it to call the Weather-Temperature service. The SOAP::Lite client application built using the contents of the RPC profile is shown in Listing 10.1.

Listing 10.1 **SOAP::Lite-based client application to retrieve temperature based on a zip code. (Filename: ch10_soap_retrieve_temp_app.pl)**

```
use strict;
use SOAP::Lite;

# Instantiate a new SOAP::Lite object
my $service = new SOAP::Lite
          ->uri('urn:xmethods-Temperature')
          ->proxy('http://services.xmethods.net/soap/servlet/rpcrouter');

# Remotely call the getTemp method
my $result = $service->getTemp(SOAP::Data->type(string => '08736'));

unless ($result->fault) {
  print $result->result();
} else {
  print join ', ',
```

```
16.         $result->faultcode,
17.         $result->faultstring,
18.         $result->faultfactor,
19.         $result->faultdetail;
20.  }
```

**1–7** In this section of the application, we start off by using the standard `use strict` pragma statement. Because we're using SOAP::Lite, we also need the `use SOAP::Lite` pragma statement to load the module. The first step after loading the module is to instantiate a SOAP::Lite module by using the `new()` method.

After we create a SOAP::Lite object, we call the `uri()` and `proxy()` methods. The `uri()` method is actually a shortcut to the `serializer->uri()` method. The `uri()` method enables us to specify the URI for SOAP methods. In our case, the URI is the method namespace specified in the namespace profile. Note that URIs may look similar to URLs, but aren't required to actually point anywhere. URIs will, however, be unique within the space of XML documents.

The `proxy` method is actually a shortcut to the `transport->proxy()` method. The `proxy` method enables us to specify an endpoint (or service address) for the web service. Note that the name of the module is prepended with the transport protocol that we'll be using.

The prefix SOAP::Transport is also prepended to the name, so the module will be loaded and an object (also with an appended "::Client") will be created. So, the class that creates objects will look for the name "SOAP::Transport::HTTP::Client."

In this example, we're not using any transport-specific parameters, but the `proxy()` method can also accept any transport-specific parameters that may be required. For example, we can specify an HTTP timeout or any required cookie-specific parameters.

```
1.   use strict;
2.   use SOAP::Lite;
3.
4.   # Instantiate a new SOAP::Lite object
5.   my $service = new SOAP::Lite
6.             ->uri('urn:xmethods-Temperature')
7.             ->proxy('http://services.xmethods.net/soap/servlet/rpcrouter');
```

**Note**

The context of the calls may look a little strange (that is, no commas between the `new()`, `uri()`, and `proxy()` methods). That's because all the methods with parameters will return the current object. The SOAP::Lite Perl module author says that the module supports method "stacking."

**9–10** After we have created our service object, we can proceed to call the `getTemp` method available through the web service and pass it the `zip_code` argument (in our case `08736`). After the call is processed by the web service, it returns the current temperature (in degrees Fahrenheit) in a float data type. Because Perl does not have strong typing, the temperature is returned as a scalar. Note that the result is returned in a result object instead of just a value. This object can then be used to retrieve the returned value or print out an error message if an error was returned by the web service.

```
9.  # Remotely call the getTemp method
10. my $result = $service->getTemp(SOAP::Data->type(string => '08736'));
```

**12–19** If the remote method didn't encounter any errors and no faults have been returned, we can print the result. The result is retrieved from the object by using an access method named `result()`. If an error occurred, it is returned as a `SOAP Fault` element. Each `SOAP Fault` element contains the following four child elements:

- **`faultcode`**—This element is intended to be used by your software to provide a mechanism to identify the fault. The `faultcode` is required to appear in a `SOAP Fault` element, and it must be an XML-qualified name. The SOAP standard has defined a few SOAP faultcodes that cover basic faults.
- **`faultstring`**—This element is supposed to provide a human-readable string that describes the fault. The `faultstring` element is required to appear in a `SOAP Fault` element.
- **`faultfactor`**—This element is intended to provide additional information about who caused the fault to occur throughout the message path.
- **`faultdetail`**—This element is intended to carry application-specific fault information.

```
12. unless ($result->fault) {
13.   print $result->result();
14. } else {
15.   print join ', ',
16.     $result->faultcode,
17.     $result->faultstring,
18.     $result->faultfactor,
19.     $result->faultdetail;
20. }
```

When you run the example shown in Listing 10.1, the temperature for your zip code is returned. Before we move on to the next example, take a look at Listing 10.2. Listing 10.2 contains the SOAP request that we sent out to the temperature web service.

Listing 10.2 **Example SOAP weather request to retrieve the temperature for a particular zip code. (Filename: ch10_soap_request.xml)**

```
<SOAP-ENV:Envelope xmlns:SOAP-ENV="http://schemas.xmlsoap.org/soap/envelope/"
                   xmlns:xsi="http://www.w3.org/1999/XMLSchema-instance"
                   xmlns:xsd="http://www.w3.org/1999/XMLSchema">
<SOAP-ENV:Body>
<ns1:getTemp xmlns:ns1="urn:xmethods-Temperature"
             SOAP-ENV:encodingStyle="http://schemas.xmlsoap.org/soap/encoding/">
<zipcode xsi:type="xsd:string">08736</zipcode>
</ns1:getTemp>
</SOAP-ENV:Body>
</SOAP-ENV:Envelope>
```

As you can see, the SOAP request contains the required SOAP `<Envelope>` and `<Body>` elements. You can see that we are calling the `xmethods-Temperature` service and executing the `getTemp` method with the `zip_code` argument.

After the server receives this call, it is responsible for parsing the request and providing the information requested as a SOAP response. The simple return message for this RPC is shown in Listing 10.3.

Listing 10.3 **Example SOAP weather reply. (Filename: ch10_soap_response.xml)**

```
<SOAP-ENV:Envelope xmlns:SOAP-ENV="http://schemas.xmlsoap.org/soap/envelope/"
                   xmlns:xsi="http://www.w3.org/1999/XMLSchema-instance"
                   xmlns:xsd="http://www.w3.org/1999/XMLSchema">
<SOAP-ENV:Body>
<ns1:getTempResponse xmlns:ns1="urn:xmethods-Temperature"
                     SOAP-
ENV:encodingStyle="http://schemas.xmlsoap.org/soap/encoding/">
<return xsi:type="xsd:float">79.0</return>
</ns1:getTempResponse>
</SOAP-ENV:Body>
</SOAP-ENV:Envelope>
```

### WSDL

Another technology that is quickly emerging along with SOAP is the WSDL specification that is used to describe web services. WSDL describes all functions available for the web service, all the data types for response and request messages, web service location information, and the transport protocol binding information. WSDL facilitates web service invocation by providing both descriptive and connectivity information about a web service in a single XML document. Using WSDL tools, you can easily construct a SOAP client that can be quickly modified to support any potential web service changes.

The service described earlier, Weather-Temperature, has an associated WSDL file that describes the web service. The WSDL file is shown in Listing 10.4.

**Note**

The WSDL file can be viewed at `http://www.xmethods.net/sd/2001/TemperatureService.wsdl`.

Listing 10.4 **Weather temperature WSDL file. (Filename: ch10_temp_service.wsdl)**

```
<?xml version="1.0"?>
<definitions name="TemperatureService"
targetNamespace="http://www.xmethods.net/sd/TemperatureService.wsdl"
xmlns:tns="http://www.xmethods.net/sd/TemperatureService.wsdl"
xmlns:xsd="http://www.w3.org/2001/XMLSchema"
xmlns:soap="http://schemas.xmlsoap.org/wsdl/soap/"
xmlns="http://schemas.xmlsoap.org/wsdl/">
   <message name="getTempRequest">
      <part name="zipcode" type="xsd:string"/>
   </message>
   <message name="getTempResponse">
      <part name="return" type="xsd:float"/>
   </message>
   <portType name="TemperaturePortType">
      <operation name="getTemp">
         <input message="tns:getTempRequest"/>
         <output message="tns:getTempResponse"/>
      </operation>
   </portType>
   <binding name="TemperatureBinding" type="tns:TemperaturePortType">
      <soap:binding style="rpc" transport="http://schemas.xmlsoap.org/soap/http"/>
      <operation name="getTemp">
         <soap:operation soapAction=""/>
         <input>
            <soap:body use="encoded" namespace="urn:xmethods-Temperature"
            ➥encodingStyle="http://schemas.xmlsoap.org/soap/encoding/"/>
         </input>
         <output>
            <soap:body use="encoded" namespace="urn:xmethods-Temperature"
            ➥encodingStyle="http://schemas.xmlsoap.org/soap/encoding/"/>
         </output>
      </operation>
   </binding>
   <service name="TemperatureService">
      <documentation>Returns current temperature in a given U.S. zipcode
      ➥</documentation>
      <port name="TemperaturePort" binding="tns:TemperatureBinding">
         <soap:address location="http://services.xmethods.net:80/
         ➥soap/servlet/rpcrouter"/>
      </port>
   </service>
</definitions>
```

Looking at the WSDL file, you'll notice some familiar contents that include the web service URL, namespace, and its method(s). Now we'll take a look at a SOAP::Lite-based example to invoke this web service with the WSDL file. The Perl application to do this is shown in Listing 10.5.

Listing 10.5 **Program that uses the SOAP::Lite module and a WSDL file to retrieve the temperature based on a zip code. (Filename: ch10_getWeather_wsdl.pl)**

```
use SOAP::Lite;

my $result = SOAP::Lite
   ->service('http://www.xmethods.net/sd/2001/TemperatureService.wsdl')
   ->getTemp(08736);

print $result;
```

Running this example, the result was 84 degrees (a warm early summer day). As you can see, this is a very short example, but I believe it is an important example. It demonstrates how to use a WSDL XML document to access a web service. Looking at the above example, we can see that the WSDL file is first loaded using the SOAP::Lite `service` method, and then the method is called. Notice that we didn't have to specify the service namespace or location because SOAP::Lite retrieves this information from the WSDL file. Also, note that we didn't need a copy of the WSDL XML document locally to access the web service; we just needed a path to the WSDL file. So far, the examples have only been SOAP clients. In the next example, I'll show you what is required to build your own web service provider application.

## Web Service Client and Server Example

Now that I demonstrated how easily SOAP clients can be built and used with the existing SOAP servers, we'll build a full SOAP application (that is, both the server and the client). So, if you wanted to register this application as a web service with a web services directory, it would be accessible through the Internet.

Because SOAP was originally designed to be platform- and language-independent, the SOAP client and SOAP server can each reside on two different platforms and can be written in two different languages. For example, Weather-Temperature service, which we accessed in our earlier SOAP client examples, was actually written using the Apache SOAP toolkit for Java. We don't need to know which platform a web service resides on, nor do we need to know which toolkit/language was used to develop the service. As long as a web service conforms to the SOAP standards, we know our client will be able to communicate with the web service.

In this example, both the SOAP client and the SOAP server will reside on the same platform (that is, we will connect to a service located on localhost/127.0.0.1).

> **Note**
>
> To run this example, you'll need a web server (for example, Apache) installed, running, and configured to accept incoming connections on port 80. Precompiled Apache web server binaries for a number of platforms are available at `http://www.apache.org`.

### Web Service Description

Let's pretend that you work for an online reseller, and you've been asked to develop a web service application that provides real-time access to the current book inventory. Currently, the book inventory is stored in an XML document that contains the following information for each book: name, publisher, author, pages, and price.

Our SOAP-based application is a web services client that retrieves information about any published book. The only input required is the International Standard Book Number (ISBN) number that has been assigned to the book. Listing 10.6 shows the DTD for the XML document that contains the inventory information.

> **Note**
>
> In case you're not familiar with it, the ISBN is almost like a social security number for books—each book is assigned a unique number. Keep this in mind in case you ever need to build a real-life application to track books; the ISBN number provides a perfect unique key.

Listing 10.6 **DTD for the book inventory. (Filename: ch10_book_inventory.dtd)**

```
<?xml version="1.0" encoding="UTF-8"?>
<!ELEMENT books (book+)>
<!ELEMENT book (name, publisher, author+,pages,price)>
<!ATTLIST book
      isbn CDATA #REQUIRED>
<!ELEMENT name (#PCDATA)>
<!ELEMENT publisher (#PCDATA)>
<!ELEMENT author (#PCDATA)>
<!ELEMENT pages (#PCDATA)>
<!ELEMENT price (#PCDATA)>
```

Listing 10.7 contains the XML schema that defines the XML book inventory document.

Listing 10.7 **XML schema for the book inventory. (Filename: ch10_book_inventory.xsd)**

```
<?xml version="1.0" encoding="UTF-8"?>
<xs:schema xmlns:xs="http://www.w3.org/2001/XMLSchema"
elementFormDefault="qualified">
   <xs:element name="author" type="xs:string"/>
   <xs:element name="book">
      <xs:complexType>
         <xs:sequence>
            <xs:element ref="name"/>
            <xs:element ref="publisher"/>
            <xs:element ref="author" maxOccurs="unbounded"/>
            <xs:element ref="pages"/>
            <xs:element ref="price"/>
         </xs:sequence>
         <xs:attribute name="isbn" type="xs:string" use="required"/>
      </xs:complexType>
   </xs:element>
   <xs:element name="books">
      <xs:complexType>
         <xs:sequence>
            <xs:element ref="book" maxOccurs="unbounded"/>
         </xs:sequence>
      </xs:complexType>
   </xs:element>
   <xs:element name="name" type="xs:string"/>
   <xs:element name="pages" type="xs:string"/>
   <xs:element name="price" type="xs:string"/>
   <xs:element name="publisher" type="xs:string"/>
</xs:schema>
```

The XML document containing all the book information is shown in Listing 10.8. As you can see, this is a fairly simple XML document that contains the important information for several books.

Listing 10.8 **Book inventory information stored in XML. (Filename: ch10_book_inventory.xml)**

```
<?xml version="1.0"?>
<books>
  <book isbn="0596000952">
    <name>Programming Web Services with SOAP</name>
    <publisher>O'Reilly</publisher>
    <author>James Snell</author>
    <author>Doug Tidwell</author>
    <author>Pavel Kulchenko</author>
    <pages>244</pages>
    <price>34.95</price>
```

*continues*

Listing 10.8 **Continued**

```
  </book>
  <book isbn="0201615711">
    <name>Network Programming with Perl</name>
    <publisher>Addison Wesley</publisher>
    <author>Lincoln D. Stein</author>
    <pages>754</pages>
    <price>39.99</price>
  </book>
  <book isbn="020170353X">
    <name>Accelerated C++</name>
    <publisher>Addison Wesley</publisher>
    <author>Andrew Koenig</author>
    <author>Barbara E. Moo</author>
    <pages>336</pages>
    <price>33.95</price>
  </book>
</books>
```

Now that we've looked at the data that our web service needs to provide, let's take a look at how we build a SOAP server.

### SOAP Server Implementation

In this section, we're going to design and build our SOAP server that provides access to the data in the XML inventory file. Our SOAP server will provide one method named `getInfo`. The SOAP server `getInfo` method will take the ISBN of the book that the web services client is interested in as an argument. It will then parse the XML document shown in Listing 10.8 (ch10_book_inventory.xml) and search for the desired ISBN number. If the SOAP server's `getInfo` method finds the desired book, it will return the book information; otherwise, it will return the "`ISBN: ##### Not Found`" message. The source code for the Perl module is shown in Listing 10.9.

Listing 10.9 **Perl module Books.pm containing the `getInfo` method. (Filename: Books.pm)**

```
package Books;
use XML::SAX::ParserFactory;

# This is the method that will be available as a Web service.
sub getInfo {
  shift;  # get the class name
  my $isbn = shift;
  my $return_message = "";

  # Instantiate a new handler object.
  my $handler = Books::Handler->new(ISBN => $isbn,
                                    RETURN_MESSAGE => \$return_message);
```

```
  my $p = XML::SAX::ParserFactory->parser(Handler => $handler);
  $p->parse_uri("ch10_book_inventory.xml");
  return $return_message;
}

# Handler package definition
package Books::Handler;

my $flag = 0;
my $elem = "";
my $data = "";

sub new {
  my $class = shift;
  die "Usage: new(ISBN => '3429493', RETURN_MESSAGE => \$mess)" if @_ != 4;
  return bless {@_}, $class;  ## This will bless and
                              ## return a Book::Handler class
}

# start_element event handler
sub start_element {
  my ($self, $element) = @_;

  if ($element->{Attributes}->{'{}isbn'}->{Value} eq $self->{ISBN}) {
    $flag = 1;
    $elem = $element->{Name};
  }
}

# characters event handler
sub characters {
  my ($self, $char) = @_;
  $data = $char->{Data};
}

# end_element event handler
sub end_element {
  my ($self, $element) = @_;

  if ($flag and $element->{Name} eq $elem) {
    $flag = 0;
    $elem = "";
  }

  if ($flag) {
    ${$self->{RETURN_MESSAGE}} .= "$element->{Name}: $data\n";
  }
}
```

This Perl module is very similar to the SAX examples that we discussed in Chapter 3, "Event-Driven Parser Modules," so we won't go through it in great detail. As you can see, Books.pm uses a SAX2 parser to iterate through the ch10_book_inventory.xml file and retrieve the information based on the ISBN number that was provided. After the ISBN number is found, the module Books::Handler collects the data and appends it to the string that is later returned in the `getInfo` method. If you are having difficulties, refer to Chapter 3 for more information.

The next step is to create a SOAP server that accepts incoming RPCs from the SOAP client. After the RPCs are accepted, they must be routed to the appropriate module and methods. The SOAP server is shown in Listing 10.10.

Listing 10.10 **SOAP server. (Filename: ch10_book_service.cgi)**

```
1.  #!perl
2.
3.  use SOAP::Transport::HTTP;
4.  SOAP::Transport::HTTP::CGI
5.     ->dispatch_to('Books::(?:getInfo)')
6.     ->handle;
```

Yes, that's all there is to it. You can see how easily and quickly you can create a SOAP server. The SOAP server can accept and forward incoming requests to the methods of any module. So, it is fair to say that Perl web service programming with the SOAP::Lite module can be accomplished using only six lines of code by anyone who can type the preceding program without any typing mistakes. Let's discuss a few subtle points about this example.

**1** The construct on the first line (`!#perl`) is the shebang line, and it specifies that the Perl interpreter should run this program as a Common Gateway Interface (CGI) script. Although it is not mandatory to include the shebang to run non-CGI programs, the server's CGI execution environment requires this line to execute the script with the correct interpreter.

**3** In this example, we're using SOAP and the HTTP protocol on the standard port 80. So, we need the `use SOAP::Transport::HTTP` pragma. The SOAP::Lite Perl module supports a number of other protocols. In addition to HTTP, the SOAP::Lite Perl module supports POP3, TCP, or SMTP. For additional information on support for these transport protocols, please see the perldoc SOAP::Lite documentation.

**4–6** This section of the Perl application is where our SOAP web service server handles the incoming RPC calls. There are two steps to the incoming RPC calls. First, we use the `dispatch_to` method to specify the module (that is, namespace) we are using to make the calls, as well as the methods we want to allow to be invoked. Second, we call the `handle()` method that receives and parses the SOAP request message and processes the RPC. After the method returns, the SOAP response message is sent back to the client.

That's about it for the server side. Not too bad, right? So far, we have developed the following server-side components:

- A Perl module to locate and return the book inventory information
- The XML document that contains the book inventory information
- The SOAP server to handle the RPCs and process all web service requests

These are all the components required on the server side. The last piece of our web service example that we need is a web service client. The SOAP client is discussed in the next section.

### SOAP Client

This section discusses the SOAP client that communicates with our web services server that reads the book inventory. Our web services client application is very similar to the application we discussed earlier that accessed the Weather-Temperature web service. This is an important point because after you're familiar with the structure of a SOAP client, chances are that you will only need minor modifications to use any web service. The book inventory web service client is shown in Listing 10.11.

Listing 10.11 **SOAP client to access the book inventory. (Filename: ch10_soap_book_client.pl)**

```
use strict;
use SOAP::Lite;

# ISBN come in as a command line argument
my $isbn = shift ||
  die "Must start the service with ISBN number\n";

print "Now searching for a book with ISBN # $isbn\n\n";

# Instantiate a SOAP::Lite object, passing in the ISBN
# number as an argument.
my $result = new SOAP::Lite
  ->uri('urn:Books')
  ->proxy('http://localhost/cgi-bin/book_service.cgi')
  ->getInfo($isbn);

# Print the result or error.
unless ($result->fault) {
```

*continues*

Listing 10.11 **Continued**

```
19.     print $result->result();
20.  } else {
21.     print join ', ',
22.       $result->faultcode,
23.       $result->faultstring,
24.       $result->faultfactor,
25.       $result->faultdetail;
26.  }
```

**1–8** Our book client starts with the standard `use strict` pragma statement. Because we're using the SOAP::Lite module, we also need the `use SOAP::Lite` pragma statement. Our application requires an ISBN number as a command-line argument and proceeds to invoke the web service. We assign the command-line argument to `$isbn`, or terminate the application if a command-line argument isn't provided. A message is generated that provides some feedback to the user that indicates that the search is in progress.

**Other Sources of Input**

Note that this input can easily be modified to come from a source other than the command line. For example, let's say that you have a database containing book information and have all the fields in the XML document except the price. So, you can easily use the Perl DBI to walk through the database, extract the ISBN of each book, and use the web service to retrieve the price of each book.

**10–15** In this section of the application, we instantiate a SOAP::Lite object and actually send a request to the web service. This application is very similar to the SOAP client that accessed the Weather-Temperature service back in Listing 10.1. We first call the `uri()` method and specify the namespace, or in our case, the Perl module we are invoking. Next, we specify the location of the web service server script using `proxy()` method. At this point, we're ready to actually invoke the `getInfo()` method and pass in the `$isbn` variable.

**17–26** After calling the `getInfo()` method, we check the return value (named `$result`) to see if any faults were returned by the SOAP server. If no faults were returned, we print the returned values from the `getInfo()` method. If a fault was returned, we print out the following fault information: `faultcode`, `faultstring`, `faultfactor`, and `faultdetail`. These fault elements were discussed earlier in this chapter.

### Running the Web Service

After we have developed all the components that comprise the web service, we need to install it onto a machine. However, before we can offer a web service, we need to have a web server installed and listening on the default port 80. After installing the web server, we place our SOAP server script shown in Listing 10.10 (ch10_book_service.cgi) into the cgi-bin directory of the web server.

> **Note**
>
> For testing in this chapter, we used the Apache web server. The Apache web server from the Apache Software foundation is an open source product and available for free download from `http://httpd.apache.org`. Note that if you're using a different web server, our web service setup and installation instructions will have to be adjusted.

Any web server should work for this example as long as it supports CGI scripts. However, the instructions for installation may not apply to different web servers. I assumed the scripts will be placed into the cgi-bin directory, but any directory capable of executing CGI scripts is fine as long as you modify the `proxy()` call argument in all the scripts that we've created and pass the correct URL to the SOAP server. The rest of the installation instructions assume that you have a cgi-bin directory and are running the Apache web server with default installation settings.

1. Place the files from listings 10.8 (ch10_book_inventory.xml), 10.9 (Books.pm) and 10.10 (book_service.cgi) into the cgi-bin directory. Based on the default installation, the cgi-bin directory is located in the root Apache installation folder.
2. Verify that files ending with a .cgi extension are executable. Standard Apache installations assume that .cgi extensions are executable files.
3. Change book_service.cgi's permissions to allow it to be executed. If you are using a Linux or a *NIX-like system, you should execute this command: `chmod 755 book_service.cgi`. If you are using Windows, the default permission settings usually allow it to be executed, and you don't have to change any permissions. You should be familiar with your system and the HTTP server and set the permissions accordingly. If not, ask your local system administrator; he or she should be able to help you with this.

After the installation is complete, place the client script in any user directory, so that you can execute the client application.

### Accessing the Web Service

After our web service is installed and the local web server is running, we're ready to try and access our web service. Remember, the web service client requires a command-line argument that contains an ISBN number. So, we can access the web service by launching the client and passing in a command-line argument:

```
ch10_soap_client.pl 0201615711
```

As expected, we receive the following reply after executing the web service client:

```
Now searching for a book with ISBN # 0201615711

name: Network Programming with Perl
publisher: Addison Wesley
author: Lincoln D. Stein
pages: 754
price: 39.99
```

Note that the web service client can easily be modified to access a different web service. In this example, the location of the web service was hard coded in the client using the following line:

```
http://localhost/cgi-bin/book_service.cgi
```

It would be a very simple change to extend our client application to access a different web service, perhaps passed in as a second command-line argument.

As you can see, web services using the SOAP::Lite Perl are a very powerful technology that are easily implemented, and they don't require a lot of extra programming on either the client or server side. SOAP is by far the most popular web service technology in use today.

## Summary

In this chapter, I demonstrated how to implement web services using the Perl SOAP::Lite module. You also saw how XML is implemented in actual middleware technologies, using its data description capabilities to describe the messages and their data types. Using XML, we can easily transfer data types between two different machine architectures, as well as two different programming languages. This is one of the biggest advantages of XML as opposed to other data formats, and it is one of the reasons for the well-deserved popularity.

XML web services, although heavily advertised and discussed, are not even close to reaching their potential. Applications are only now beginning to take advantage of the web services facilities that are currently available. As we all know (especially with web-related technologies), the biggest changes happen for the better as the number of implementations increase and people gain experience working with the technology. We can only imagine how web services will transform information sharing between applications.

## Exercises

1. Look at the web site `http://www.xmethods.net` and find another interesting web service. Modify our web service client to access another web service. Was it easy to do? Will you be able to use our web service client as a template for future applications?
2. Develop your own web service. Do you have an XML document that you would like to provide to users through a web service? Again, you can use our example as a template for future applications.

For suggested solutions to this exercise, be sure to check out the web site:
`http://www.xmlproj.com/book/chapter10`

## Relevant Links

Apache Web Server: `http://www.apache.org`
SOAP specification: `http://www.w3.org/TR/SOAP/`
UDDI homepage: `http://www.uddi.org/`
W3C XML Protocol Working Group: `http://www.w3.org/2000/xp/Group/`
WSDL specification: `http://www.w3.org/TR/wsdl`
Xmethods—list of publicly available web services: `http://www.xmethods.net`

# V

# Appendices

# What Is XML?

## Introduction to the eXtensible Markup Language

If you've been online or to a bookstore recently, you know that XML is everywhere. What is XML? Why is XML so important? Is XML something I should learn and use? Let's see if I can answer these questions for you in this Appendix. I will provide an introduction to the eXtensible Markup Language (XML) and discuss all the basics of the language. This Appendix should provide a beginner with enough information to get started with this important language and to work through the concepts in this book.

## History of XML

Before discussing XML and what it can do for you, let's go back a few years and look into the history of XML. Back in 1986, the International Organization for Standardization (ISO) published the Standard Generalized Markup Language (SGML) standard. SGML is a meta-language that describes how to embed formatting commands inside of a document. It was purposely designed to be very general to provide maximum flexibility. However, this came at the price of a very complicated standard. As a result, it became a very powerful and complicated language—in fact, one of my references stated that very few (if any) software packages were ever able to completely implement the SGML standard. SGML achieved some success in government and the aerospace industry and other business sectors that required an efficient method to organize thousands of pages of detailed technical documentation.

A successful byproduct of SGML (actually an application of it) is the HyperText Markup Language (HTML). HTML is a markup language that has been widely adopted by web browsers, even though the language is limited. HTML is limited because it is comprised of a finite set of tags. The original version 1.0 of the HTML standard only supported about a dozen tags, while version 4.01 supports nearly a hundred tags. Although a hundred tags sounds like a lot, it isn't enough of a variety to support anything other than the creation of web pages. So, you will never see anyone use HTML as a format to exchange data. It will, however, continue to be used to display web pages until it is eventually phased out by XHTML.

**Note**

Additional information on XHTML can be found at `http://www.w3.org/MarkUp/`.

Several individuals in 1996 started development of a new scaled down version of SGML that would remove the complicated and rarely used portions of the nearly 20-year-old SGML standard. The first draft of the XML standard, version 1.0, was released in February 1998 and users immediately saw the benefits of XML.

## What Exactly Is XML?

To get a good idea of what XML is, you also need to know what XML is not. I'll cover some of those misconceptions in the following section, but for now, let's cover what XML is—a language that was designed to facilitate the exchange of information.

**Note**

One of the best sources for XML information is at the World Wide Web Consortium (W3C) web site (`http://www.w3.org`). The W3C publishes the XML standards as well as most (if not all) of the World Wide Web-related standards.

## XML Applications

XML and the related technologies can be applied to a number of applications. Before I actually start discussing some of the characteristics of XML, let's take a moment and look at some of the important applications of XML. Currently, three of the main applications of XML are

- **Data Interchange**—XML is widely utilized to facilitate the exchange of data between organizations. Different organizations can develop a DTD or XML schema that defines the contents of an XML document. A DTD or XML schema acts as a contract between the participating organizations. An XML parser can easily verify that the XML document is valid, that is, conforms to the DTD or XML schema.
- **Defining Custom Documents**—Unlike HTML, which has a finite set of tags, XML doesn't have any defined tags, so users are free to define their own (provided they follow the XML formatting and structure rules). XML enables users to easily define application-specific XML documents for standardized communication.
- **Generate Easily Transformed Data**—XML provides a very flexible initial data format, especially when combined with the XSL facilities. By employing an XSLT stylesheet, you can easily transform an XML document into a plain text format (for example, tab-delimited, CSV), an HTML document, or another XML document. As you can see, this provides the end user with a great deal of flexibility to use the same data in a number of different formats.

## Characteristics of XML

XML can be easily described by a few key characteristics that provide a clear, high-level description. This section provides a short list of the more important characteristics.

- An XML document is stored as a plain text file. This means that you can open an XML document with any editor. Text files are portable across platforms, while binary files can be platform-specific. In addition, because an XML document is stored as plain text, it is easier to find errors in the XML document—nearly an impossible task with a binary file.
- XML was designed for and works best with structured data. An example of structured data is a database table or the contents of a spreadsheet. These data sources are called structured because they can be broken down into records (or rows), and each row is made up of multiple columns (or cells). Because XML is hierarchical, complex data structures can be defined within the XML document.

- XML separates data and presentation. Unlike HTML that mixes data and formatting of the data, XML was designed to consist of data only. This leaves you, as the developer, free to present the data in the best way you see fit. This is also important because it enables you to format the same data several different ways. For example, the same data can be formatted for presentation on both a Personal Computer (PC) and a handheld Personal Digital Assistant (PDA).
- XML is self-describing. A well-designed XML document with clearly defined element names is easy to read and understand. This means that when you open up an XML document in a text editor, you should be able to easily see all the elements in an XML document and the relationship between the elements (that is, the element hierarchy). If the elements in an XML document are assigned descriptive names, you may not even need to insert any comments into the XML document.
- XML is publicly available and very popular. You don't need to worry about any licensing issues with XML, and, because XML is so popular, it's easy to find a lot of documentation, both in print and online. Books, magazines, web pages, mailing lists, and newsgroups are dedicated to XML. Look at the section, "Additional Sources of XML Information" at the end of this Appendix for a list of resources.
- XML has launched an entire series of related standards. A number of important related standards are built upon XML. Some of the more popular XML-based standards include XLink, XPointer, XSL, and XSLT. Full definitions of these terms can be found in the Glossary.

## What XML Isn't

Now that I've shown a few characteristics of XML, let's reverse things a bit and clarify a few misconceptions that exist about XML.

- XML is not a transport protocol. Sometimes, XML is confused with a transport protocol, and developers mistakenly believe that they can communicate between two processes using XML. XML cannot be used as a transport protocol. You can, however, send XML between two processes using a transport protocol (for example, TCP or UDP). An example of this would be a TCP server that is waiting for incoming connections from clients. A client can open a socket and connect to the server, and send (or receive) an XML document.
- XML is not a programming language. XML was designed as a common language to support the sharing of data between applications. Perhaps people sometime confuse XML and XML parsers. An XML parser is used to read an XML document, and XML parsers are available in a number of languages including C/C++, Java, and Perl.

- XML is not a replacement for HTML. Both XML and HTML have the same ancestor, SGML. They perform different tasks. Remember, HTML combines data with the presentation of the data, while XML separates the data from the presentation.

# Components of an XML Document

So far, I have provided some background material and discussed some of the characteristics of XML, but you still don't really know what makes up an XML document. In this section, I'll discuss the components required to build an XML document and then present an XML document that illustrates these various components.

## Types of Markup

An XML document is a text file that consists of character data and markup. In the case of XML, there are several different constructs that are considered to be markup. A summary of these different constructs is shown in Table A.1.

Table A.1 **Summary of XML markup.**

| Markup | Description |
|---|---|
| Start tag | Used to mark the beginning of a non-empty XML element (for example, `<address>`). Note that in an XML document, all start tags must have a corresponding end tag. |
| End tag | Used to mark the end of a non-empty XML element (for example, `</address>`). Note the forward slash before the element name, which distinguishes an end tag from a start tag. Note that in XML, all end tags must have a corresponding start tag. |
| Empty element tag | Identifies an empty element (for example, `<address/>`). Note that the forward slash appears after the element name. |
| Character reference | Characters of languages that cannot be displayed with the standard ASCII character set can be represented using Unicode. Unicode is a list of unique numbers that map to characters in just about any language. This enables you to insert native language characters into an XML document by using Unicode. For additional Unicode information, see `http://www.unicode.org`. |

*continues*

Table A.1 **Continued**

| | |
|---|---|
| Entity reference | Certain characters cannot appear between the start and end tags of an element. For example, the less than character “<” is used to delimit the start and end tags, so it would cause confusion to XML parsers if it appeared within the character data. So, inside an XML document, the offending characters are mapped to these. When the XML document is parsed, the entity references are replaced with their real values. For example, an element containing the following string:<br><inventory>Mark's computer</inventory><br>would need to actually contain the following markup inside an XML document:<br><inventory>Mark"s computer</inventory><br>Currently, the five valid entity references are<br>& The ampersand character “&”.<br>' The apostrophe character “'“.<br>> Closing tag bracket and greater than sign “>”.<br>< Opening tag bracket and less than sign “<”.<br>" Double quote character “"”. |
| Comment | Comments can be inserted into XML documents by the authors as notes to themselves or notes to other users. A comment starts with <! – and ends with the first occurrence of –>. For example, the following would appear as a comment in an XML document:<br><!–This is a comment. –> |
| CDATA Section | A CDATA section of an XML document enables a user to include markup data without having to use entity references. This is helpful when the XML document contains data from other formats. You can enclose an HTML or Scalable Vector Graphics (SVG) document within an XML document and not have to worry about entity references. For example, you would use the following notation to enclose an HTML document:<br><![CDATA[<br><html><br><head><br><meta http-equiv="content-type"<br>➥content="text/html; charset=ISO-8859-1"><br></head><br><body><br><div align="Center"><br><div align="Left">This is an HTML document.<br><br></div><br></div><br></body><br></html><br>]]> |

| Markup | Description |
|---|---|
| Document Type Declaration | A Document Type Definition (DTD) defines the format and content of an XML document and can be either internal or external to the XML document. I'll discuss DTDs in more detail later in this Appendix. |
| Processing Instruction | Processing instructions (PIs) are used to pass instructions to applications that are working with XML documents. All PIs start with the characters "<?" and end with the characters "?>". |
| XML Declaration | The XML declaration must always appear at the top of a well-formed XML document, starting at the first column. Any whitespace before the XML declaration in an XML document would render it invalid. There is one required parameter and two optional parameters in the XML declaration. An example of the required XML declaration is <?xml?>. Remember, this must be the first line of an XML document, and it must start in the first column. The other parameters that can appear with the XML declaration are XML version, encoding parameter, and standalone. |
| XML version | The required version parameter identifies the version of XML used in this XML document. Currently, there is only one version of XML and the version is 1.0. An example of the XML version parameter (appearing with the XML declaration) is <?xml version="1.0"?>. |
| Encoding Parameter | The optional encoding parameter identifies the character encoding method for the characters in this XML document. All XML processors are required to support Universal Character Set (UCS) Transformation Formats (UTF)-8 or -16. The encoding scheme UTF-8 is used to represent 7-bit ASCII characters while UTF-16 provides access to 63,000 characters as a single Unicode 16-bit unit. If the encoding parameter isn't provided, the Unicode character set is the default encoding scheme. An example of the encoding parameter encoding is <?xml version="1.0" encoding="UTF-8"?>. |
| standalone Parameter | The optional standalone parameter indicates whether this XML document has an internal or external DTD. If it has an internal document, then this value would be set to "yes," otherwise if it requires an external DTD, the value is set to "no." External in this context means that the DTD resides in a different file. If the standalone parameter isn't provided, the default value is "no." An example of the standalone encoding parameter is <?xml version="1.0" encoding="UTF-8" standalone="no"?>. |
| Text Declaration | A text declaration looks similar to the XML declaration; however, it has a different purpose. The text declaration is used to tell the parser if an external entity uses a different encoding scheme than the one used in the current XML document. |

## Elements

The most fundamental structure of an XML document is the element. A well-formed XML document must contain at least one element, although an XML document usually contains many elements. An element typically surrounds character data with start and end tags. A sample of an element is

```
<address>1106 River Avenue</address>
```

This is a single element named `<address>` and it contains the character data "`1106 River Avenue`." Note that in an XML document, an element always uses the following syntax:

- Start tags begin with a less than sign "<"
- End tags begin with a less than sign followed by a forward-slash "</".

Instead of containing character data, elements can also contain other elements called child elements. When we begin to discuss elements containing other elements (that is, nested elements), you can start to visualize the XML document almost as a tree. As you can see in Figure A.1, we have a tree that has a `<record>` element at the root and two child elements named `<name>` and `<address>`.

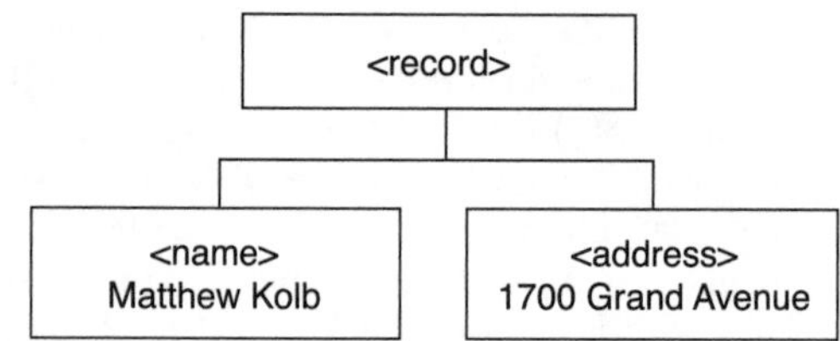


**Figure A.1** Tree representation of a simple XML document.

The XML document that corresponds to the XML tree shown in Figure A.1 is

```
<?xml version="1.0" encoding="UTF-8"?>
<record>
   <name>Matthew Kolb</name>
   <address>1700 Grand Avenue</address>
</record>
```

In this example, the `<record>` element has two child elements, `<name>` and `<address>`. The `<name>` element contains the character data "`Matthew Kolb`" and the `<address>` element contains the character data "`1700 Grand Avenue`." Note that the child elements follow the same rules for start and end tags (that is, each element must have matching start and end tags).

Elements can also be empty, and of course, they're called empty elements. We can use the standard notation without any character data, such as `<book> </book>`, or we can use a shorthand notation that consolidates the start and end tags into one tag, such as `<book/>`. Note that the forward slash appears after the element name in an empty element; it usually appears before the element name in an end tag.

XML is case sensitive, so opening and closing tags for elements must use the same case. Either lower case or all capital letters can be used (and even mixed case), however you must be consistent. For example, `<account>data</ACCOUNT>` isn't valid.

## Attributes

Each element can also have one or more attributes associated with it. Attributes are usually used to store data that is relative to a particular instance of an element. An attribute has a name and value associated with it, and it appears as part of the element's start tag. For example, the following is a valid attribute:

```
<book isbn="0735712891">XML and Perl</book>
```

As you can see, the `<book>` element has one attribute named `isbn`, and the value of the `isbn` attribute is "`0735712891`." As I mentioned earlier, the attribute is applicable to this particular element—another book element would have a different `isbn` attribute value. Elements can have several attributes if required. Attributes within the start tag must be separated by at least one space:

```
<book isbn="0735712891" price"$39.99">XML and Perl</book>
```

Attribute values have to be quoted (either single or double quotes are allowed). The quotes must match (that is, be the same) for each attribute. For example, `isbn="0735712891" price='$39.99'` is ok, but `isbn='0735712891" price="$39.99'` isn't.

### Use of Attributes Versus Elements

You could have easily created `<isbn>` and `<price>` elements in the previous section and stored the values as character data rather than attributes. Why would you use an attribute instead of an element (or vice versa)? Well, there isn't an easy answer to the question, and it is a popular topic on newsgroups or forums that always provokes a lot of strong opinions about when to use an element versus when to use an attribute. I might not be able to provide a definitive answer, but I can certainly provide a few suggestions. As you become more familiar with XML, you will get more comfortable with designing XML documents and the best approach is usually obvious. Let's take a look at a few examples that will help you determine when to store data as an element or an attribute.

***Storing Data as an Element***

If there is more than one occurrence of a data item, then you will need to store the data in an element rather than in an attribute. For example, let's say that you need to store a list of employee names. One option would be to use a root element named `<employees>` that has multiple `<employee>` elements. Each employee element has two child elements, `<name>` and `<phone>`, and each of these elements contains character data. Here is an example of that hierarchy:

```
<?xml version="1.0" encoding="UTF-8"?>
<employees>
   <employee>
      <name>Joseph</name>
      <phone>112</phone>
   </employee>
   <employee>
      <name>Kayla</name>
      <phone>114</phone>
   </employee>
   <employee>
      <name>Sean</name>
      <phone>116</phone>
   </employee>
   <employee>
      <name>Matthew</name>
      <phone>118</phone>
   </employee>
</employees>
```

This example can easily be extended to include additional information for each employee, such as an employee number, department, or home address.

***Storing Data as an Attribute***

A good example of when to use an attribute to store data is when you need to assign a unique identifier to each element, or the data describes the element itself. Let's take a look at the list of employees again, and let's say that you want to associate an employee number to each name. An example is shown in the following:

```
<?xml version="1.0" encoding="UTF-8"?>
<employees>
   <employee id="100">
      <name>Joseph</name>
      <extension>112</extension>
   </employee>
   <employee id="101">
      <name>Kayla</name>
      <extension>114</extension>
   </employee>
   <employee id="102">
      <name>Sean</name>
      <extension>116</extension>
   </employee>
   <employee id="103">
      <name>Matthew</name>
      <extension>118</extension>
   </employee>
</employees>
```

As you can see, without reorganizing your XML document, you uniquely associated each `employee` element with an employee identification number. Depending on what you are going to do with the XML document will help drive the design of the XML document. For example, you would need a document structure similar to this if you plan to search the XML document and find employee `<name>` elements based on the employee identification numbers.

Another example of when it is beneficial to use attributes involves data that requires units (for example, kilograms, degrees Celsius, kilometers, and so forth). For example, the following XML element would require an additional step (a Perl `split` function call) to separate the data from the units of the data:

```
<weight>75 kg</weight>
```

An alternative to mixing the data and units in the character data would be to store the data unit in an attribute. For example, the following element and attribute would be easier to parse:

```
<weight unit="kg">75</weight>
```

Attributes can also be used when you want to limit the possible range of values to an enumerated list or range of valid values. This will be demonstrated a little later in this Appendix when we discuss DTDs and XML schemas.

# Defining the Structure and Content of an XML Document

Two main approaches to defining the format and contents of XML documents are Document Type Definitions (DTDs) and XML schemas. However, before discussing DTDs and XML schemas, let's discuss the format of an XML document.

## Well-Formed and Valid XML Documents

XML documents are considered well-formed if they follow the rules in the XML specification regarding document structure. Let's take a look at some of the more important points related to well-formed documents.

An XML document can only have one root element, that is, the top level of the document tree. For example, in the following XML document, the root element is named `<employees>`:

```
<?xml version="1.0" encoding="UTF-8"?>
<employees>
   <name employee_id="100">Joseph</name>
   <name employee_id="101">Kayla</name>
   <name employee_id="102">Sean</name>
   <name employee_id="103">Matthew</name>
</employees>
```

All elements (including the root element) must have matching start tags and end tags. In the following case, the XML document isn't well-formed because the `<name>` element containing the character data `Matthew` element is missing the end tag.

```
<?xml version="1.0" encoding="UTF-8"?>
<employees>
   <name employee_id="100">Joseph</name>
   <name employee_id="101">Kayla</name>
   <name employee_id="102">Sean</name>
    <!—Missing closing tag here —>
   <name employee_id="103">Matthew
</employees>
```

Another important rule regarding XML document structure is nesting. All elements XML document, the root element is `<employees>`, and it is made up of multiple `<employee>` elements. Each `<employee>` element has `<name>` and `<employee_num>` child elements. For the nesting to be correct, the closing tag for each child (for example, `<employee>`) must be closed with an end tag before you can start the next `<employee>` element. You can see that the end tag for the

<employee> element containing the character data "Sean" is missing. In this case, I've illegally tried to start a new <employee> element containing the character data "Matthew" before properly closing the <employee> element containing the character data "Sean."

```
<?xml version="1.0" encoding="UTF-8"?>
<employees>
   <employee>
      <name>Joseph</name>
      <employee_num>100</employee_num>
   </employee>
   <employee>
      <name>Kayla</name>
      <employee_num>101</employee_num>
   </employee>
   <employee>
      <name>Sean</name>
      <employee_num>102</employee_num>
<!—Missing </employee> closing tag here —>
   <employee>
      <name>Matthew</name>
      <employee_num>103</employee_num>
   </employee>
</employees>
```

A stricter check of an XML document verifies that the XML document is valid. An XML document is considered valid if it follows the rules defined in a DTD or XML schema regarding structure and content. For example, a DTD or XML schema may specify that each of the <employee> elements must contain a name <element> and an <employee_num> element, and in this case, the preceding document (with the missing </employee> end tag replaced) would be considered valid. If the DTD or XML schema specified that each <employee> element is required to have a <telephone_number> element, then the XML document would be considered invalid.

Some XML parsers are validating parsers. A validating parser compares an XML document against a DTD or XML schema and verifies that the XML document contains the required elements and is properly structured according to the DTD or XML schema. If a validating parser finds that an XML document doesn't correspond to a DTD or XML schema, it notifies the user of the problem.

An XML document can be well-formed but invalid (that is, it is syntactically correct, but it just doesn't match your DTD or XML schema). However, if an XML document is valid, that implies that it is also well-formed.

All XML documents need to be well-formed, but they don't necessarily need to be valid. It is good XML practice to develop and use a DTD or XML schema that defines your XML document whenever XML documents are being exchanged. Let's say that your company exchanges sales information with other companies. In a situation such as this, it is critical to first agree on the data that will be exchanged, and then define a set of rules that govern the structure of the data in an XML document. After these rules are defined by a DTD or XML schema, then the two companies can begin to exchange information in XML.

Think of a DTD or XML schema as a contract between the companies that defines the structure and content of the XML document. This contract will help you verify that the XML documents you send to other companies are in the proper format (so that they'll be able to process your XML documents with their applications). Also, this contract verifies that the XML documents you receive from other companies are in the proper format (so that your applications will be able to process their XML documents). It may take some negotiating between the organizations to agree on document structure and content, but all the benefits provided by XML make it worth the trouble.

You can use XML documents in a number of cases that aren't defined by a DTD or XML schema. For example, if you're using XML for simple or small XML documents (for example, configuration/startup files) that aren't exchanged between organizations, you may not need to develop a DTD or XML schema. As long as the XML documents are well-formed, they will suffice for particular applications.

> **Note**
>
> An interesting question that occasionally pops up is, "Are XML documents that don't have a DTD or XML schema considered invalid?" The answer is no. An XML document is considered invalid if it doesn't follow the corresponding DTD or XML schema. So, if an XML document doesn't have a DTD or XML schema, it can't be invalid.

Let's take a look at DTDs and XML schemas and how the rules that control the structure and contents of XML documents are specified. Both DTDs and XML schemas have advantages and disadvantages associated with them, and which one you use depends on your requirements. After I discuss DTDs and XML schemas, I will present a few advantages and disadvantages that will aid you in deciding which approach to use.

## Document Type Definition

A DTD is a set of rules in non-XML format that defines the content and the structure of an XML document. The DTD describes the elements that appear in the XML document, parent-child relationships (that is, nesting), and also specifies which elements are required and which elements are optional.

### XML Document Type Definition

The easiest way to describe the structure of a DTD might be to walk through an example, starting with the input data, describing a DTD, and then building the corresponding XML document. For this example, let's assume that you work for a financial institution and you're working with the data generated by a series of daily bank transactions. Each transaction will contain the following information:

Account number

Name

Amount

Date

Transaction type: withdrawal or deposit

#### *Tree Representation of Data*

Figure A.2 contains a tree structure that shows the relationship between several data elements. As you can see, each transaction has an attribute type (that is, withdrawal or deposit) associated with it and four child elements (`<account_number>`, `<name>`, `<amount>`, and `<date>`). If you describe the data in terms of an XML document, the root element would be `<daily_activity>`, and it has multiple `<transaction>` child elements. The `<transaction>` element has a `type` attribute associated with it, and it has three child elements: `<account_number>`, `<name>`, and `<amount>`. Now that you know the parent-child relationships between the data elements, let's take a look at how to describe this in a DTD.

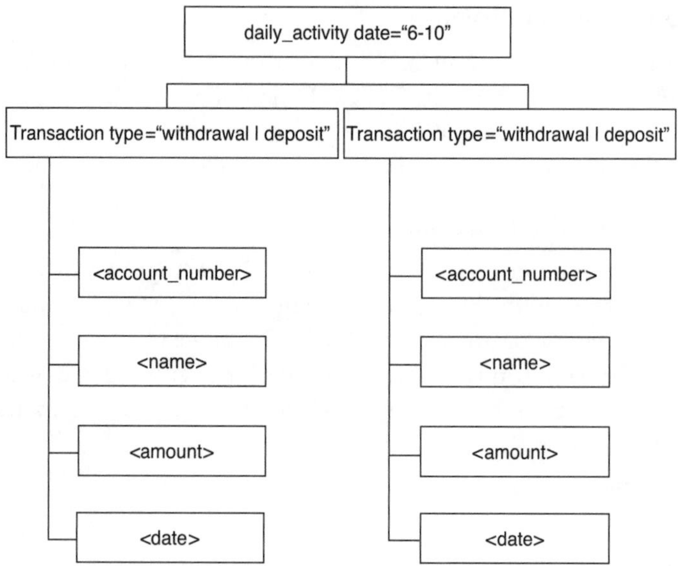


**Figure A.2** Relationship between the data associated with a bank transaction.

### *Structure of an XML Document Type Definition*

The DTD that corresponds to the data represented by Figure A.2 is shown in Listing A.1. Let's take a closer look at the DTD and explain the format. Several important points need to be made.

Listing A.1 **A simple DTD that contains bank transaction information. (Filename: app_a_daily_activity.dtd)**

```
<!ELEMENT daily_activity (transaction+)>
<!ATTLIST daily_activity
   branch CDATA #REQUIRED>
<!ELEMENT transaction (account_number, name, amount, month, day)>
<!ATTLIST transaction type (withdrawal¦deposit) #REQUIRED>
<!ELEMENT account_number (#PCDATA)>
<!ELEMENT name (#PCDATA)>
<!ELEMENT amount (#PCDATA)>
<!ELEMENT month (#PCDATA)>
<!ELEMENT day (#PCDATA)>
```

The data shown in Figure A.2 follows the structure of the DTD hierarchy. At the top of the DTD is the declaration for the `<daily_activity>` element:

```
<!ELEMENT daily_activity (transaction+)>
```

Whenever you declare an element in a DTD, you use the following format:

```
<!ELEMENT element_name contents>
```

In this case, you're declaring the element name is `<daily_activity>`, and the content of the `<daily_activity>` element is multiple `<transaction>` child elements. Also, the `<daily_activity>` element is the root of your XML document because it is the first element to appear in the DTD. Note the plus sign "+" in the declaration of the `<daily_activity>` element. That is an indicator of the number of children that the `<daily_activity>` element is permitted to have. The valid element suffixes are

* zero or more occurrences of the element

? zero or one occurrence of the element

\+ one or more occurrences of the element

In the absence of one of the suffix characters, the DTD allows only one occurrence of the child element.

The next declaration in your DTD is

```
<!ATTLIST daily_activity
   branch CDATA #REQUIRED>
```

This is the declaration for an element attribute that uses the following format:

```
<!ATTLIST element_name attribute_name attribute_type default>
```

The `element_name` and `attribute_name` parameters are self-explanatory, but let's take a closer look at their types and the default parameters. In your case, you have one attribute associated with the `<daily_activity>` element named `branch` and the attribute type is `CDATA`. Note that several attributes can be declared as part of each `ATTLIST` declaration. The `attribute_type` parameter specifies the type of the attribute. Currently, 10 attribute types are supported:

- **CDATA**—Attribute value data is character data.
- **ENTITIES**—Attribute value data is made up of multiple entities that are defined elsewhere in the DTD.
- **ENTITY**—Attribute value data is a single entity that is defined elsewhere in the DTD.
- **Enumeration**—Attribute data must be selected from an enumerated list. This bounds the possible user inputs (for example, an enumerated list containing days of the week would only contain Monday, Tuesday, Wednesday, Thursday, Friday, Saturday, and Sunday, thereby limiting the possible values to only valid values). Note that the `enumeration` type is the only attribute type that doesn't have a DTD keyword, hence the lowercase name.

- **ID**—Attribute data value must be unique within the XML document (that is, the value can appear in the XML document, but not as the value assigned to an attribute of type ID).
- **IDREF**—Attribute data value is the ID type attribute of another element in the XML document.
- **IDREFS**—Attribute data value is a list of multiple ID type attributes of other elements in the XML document.
- **NMTOKEN**—Attribute data value must follow a specific naming convention that is similar, but not identical to, XML names. A valid NMTOKEN can consist of alphanumeric characters and the punctuation marks _, -, ., and :.
- **NMTOKENS**—Attribute data value consists of multiple NMTOKENS separated by whitespace.
- **NOTATION**—Attribute contains the name of a notation that is declared in the DTD. Note that this is very rarely used.

The next declaration is for the transaction element:

```
<!ELEMENT transaction (account_number, name, amount, month, day)>
```

This declaration says that the <transaction> element has five child elements: <account_number>, <name>, <amount>, <month>, and <day>. The <transaction> element also has an attribute that is declared by the following statement:

```
<!ATTLIST transaction type (withdrawal¦deposit) #REQUIRED>
```

As you can see, the transaction element has one attribute named type. The type attribute is an enumerated attribute, and the only valid values are withdrawal or deposit. Because the default declaration for the type attribute is #REQUIRED, this means that a value for the type attribute must be present, and it must be one of the values that appears in the enumerated list.

The valid values for the attribute default declarations are shown in the following.

- **#FIXED**—The #FIXED attribute default declaration means that the attribute is a constant value.
- **#IMPLIED**—The #IMPLIED attribute default declaration means that the attribute is optional.
- **Literal**—The attribute default value is provided as a quoted string. Similar to the enumeration attribute type, there isn't a reserved word for the literal default declaration.
- **#REQUIRED**—The #REQUIRED attribute default declaration means (as you may have already guessed from the name) that the attribute is required.

The last portion of our DTD contains the declaration for the child elements and is shown in the following.

```
<!ELEMENT account_number (#PCDATA)>
<!ELEMENT name (#PCDATA)>
<!ELEMENT amount (#PCDATA)>
```

The declarations for the `<account_number>`, `<name>`, and `<amount>` elements are basically the same, all specifying that the respective elements will contain only `#PCDATA`. The notation `#PCDATA` tells us that the elements will not contain any child elements, only character data.

PCDATA stands for parsed character data; basically, that is the remaining character data after all entity references have been resolved. Be careful not to confuse PCDATA with CDATA. Remember, CDATA denotes a section of an XML document that may contain characters (for example, "<" and ">") that are normally encoded as < and >, respectively.

### *Document Type Definition Example*

Now that you have specified the format of the XML document by designing a DTD, let's take a look at the XML document shown in Listing A.2. As you can see, the sample XML document has two `<transaction>` elements. Note that the `standalone` is equal to "`no`", which means that this XML document relies on the existence of an external DTD.

Listing A.2 **XML document containing bank transactions using an external DTD. (Filename: app_a_daily_activity_ext.xml)**

```
<?xml version="1.0" encoding="UTF-8" standalone="no"?>
<!DOCTYPE daily_activity SYSTEM "app_a_daily_activity.dtd">
<daily_activity branch="Manasquan, NJ">
<transaction type="withdrawal">
   <account_number>11-22-33-4444</account_number>
   <name>Mark Riehl</name>
   <amount>100.00</amount>
   <month>6</month>
   <day>8</day>
</transaction>
<transaction type="deposit">
   <account_number>22-11-44-1111</account_number>
   <name>Joseph Burns</name>
   <amount>50.00</amount>
   <month>6</month>
   <day>10</day>
</transaction>
</daily_activity>
```

The last DTD-related item that we need to discuss is the DOCTYPE declaration in the DTD. The following DOCTYPE declaration is used in your DTD:

```
<!DOCTYPE daily_activity SYSTEM "daily_activity.dtd">
```

The DOCTYPE declaration must appear after the XML declaration, but before the root element of the document. The format of the DOCTYPE declaration is as follows:

```
<!DOCTYPE root_element SYSTEM "DTD name">
```

This is fairly straightforward—the DOCTYPE declaration needs to include the root element name and the location of the external DTD file. The location can include a path on the local machine to the DTD or a URL if the DTD is available on another machine.

In addition to the SYSTEM identifier, you can also use the PUBLIC identifier. PUBLIC provides a globally unique string that identifies the version of the DTD being used and other information, but this string doesn't specify the filename of the DTD. The PUBLIC keyword is rarely used.

A slight variation on the XML document is shown in Listing A.3. As you can see, we've changed the value of the standalone parameter to "yes" and included the entire DTD in place of the SYSTEM identifier. Now, you have a standalone XML document. It is often beneficial to include the DTD at the top of the XML document, so that when you make changes to the DTD or the XML document, you can easily make any required changes to synchronize the DTD and the XML document. One potential drawback of storing the DTD in an XML file is that the DTD can't be used during the validation of another XML document. Remember, a validating XML parser needs access to the DTD (or an XML schema) to perform the validation.

Listing A.3 **XML document containing bank transactions using an external DTD. (Filename: app_a_daily_activity_ext.xml)**

```
<?xml version="1.0" encoding="UTF-8" standalone="yes"?>
<!DOCTYPE daily_activity [
<!ELEMENT daily_activity (transaction*)>
<!ATTLIST daily_activity date CDATA #REQUIRED>
<!ELEMENT transaction (account_number, name, amount)>
<!ATTLIST transaction type (withdrawal¦deposit) #REQUIRED>
<!ELEMENT account_number (#PCDATA)>
<!ELEMENT name (#PCDATA)>
<!ELEMENT amount (#PCDATA)>
]>
<daily_activity month="6" day="10">
<transaction type="withdrawal">
   <account_number>11-22-33-4444</account_number>
   <name>Mark Riehl</name>
   <amount>100.00</amount>
```

```
</transaction>
<transaction type="deposit">
   <account_number>22-11-44-1111</account_number>
   <name>Joseph Burns</name>
   <amount>50.00</amount>
</transaction>
</daily_activity>
```

**Note**

Please see `http://www.w3.org/TR/REC-xml` for additional information on DTDs.

## XML Schemas

XML schemas are XML documents that are similar to DTDs in that they are used to specify the content and structure of an XML document. However, that is where the similarities end. XML schemas were developed by the W3C in response to complaints about DTDs. For example, DTDs don't support namespaces. Also, DTD data typing is weak and it only applies to attributes. Unfortunately, XML schemas are much more complicated than DTDs. Fortunately, XML schemas are much more powerful than DTDs, so their additional complexity has a benefit, and their benefits are worth the extra work.

Although a DTD will enable you to verify that a particular element contains data or that an attribute must be selected from an enumerated list, XML schemas enable you to specify that an element must contain a particular data type. For example, you can specify that a `<title>` element in a report must contain a string, the `<price>` element of an XML catalog must be a value that is greater than zero, or a `<date>` element must be an integer between 1 and 31. As you can see, XML schemas enable a finer grain of resolution when it comes to defining contents of an XML document.

The subject of XML schemas is complex and cannot be thoroughly discussed in the pages available in this appendix. However, I will present an example of an XML schema and discuss all its major components.

### Simple Types

One of the major concepts behind XML schemas is using simple and complex types to describe elements. A simple type is just that—it cannot have any attributes or enclose any other elements. A complex type can do those things the simple cannot—that is, support attributes and enclose other elements. One of the tasks that you will be doing quite often when working with XML schemas is building complex types. A number of simple types are available to use as part of XML schema. Table A.2 shows all the simple types built into XML schema.

**Note**

Additional information on simple types in XML schema can be found at `http://www.w3.org/TR/xmlschema-0/`.

Table A.2 **Simple types defined in XML schema.**

| Simple Type | Description |
|---|---|
| `anyURI` | Contains a standard URI, such as `http://www.w3c.org`. |
| `base64Binary` | Contains Base64-encoded binary data. |
| `boolean` | Contains either true, false, 0, or 1. |
| `byte` | Contains a small integer, such as –1 or 126. |
| `date` | Contains the date, such as 2000-08-12. |
| `dateTime` | Contains time and date using the following format: 2000-08-12T10:00:00.000-05:00, which corresponds to August 12, 2000 at 10:00 a.m. Eastern. |
| `decimal` | Contains decimal data. |
| `double` | Contains the equivalent of a 64-bit floating-point number. |
| `duration` | Contains a time-duration as a string. For example, P1Y2M3DT10H30M12.3S represents 1 year, 2 months, 3 days, 10 hours, 30 minutes, and 12.3 seconds. |
| `ENTITIES` | Contains an XML version 1.0 specification `ENTITIES` attribute type. |
| `ENTITY` | Contains an XML version 1.0 specification `ENTITY` attribute type. |
| `float` | Contains the equivalent of a 32-bit floating-point number. |
| `gday` | Contains a day of the month, for example 12. |
| `gMonth` | Contains a month number in the Gregorian calendar. For example, 08 represents the month of August. |
| `gMonthDay` | Contains a month and a day from the Gregorian calendar. For example, 08–12 represents August 12. |
| `gYear` | Contains a year in the Gregorian calendar, for example, 2000. |
| `gYearMonth` | Contains a year and a month in the Gregorian calendar. For example, 2000–08 represents August of 2000. |
| `hexBinary` | Contains hexadecimal encoded binary data. |
| `ID` | Contains an XML version 1.0 specification `ID` attribute type. |
| `IDREF` | Contains an XML version 1.0 specification `IDREF` attribute type. |
| `IDREFS` | Contains an XML version 1.0 specification `IDREFS` attribute type. |
| `int` | Contains an integer that ranges from –2147483648 to 214748367. |
| `integer` | Contains a type derived from decimal—that is, decimal digits with an option sign. |
| `language` | Contains the xml:lang value that is defined in the XML version 1.0 specification. |

| Simple Type | Description |
|---|---|
| long | Contains a long integer. |
| Name | Contains a valid XML 1.0 Name type. |
| NCName | Contains a XML Namespace NCName. Note that this is the same as an XML Namespace Qname without the prefix and colon. |
| negativeInteger | Contains a negative integer with a valid range of –126789 to –1. |
| NMTOKEN | Contains an XML version 1.0 specification NMTOKEN attribute type. |
| NMTOKENS | Contains an XML version 1.0 specification NMTOKENS attribute type. |
| nonNegativeInteger | Contains a non-negative integer. |
| nonPositiveInteger | Contains a negative integer. |
| normalizedString | New lines, tabs, and carriage returns are converted to spaces before processing. |
| NOTATION | Contains an XML version 1.0 specification NOTATION attribute type. |
| positiveInteger | Contains a positive integer. |
| QName | Contains a valid XML Namespace QName. |
| short | Contains a short integer, such as 1 or 12678. |
| string | Indicates a normal string. |
| Time | Contains a string representing time as either 13:20:00.000 or 13:20:00.000-05:00. Note the –05:00, which is for a conversion to Eastern Standard Time, 5 hours behind Universal time. |
| token | Similar to a normalizedString; however, leading and trailing whitespace is removed and multiple adjacent space characters are reduced to a single space character. |
| unsignedByte | Valid range is from 0 to 126. |
| unsignedInt | Derived from an unsigned long, and the maximum inclusive value is 4294967295. |
| unsignedLong | Derived from the nonNegativeInteger type, the max value is 18446744073709551615. |
| unsignedShort | Derived from an unsigned integer, the max inclusive value is 65535. |

As you can see, there are a large number of data types already defined for you in XML schema. As mentioned earlier, you can use these types to limit the valid values of element character data in an XML document.

### XML Schema Example

Now that I've provided a little bit of a background to XML schema, let's take a look at an actual XML schema. To make things a little easier, let's reuse the XML document that you created for the DTD section as your input data. I'll show it again here for your convenience in Listing A.4.

Listing A.4 **XML document containing daily bank transactions. (Filename: app_a_daily_activity_ndc.xml)**

```
<?xml version="1.0" encoding="UTF-8"?>
<daily_activity branch="Manasquan, NJ">
   <transaction type="withdrawal">
      <account_number>11-22-33-4444</account_number>
      <name>Mark Riehl</name>
      <amount>$100.00</amount>
      <month>6</month>
      <day>8</day>
   </transaction>
   <transaction type="deposit">
      <account_number>22-11-44-1111</account_number>
      <name>Joseph Burns</name>
      <amount>$50.00</amount>
      <month>6</month>
      <day>10</day>
   </transaction>
</daily_activity>
```

Remember, XML schemas have basically the same function as a DTD. Their purpose is to help us define the structure and contents of an XML document. As mentioned earlier, some XML parsers can compare an XML document to an XML schema to verify that the XML document is valid, that is, conforms to the XML schema.

Take a look at the XML document shown in Listing A.4. Which elements, attributes, and child relationships do you need to define, so that you can describe the XML document? Looking at the XML document in Listing A.4, let's make a list of what you need. First, you need the following elements:

- **`<daily_activity>`**—Root element that has an attribute named `branch`.
- **`<transaction_type>`**—Complex element that has an attribute named `type`. The `<transaction_type>` element has the following child elements: `<account_number>`, `<name>`, `<amount>`, `<month>`, and `<day>`.

Now that you know what you need to define, let's take a look at the XML schema in Listing A.5 that defines this XML document.

Listing A.5 **XML schema for the daily bank transactions. (Filename: app_a_daily_activity.xsd)**

```
<?xml version="1.0" encoding="UTF-8"?>
<xs:schema xmlns:xs="http://www.w3.org/2001/XMLSchema"
➥elementFormDefault="qualified">

  <!— account_number element definition —>
  <xs:element name="account_number" type="xs:string"/>

  <!— amount element definition —>
  <xs:element name="amount" type="xs:string"/>

  <!— name element definition —>
  <xs:element name="name" type="xs:string"/>

  <!— day element definition —>
  <xs:element name="day">
    <xs:simpleType>
      <xs:restriction base="xs:integer">
        <xs:minInclusive value="1"/>
        <xs:maxInclusive value="31"/>
      </xs:restriction>
    </xs:simpleType>
  </xs:element>

  <!— month element definition —>
  <xs:element name="month">
    <xs:simpleType>
      <xs:restriction base="xs:integer">
        <xs:minInclusive value="1"/>
        <xs:maxInclusive value="12"/>
      </xs:restriction>
    </xs:simpleType>
  </xs:element>

  <!— root element definition —>
  <xs:element name="daily_activity">
    <xs:complexType>
      <xs:sequence>
        <xs:element ref="transaction" minOccurs="0"
        ➥maxOccurs="unbounded"/>
      </xs:sequence>
      <xs:attribute name="branch" type="xs:string" use="required"/>
    </xs:complexType>
  </xs:element>

  <!— transaction element definition —>
  <xs:element name="transaction">
    <xs:complexType>
```

*continues*

```
46.         <xs:sequence>
47.           <xs:element ref="account_number"/>
48.           <xs:element ref="name"/>
49.           <xs:element ref="amount"/>
50.           <xs:element ref="month"/>
51.           <xs:element ref="day"/>
52.         </xs:sequence>
53.         <xs:attribute name="type" use="required">
54.           <xs:simpleType>
55.             <xs:restriction base="xs:string">
56.               <xs:enumeration value="withdrawal"/>
57.               <xs:enumeration value="deposit"/>
58.             </xs:restriction>
59.           </xs:simpleType>
60.         </xs:attribute>
61.       </xs:complexType>
62.     </xs:element>
63.
64.   </xs:schema>
```

**1–2** The first important point about the XML schema is the XML declaration on the first line. Remember, XML schemas are well-formed, valid XML documents. You will also notice that we're using a W3C schema namespace, and all our element names will be prefixed with `xs`.

**4–11** The first three elements that we declare in the XML schema also happen to be the simplest. The `<account_number>` element is declared by `type` string; that's because our account number was of the form "11-22-33-4444."

We declare the `<amount>` element as a `type` string also because it contains the transfer amount as a string (for example, $100.00, including the dollar sign). The `<name>` element is also declared as a `type` string in this block.

**13–21** XML schemas have a feature called facets that enable you to limit the data that a simple type can store. We're defining the `<day>` element as a type `positiveInteger`. In addition to the type definition, we're going to use the `minInclusive` and **`maxInclusive`** facets to restrict the valid values for the `<day>` element. Because this is a day of the month, we're going to limit the valid values to between 1 and 31.

**Note**

Additional information on XML schema simple types and their allowable facets can be found at `http://www.w3.org/TR/xmlschema-0/#SimpleTypeFacets`.

**23–31** The declaration for the <month> element is just about identical to the declaration for the <day> element. Both are declared as positiveInteger types, and both are using the minInclusive and maxInclusive facets to restrict the valid values for this element. The only difference is the range of valid values. Because this is a declaration for a month, the valid range of values is from 1 to 12.

**33–41** The declaration for the root <daily_activity> element has a few different constructs that we need to discuss. First, note that the <daily_activity> element is being declared as a complex type by the <complexType> element. Remember, because the root element will have child elements, it must be declared as a complex type. Also, note the <sequence> element; it will contain all the child elements of our root <daily_activity>. Here, we can also specify the minimum and the maximum number of occurrences of the transaction element by using the minOccurs and maxOccurs attributes, respectively. In this block, we're also defining the <daily_activity> element attribute named branch. The required branch attribute has been defined as type string because it will contain a town name.

**43–62** The declaration of the <transaction> element is the longest declaration in the XML schema. First, we're declaring that the <transaction> element is a complex type. The <transaction> element is a complex element because it has several child elements and an attribute. Each of the child elements appears in the <sequence>.

In addition to declaring the child elements in this block, we're also declaring the type attribute for the <transaction> element. Note that the attribute is being declared as a simple type, and that the type is a string. We are also limiting the potential values for the attribute by using the <restriction> element and specifying the valid values ("withdrawal" or "deposit").

## Comparing Document Type Definitions and XML Schemas

Before we finish up this section, let's discuss some of the advantages and disadvantages of DTDs and XML schemas.

### Advantages and Disadvantages of DTDs

Several advantages to using DTDs exist. First, DTDs are easy to learn and work with, and therefore, you have a relatively short learning curve. So, you can be working with DTDs in a short amount of time. As you have seen from the examples, DTDs can be very compact, even for fairly complicated XML documents. If you're new to XML, DTDs might initially be a little easier to work with compared to XML schemas.

DTDs do have quite a few shortcomings. First, DTDs are not in XML, so you need to become familiar with the format used by DTDs in addition to learning XML. Also, DTDs have limited capabilities. For example, using a DTD, you can't specify that elements must contain a particular data type. All you can do is specify that some type of data is present in an element. Remember, one of the main uses for XML is to facilitate the exchange of data. DTDs don't allow you to specify data types. As a result, you will need to add additional error checking to your application to validate the input data in the XML document whenever you're using DTDs (because they can create unnecessary, additional work).

**Advantages and Disadvantages of XML Schemas**

XML schemas have several advantages. First, contrary to DTDs, XML schemas are written in XML. It's easier to work in XML, especially if you're learning XML for the first time. Another advantage of XML schemas is that they are much stricter than DTDs. For example, you can specify data types for elements. This allows for more control over input data and enables you to reduce the input type checking required in your application.

The major disadvantage of XML schemas is their complexity and size. Initially, they can be overwhelming. In our example, the XML schema is approximately four times the size of the DTD that describes the same XML document. However, a number of commercial and freely available tools and editors are available to help automate the process of XML schema development. One of the more popular commercial tools used throughout the development of the book is XML Spy (`http://www.xmlspy.com`).

As you become more familiar with XML, you will begin to see that the extra work required by XML schemas is well worth the effort.

## Additional Sources of XML Information

Numerous sources of XML information exist, and it definitely isn't hard to find information. A recent web search on Google found approximately 12 million matches on "XML." With that many matches, it is sometimes difficult to find good information. So, I've put together a listing of some useful sources of information, both in print and online.

### Books

*Inside XML* by Steven Holzner (New Riders Publishing, ISBN 0-7357-1020-1)

### Mailing Lists

`http://www.w3.org/Mail/Lists.html`

### Newsgroups

comp.text.sgml
comp.text.xml

### Web Sites

Main W3C page: `http://www.w3.org/`
Main W3C XML page: `http://www.w3.org/XML/`
Unicode Home Page: `http://www.unicode.org/`
XLink Specification: `http://www.w3.org/TR/xlink/`
XML Specification: `http://www.w3.org/TR/2000/REC-xml-20001006`
XPointer Specification: `http://www.w3.org/XML/Linking`
XML schema: `http://www.w3.org/XML/Schema`

# B

# Perl Essentials

## Perl Module Installation

The installation of Perl modules varies by Perl distribution. If you're using an ActiveState Perl distribution, the installation is very easy. If you're using another distribution of Perl, such as a version that was delivered with your operating system or a Perl binary that you compiled from source, there may be an additional step or two in the process, but it is still fairly straightforward. Let's take a look at these two cases and discuss how to install a Perl module.

### Standard Perl Module Installation

Standard module installation can be performed in two ways: either with a manual install or by using the CPAN.pm module. Let's take a look at the manual installation first.

#### Manual Perl Module Installation

The standard module installation process requires you to use the same compiler that was used to compile the Perl binary for your operating system. In addition to the compiler, you must also have the `make` utility available.

> **Note**
>
> The `make` utility name may vary between operating systems. Microsoft Visual C++, for example, comes with the `nmake` utility, and Borland C++ comes with `dmake`. Be sure to use the utility that corresponds to the compiler that was used to build the Perl binary.

Provided that your compiler is properly installed, the first step in the process is to download the module. Most Perl modules are available at CPAN (`http://www.cpan.org`). Some specialized Perl modules not available on CPAN may be offered at different sites.

Perl modules are usually downloaded in a compressed format. The following assumes that the module is compressed using either `tar` or `gzip`.

> **Note**
>
> The `tar` and `gzip` utilities are freely available at `http://www.gnu.org`. Although initially developed for Unix-like platforms, they have now been ported to other operating systems, including Windows. You can get the Microsoft Windows version of both utilities from `www.cygwin.com`. Microsoft Windows compression utilities may also extract tar and gzip files.

Let's assume that we just downloaded the XML::SAX module to the current directory. The following are the commands we need to execute to compile and install the modules. We'll first need to decompress the package, *cd*, to the top-level directory where the unzipped files reside and execute the following commands:

1. >`perl Makefile.PL`
2. >`make` (or *`nmake`* if you are on win32)
3. >`make test` (or *`nmake test`* if you are on win32)
4. >`make install` (or *`nmake test`* if you are on win32)

Note the capital letters (`Makefile.PL`) in the first step. These are very important on a Unix system.

These steps decompress, compile, and install the module. If a prerequisite is not met (for example, the module you're trying to install is expecting that another module was already installed), the installation will fail.

For more accurate installation instructions, be sure to read the README file that is distributed with every Perl module. Usually, any platform-specific instructions are included in the README file.

### Installing Perl Modules Using CPAN.pm

Another method of installing Perl modules is to use the CPAN.pm module. To use the CPAN.pm module, you must first install the CPAN.pm Perl module using the manual installation procedure previously discussed (if it isn't already included with your Perl distribution).

Using the CPAN.pm Perl module to install other modules is very easy and straightforward. Modules are retrieved from any number of CPAN mirror sites. An added benefit is that the CPAN.pm Perl module also takes care of the prerequisites for you. Therefore, when you install a module, the CPAN.pm Perl module will compile and install all its prerequisites first, as well as their requisites, before proceeding.

Here is how you would install XML::SAX using CPAN.pm in the shell mode:

```
>perl -MCPAN -e shell
CPAN>install XML::SAX
```

The first line starts the CPAN shell prompt. Typing **`install XML::SAX`** retrieves and installs all the required Perl modules (assuming you have a network connection to the Internet).

After you're finished with the installation, type **`exit`** to leave the CPAN shell.

> **Note**
> The CPAN.pm module has a large number of commands and options. Unfortunately I can't discuss all of them here. For additional information on the CPAN.pm Perl module, please see perldoc CPAN.pm.

## ActiveState Module Installation

The ActiveState distribution of Perl provides the Perl Package Manager (PPM) tool. PPM provides an easy-to-use interface that enables you to locate, install, upgrade, and remove Perl modules. The first thing you'll need to do is type **`ppm`** to enter the PPM shell. Note that you can call `ppm` from any directory on your machine—the installed modules will be installed in the proper location. During the ActiveState Perl installation, modifications are made to your `PATH` statement, so that the `ppm` utility is accessible from anywhere on your machine.

Now that we've started the PPM shell, the first thing we need to do is identify PPM repositories (PPM equivalents of File Transfer Protocol (FTP) sites). These repositories are mirror sites used to distribute Perl modules.

Let's add a few of our favorite repositories. At the prompt, type the following:

- **set XMLPROJ** `http://www.xmlproj.com/PPM`
- **set JENDA** `http://jenda.krynicky.cz/perl`
- **set THEORYX5** `http://theoryx5.uwinnipeg.ca/cgi-bin/ppmserver?urn:/PPMServer`
- **set save**

What we've done is create links to Perl module repositories that can now be referred to by the location name (for example, `XMLPROJ`, `JENDA`, and `THEORY5`). The `set save` statement is important—it saves the repositories that you've just added, so that they're available next time you run `ppm`. Now, our PPM executable knows which repositories to use when looking for Perl modules. To install a module, type

```
install module_name
```

That's it. PPM will now look at the repositories that have been defined and install the requested module.

**Note**

For additional information on the Perl Package Manager, please look at perldoc ppm or visit the ActiveState PPM page at `http://aspn.activestate.com/ASPN/Downloads/ActivePerl/PPM/`.

# Acronym List

The following is a list of the acronyms used throughout the book. For definitions, be sure to check out this book's Glossary.

| Acronym | Definition |
|---|---|
| ANSI | American National Standards Institute |
| API | Application Programming Interface |
| ASCII | American Standard Code for Information Interchange |
| ASP | Active Server Pages |
| CEO | Chief Executive Officer |
| CGI | Common Gateway Interface |
| CORBA | Common Object Request Broker Architecture |
| CPAN | Comprehensive Perl Archive Network |
| CSS | Cascading Style Sheet |
| CSV | Comma Separated Value |
| DBI | Database Interface |
| DCOM | Distributed Component Object Model |
| DNS | Domain Name Server |
| DOM | Document Object Model |
| DTD | Document Type Definition |

| Acronym | Definition |
|---|---|
| FAQ | Frequently Asked Question(s) |
| FTP | File Transfer Protocol |
| GUI | Graphical User Interface |
| HTML | HyperText Markup Language |
| HTTP | HyperText Transfer Protocol |
| IIOP | Internet Inter-ORB Protocol |
| IMAP4 | Internet Message Access Protocol version 4 |
| IP | Internet Protocol |
| ISBN | International Standard Book Number |
| ISO | International Organization for Standardization |
| ISP | Internet Service Provider |
| IT | Information Technology |
| JRMP | Java Remote Method Protocol |
| JSP | JavaServer Pages |
| OO | Object-Oriented |
| ORPC | Object Remote Procedure Call |
| PDA | Personal Digital Assistant |
| PDF | Portable Document Format |
| Perl | Practical Extraction and Reporting Language |
| PHP | PPHP HyperText Processor |
| PI | Processing Instruction |
| POC | Point of Contact |
| PPM | Perl Package Manager |
| RFC | Request for Comment |
| RMI | Remote Method Invocation |
| RPC | Remote Procedure Call |

| Acronym | Definition |
|---|---|
| RTF | Rich Text Format |
| SAX | Simple API for XML |
| SAX2 | Simple API for XML version 2 |
| SGML | Standard Generalized Markup Language |
| SMTP | Simple Mail Transfer Protocol |
| SOAP | Simple Object Access Protocol |
| SQL | Structured Query Language |
| SVG | Scalable Vector Graphics |
| TCP | Transmission Control Protocol |
| UCS | Universal Character Set |
| UDDI | Universal Description Discovery and Integration |
| UDP | User Datagram Protocol |
| URI | Universal Resource Identifier |
| URL | Universal Resource Locator |
| UTF | UCS Transformation Format |
| W3C | World Wide Web Consortium |
| WML | Wireless Markup Language |
| WSDL | Web Services Description Language |
| XHTML | eXtensible HyperText Markup Language |
| XLink | XML Linking Language |
| XML | eXtensible Markup Language |
| XML-RPC | XML Remote Procedure Call |
| XPointer | XML Pointer Language |
| XSL | eXtensible Stylesheet Language |
| XSL-FO | eXtensible Stylesheet Language Formatting Objects |
| XSLT | eXtensible Stylesheet Language Transformation |

# References

## Books


*CGI Programming with Perl* – Guelich, Gundavaram, Birznieks/O'Reilly

*Inside XML* – Steve Holzner/New Riders

*MySQL* – Paul DuBois/New Riders

*XML By Example* – Sean McGrath/Prentice Hall

*XML Companion* – Neil Bradley/Addison Wesley

*XML in a Nutshell* – Harold & Means/O'Reilly

*SAX2* – David Brownell/O'Reilly

*TCP/IP Illustrated Vol 1.* – Richard Stevens/Addison Wesley

*XSLT* – Tidwell/O'Reilly

## RFC 2616—HyperText Transfer Protocol

http://www.xml.org

http://www.sun.com/software/xml/faqs.html#2

http://www.w3.org/XML/1999/XML-in-10-points

http://www.xml.com/pub/a/2001/11/14/xml-libxml.html

http://gnosis.cx/publish/programming/xml_models_sax.html

http://www.w3.org/TR/xlink/

http://www.w3.org/DOM/

http://www.xml.com/pub/a/2000/04/05/feature/index.html

http://www.xml.com – Kip Hampton and Michael Rodriguez articles

http://www.xml.com/lpt/a/2001/11/14/xml-libxml.html

http://www.xml.com/pub/a/2002/04/17/perl-xml.html – XPath

## WML

http://www1.wapforum.org/tech/documents/WAP-238-WML-20010626-p.pdf

# Glossary

**Active Server Pages** See ASP.

**ActivePerl** Popular, well-supported Perl distribution available for a number of platforms. Includes the Perl Package Manager (PPM) tool that simplifies Perl module installation and removal. This is the recommended Perl distribution if you are running on a Microsoft Windows-based platform. A small company named ActiveState originally developed the ActivePerl distribution. Their web site (and additional Perl development tools) can be found at `http://www.activestate.com`.

**American Standard Code for Information Interchange** See ASCII.

**API (Application Programming Interface)** An interface built into a software package that enables other applications to use the package. For example, when you use a Perl module, you are interacting with the module through an API.

**Application Programming Interface** See API.

**ASCII (American Standard Code for Information Interchange)** Standard defined by the American National Standards Institute (ANSI) that defines a coded character set based on 7-bit coded characters. Each character is assigned a unique number ranging from 0 to 127. The characters assigned to values 0–31 are non-printing control characters, and values 32–127 are assigned to letters, numbers, and other symbols.

**ASP (Active Server Pages)** Originally developed by the Microsoft Corporation for its own web servers; however, it is now available for a number of web servers. Because the ASP engine is integrated into the web server, it doesn't require another process. ASP enables the developer to merge source code within HTML pages. A Perl module named Apache::ASP supports ASP with the `mod_perl` module.

**`ATTLIST`** The keyword used in DTDs to initiate the declaration of one or more attributes for an element.

**Attribute** An XML parameter that describes data associated with an element. Attributes take name=value format. For example, to declare an attribute for an XML element, you use the following format: `<name ssn="123-45-6789">Mark Riehl</name>`. In this case, the `<name>` element has one attribute named `ssn` and the value of the attribute is "`123-45-6789`".

**Cascading Style Sheet** See CSS.

**`CDATA`** An XML keyword that describes a block of data that may legally contain XML reserved characters (for example, `< or >`) within an XML document. Usually, the reserved characters are replaced with the corresponding entity references. However, `CDATA` sections are useful when encapsulating large blocks of data inside an XML document. For example, let's say you are encapsulating an HTML document inside of an XML document. By using a `CDATA` section, you won't need to replace all the reserved characters with the corresponding entity references.

**CGI (Common Gateway Interface)** An interface that enables external programs to interact with a web server. Static web pages are basically text files that don't change. CGI scripts execute in real time, allowing you to dynamically generate web content. For example, it's very easy to build a CGI script that builds a web form, collects data from a user, queries a database, and builds a web page containing the results. CGI scripts are frequently written in Perl.

**Character data** The text in an XML document excluding markup. For example, the following XML element: `<name>Mark Riehl</name>` contains the character data "`Mark Riehl`".

**Character reference** A method of including non-printable Unicode characters in an XML document. These characters could be letters from a foreign language. The character reference contains the number of a particular Unicode character.

**Comma Separated Value** See CSV.

**Comment** Added to XML documents by using the following notation:

```
<!—Comment text here. —>
```

Note that it is a good idea to add comments throughout your XML documents. Depending on the XML parser used, you may or may not have access to the comments after parsing.

**Common Gateway Interface** See CGI.

**Comprehensive Perl Archive Network** See CPAN.

**CPAN (Comprehensive Perl Archive Network)** A mirrored web site that provides a wealth of Perl information. For example, it provides links to Perl modules, documentation, mailing lists, and Frequently Asked Questions (FAQs). Whenever you're looking for any Perl information, this is a great place to start. CPAN is at `http://www.cpan.org`.

**CSS (Cascading Style Sheet)** A simple non-XML language that was developed to support adding styles (for example, fonts, colors, and so forth) to web documents. It was originally developed to work with HTML, however it also works with XML. Support for CSS varies widely among browsers.

**CSV (Comma Separated Value)** A file that contains commas as delimiters between fields. An example of a CSV file is a database table or a spreadsheet that has been exported to a text file. In the exported text file, commas are used to separate the columns, and new lines are used to separate the rows.

**Database Interface** See DBI.

**Database Management System** See DBMS.

**DBI (Database Interface)** The Perl DBI is a widely used Perl module that provides transparent access to multiple database servers using a consistent API. The DBI module handles all the underlying differences between database servers. Some of the supported databases include Informix, Ingres, Microsoft SQL Server, mSQL, MySQL, Oracle, PostgreSQL, and all ODBC-compliant database servers. The Perl DBI homepage can be found at `http://dbi.perl.org/`.

**DBMS (Database Management System)** Typically describes a system that manages large amounts of data, optimized for easy and fast retrieval.

**Document Object Model** See DOM.

**Document Type Definition** See DTD.

**DOM (Document Object Model)** A platform and language independent standard that enables programs to access and modify the contents of a document. DOM can support HTML and XML documents and is considered to be a tree-based parser because it builds a tree of the input document in memory. Because it builds the tree in memory, DOM parsers are not recommended for parsing large documents. DOM-based XML parsers are written in a number of languages, including Java, C/C++, and Perl.

**DTD (Document Type Definition)** A non-XML file that defines the structure and content of an XML document.

**Element** An XML element is the smallest building block of an XML document. Typically, an XML element is made up of a start tag, element content, and an end tag. A typical element has the following format: `<employee>James Kennedy</employee>`. In this example, `<employee>` is the start tag, "`James Kennedy`" is the element content, and `</employee>` is the end tag.

**`ELEMENT` Declaration** The declaration of an XML element appears in a DTD. The format for the declaration is: `<!ELEMENT name (content)>`. Remember, the content of an element could be text or other elements.

**Empty element** An XML element that doesn't have any content is called an empty element. An empty XML element is represented by `<employee></employee>` or the shorthand notation `<employee/>`.

**End tag** An end tag is the closing tag required to define an XML element. For example, in the element `<city>Ocala</city>`, the tag `</city>` is the end tag of the element.

**`ENTITIES`** An attribute type that can hold a list of `ENTITY` names (see `ENTITY`) separated by spaces. For example, multiple `ENTITIES` can be defined in a DTD using the following format:

```
<!ATTLIST annual_report
charts ENTITIES #IMPLIED>
<!ENTITY sales_chart1 SYSTEM
"sales1.jpg">
<!ENTITY sales_chart3 SYSTEM
"sales2.jpg">
<!ENTITY sales_chart3 SYSTEM
"sales3.jpg">
```

In an XML document, the `ENTITIES` attribute would be used as follows:

```
<annual_report charts=
"sales_chart1 sales_chart2
sales_chart3">
```

**`ENTITY`** An attribute type that can be set to the name of an entity that is defined elsewhere in the DTD. An `ENTITY` (for example, in this case, a JPG version of a chart) can be defined in a DTD using the following format:

```
<!ATTLIST annual_report
sales_chart ENTITY #IMPLIED>
<!ENTITY sales_chart SYSTEM
"sales1.jpg">
```

Throughout the XML document, we can refer to "`sales1.jpg`" by using the attribute `sales_chart`. For example, we could use "`sales_chart`" as an attribute type in the following XML element declaration:

```
<annual_report
graphic="sales_chart">
```

**Entity reference** A markup construct used to replace a reserved character (for example, <, >, or "'") from appearing inside character data within an element. For example, the following string "`Mark's car`" would appear inside an XML element as `<name>Mark's car</name>`.

**Enumerated List** A list that contains a list of valid values. An XML attribute can be declared to specify that the only valid value must be selected from a list. For example, let's say that we're declaring a day attribute of the `<sales_report>` element in the DTD:`<!ATTLIST sales_report day (Monday | Tuesday | Wednesday | Thursday | Friday | Saturday | Sunday)`. This declaration tells us that the only valid values for `day` are the names of the days of the week—Monday through Sunday.

**Event-based XML parser** One of the major paradigms used in XML parsing. An event-based XML parser calls predefined subroutines when it encounters a particular construct inside the XML document. For example, a start handler would be called each time the parser encounters a new start tag.

**eXtensible HyperText Markup Language** See XHTML.

**eXtensible Markup Language** See XML.

**eXtensible Stylesheet Language** See XSL.

**eXtensible Stylesheet Language Transformation** See XSLT.

**File Transfer Protocol** See FTP.

**`FIXED`** A DTD keyword used in the declaration of an attribute. Use of the `FIXED` keyword means that the attribute has been assigned a constant value.

**FTP (File Transfer Protocol)** A TCP-based protocol used to transfer files between two machines. The full description of FTP can be found in Request for Comment (RFC) 959.

**HTML (HyperText Markup Language)** The de facto language standard published by the W3C that is used for publishing hypertext on the World Wide Web. HTML is a descendent of SGML. Additional HTML information can be found at `http://www.w3.org/MarkUp/`.

**HTTP (HyperText Transfer Protocol)** An Application layer protocol to transfer information to and from web servers. HTTP is a TCP-based, stateless protocol. The full description of HTTP can be found in RFC 2616 and additional information can be found at `http://www.w3.org/Protocols/`.

**HyperText Markup Language** See HTML.

**HyperText Transfer Protocol** See HTTP.

**`ID`** A keyword that is used in a DTD attribute. The `ID` keyword indicates that the value of the attribute is unique within the XML document.

**`IDREF`** An attribute type that contains the `ID` value of another element in the XML document. A common use of an `IDREF` attribute is to establish a hierarchy between elements.

**`IDREFS`** An attribute type that contains whitespace-separated `ID` values. See `IDREF`.

**`IMPLIED`** A DTD keyword used within an `<!ATTLIST>` tag to indicate that an attribute is optional.

**International Organization for Standardization** See ISO.

**International Standard Book Number** See ISBN.

**ISBN (International Standard Book Number)** A unique, machine readable identification number assigned to books (i.e., the publishing equivalent of a Social Security number). For additional information please see `http://www.isbn.org`.

**ISO (International Organization for Standardization)** A series of national standards organizations from 140 different countries. The goal is non-government development of standards to facilitate international commerce.

**Java** A programming language developed at Sun Microsystems by James Gosling and Bill Joy. Java was designed from the beginning to be platform-independent.

**JavaServer Pages** See JSP.

**JSP (JavaServer Pages)** A Java-based web technology that delivers dynamic content to a client. JSPs consist of markup text (usually HTML or XML) combined with Java. The client can be a web browser, and the data is frequently HTML or XML.

**Markup delimiter** A group of characters used to delimit text documents. In XML markup, characters are used to delimit the start and end of an element. Some markup delimiters are '<', '>', '/>', and '</'. Typically, they're used to delimit elements such as the one shown here: `<model>Chevrolet Corvette</model>`.

**`mod_perl`** An Apache web server and Perl integration project that links the Perl runtime library into the web server and provides an object-oriented Perl interface to the C API of the web server. The major reason for using `mod_perl` is that it increases the performance of a web server. Because the Perl runtime library is already linked into the web server, there is no need to launch a new Perl process to run a CGI script.

**`NMTOKEN`** A DTD attribute type. The name `NMTOKEN` stands for name token and has many of the same characteristics as an XML name. For example, an `NMTOKEN` must be made up of the same characters as an XML name (alphanumeric or the following punctuation marks _, -, ., and :). Unlike an XML name, an `NMTOKEN` can have a number or a punctuation mark as the first character. An `NMTOKEN` can be used to bound input data. For example, let's say that you have an `<employee>` element that has an employee number attribute declared as:

```
<!ATTLIST employee employee_
number NMTOKEN #REQUIRED>
```

By using the `NMTOKEN` attribute type, it will only be valid for valid `NMTOKEN`s. So, it would be valid for an employee number such as "123", and invalid for an attribute value of "1 23" (invalid because of the whitespace). However, an `NMTOKEN` won't prevent an attribute value containing a string, such as "`Mark`".

**`PCDATA`** A DTD keyword used to describe parsed character data. The term `PCDATA` is usually used to declare the contents of an element. Note that an element declared to contain `PCDATA` may contain entity references; however, it cannot contain any tags or child elements.

**PDF (Portable Document Format)** A document format that was developed by Adobe as a means of transferring documents between different platforms. Additional information can be found at `http://www.adobe.com`.

**Perl (Practical Extraction and Reporting Language)** A high-level programming language originally developed by Larry Wall. Perl is ideally suited for such tasks as text manipulation, system management, database access, networking, and web programming.

**Perl module** A self-contained piece of Perl code that performs a particular task. A module can be used by a Perl program or by other modules. Perl modules are freely available to perform just about any imaginable task. The best place to start looking for a module is CPAN, `http://search.cpan.org`.

**Perl Package Manager** See PPM.

**Personal Home Page** See PHP.

**PHP (Personal Home Page)** A programming language that is similar to Perl. Unlike Perl, PHP uses an interpreter that is embedded in the web server itself. Similar to ASP, PHP supports embedding server-side programming code in HTML pages. PHP is supported by the Apache web server. Additional information on PHP can be found at `http://www.php.net/`.

**PI (Processing Instruction)** Markup that appears in an XML document that is used to pass instructions to the XML processor. All PIs start with `<?` and end with `?>`. The only restriction is that you cannot use `<?xml?>` or `<?XML?>`. Note that because PIs are instructions being sent to the XML processor, they are processor-dependent and are not specified by the XML standard. A commonly used PI is `<?xml-stylesheet?>`.

**POP3 (Post Office Protocol version 3)** A simple protocol designed to retrieve electronic mail. Additional information on POP3 can be found in RFC 1939.

**Portable Document Format** See PDF.

**Post Office Protocol version 3** See POP3.

**PPM (Perl Package Manager)** A tool developed by ActiveState that assists in the task of Perl module management. For example, allowing a user to install, remove, or update modules from a number of Perl module repositories. Additional information is available at `http://www.activestate.com`.

**Practical Extraction and Reporting Language** See Perl.

**Processing Instruction** See PI.

**Remote Procedure Call** See RPC.

**`REQUIRED` keyword** A DTD keyword used inside the declaration of an attribute. If the `REQUIRED` keyword is used, then the attribute must be present in a valid XML document.

**RTF (Rich Text Format)** A file format originally developed by the Microsoft Corporation. An RTF file is an ASCII file that contains special format commands to define presentation characteristics, such as fonts and margin sizes.

**Rich Text Format** See RTF.

**Root element** The single XML element per XML document that contains all other elements. In an XML document, this is always the first element encountered.

**RPC (Remote Procedure Call)** A type of network programming where a client actually calls functions that reside in a server. This is a different approach to client-server programming. Typically, a client connects to a server using a socket, the client sends a request, and the server processes the request and then sends back a reply.

**SAX (Simple API for XML)** An event-based XML parsing API. The user defines a series of event handler subroutines that are called when the parser encounters a particular construct. For example, a start event handler will be called each time the parser encounters the start of an element. Unlike the DOM-based parsers, SAX is ideal for parsing large XML documents because it doesn't build a tree of the XML document in memory.

**SAX2 (Simple API for XML version 2)** Version 2 of the SAX standard. Includes bug fixes and additional functionality (for example, better namespace support than the original SAX version). The official SAX2 web site is at `http://www.saxproject.org/`.

**Scalable Vector Graphics** See SVG.

**Schematron** An XML-based language that uses XPath to query XML documents. Additional information is available at `http://www.ascc.net/xml/resource/schematron/`.

**SGML (Standard Generalized Markup Language)** A language developed to support electronic publishing of documents. SGML is the predecessor to XML.

**Simple API for XML** See SAX.

**Simple API for XML version 2** See SAX2.

**Simple Mail Transfer Protocol** See SMTP.

**Simple Object Access Protocol** See SOAP.

**SMTP (Simple Mail Transfer Protocol)** A protocol designed to deliver electronic mail. Additional information can be found in RFC 821.

**SOAP (Simple Object Access Protocol)** SOAP is a lightweight protocol designed to exchange structured information in a distributed environment. XML is used as the message format, and SOAP messages can be distributed by a number of different underlying protocols. Additional information can be found at `http://www.w3.org/TR/2001/WD-soap12-part0-20011217/`.

**SQL (Structured Query Language)** An ANSI standard language that was developed to interact with databases. SQL enables you to create, destroy, and update database tables.

**Standalone** An optional attribute in the XML declaration. The standalone attribute indicates if an XML document has an internal DTD (standalone = "yes") or if the DTD is in an external document (standalone = "no").

**Standard Generalized Markup Language** See SGML.

**Start tag** An opening tag in the declaration of an XML element. In the following declaration of an XML element `<nickname>The Chief</nickname>`, the first tag `<nickname>` is the start tag.

**Structured Query Language** See SQL.

**SVG (Scalable Vector Graphics)** A language used to describe two-dimensional graphics in XML. Currently, three types of graphic objects are supported: vector graphics, images, and text. SVG is a W3C-developed standard and additional information can be found at `http://www.w3.org/TR/SVG/`.

**UDDI (Universal Description Discovery and Integration)** An architecture that provides integration with web services. UDDI contains specifications describing services and discovery of those services. It supports multiple platforms because it is based on W3C standards such as SOAP and XML. Additional information on UDDI can be found at `http://www.uddi.org/`.

**Unicode** A universal character-encoding standard that represents text for computer processing. Unicode provides a method of encoding languages that use characters outside of the standard ASCII character set. Additional information on Unicode can be found at `http://www.unicode.org`.

**Universal Description Discovery and Integration** See UDDI.

**W3C (World Wide Web Consortium)** A group comprised of over 500 member organizations dedicated to promoting interoperability of web-based standards. The W3C is responsible for over 40 technical specifications that basically form the infrastructure of the World Wide Web. Additional information on the W3C is available at `http://www.w3c.org`.

**Web Services Description Language** See WSDL.

**Wireless Markup Language** See WML.

**WML (Wireless Markup Language)** An optimized language used for specifying presentation and user interaction on particular devices, such as mobile phones and wireless PDAs. Basically, WML provides a framework for supporting web clients that don't have access to the full suite of XHTML features due to physical constraints (for example, display size, bandwidth).

**World Wide Web Consortium** See W3C.

**WSDL (Web Services Description Language)** An XML format describing network services. These services are offered on the web and accessed using SOAP. For example, a network service could offer stock quotes, taking a stock symbol as input and returning the current stock price. For additional information on WSDL, please see `http://www.w3.org/TR/wsdl`.

**XHTML (eXtensible Hypertext Markup Language)** A major change to HTML that brings the stricter formatting rules found in XML to HTML. For example, while some browsers would display HTML that was missing end tags, all opening tags in XHTML must have a corresponding end tag. It will also enable developers to deliver web pages to a number of new devices, such as cellular phones. Additional information on XHTML can be found at `http://www.w3.org/TR/xhtml1/`.

**XLink (XML Linking Language)** Specifies a language to support linking (similar to HTML hyperlinks) in XML. For additional information, see `http://www.w3.org/XML/Linking`.

**XML (eXtensible Markup Language)** A language defined by the W3C to facilitate distribution of information on the World Wide Web. Additional information can be found at `http://www.w3.org/XML/`.

**XML Remote Procedure Call** See XML-RPC.

**XML-RPC (XML Remote Procedure Call)** A specification and implementation that defines remote procedure calling. The transport mechanism is HTTP and XML is the encoding scheme. Additional information can be found at `http://www.xmlrpc.com/`.

**XML Schema** An XML-based standard that describes the content and structure of an XML document. At a high level, it performs the same task as a DTD (that is, it can be used to validate an XML document); however, XML Schemas provide more options when it comes to specifying data types and number of element occurrences. Additional information can be found at `http://www.w3.org/XML/Schema`.

**XPath** A language that enables you to address and access specific parts of an XML document. It was originally designed for use by XSLT and XPointer. Additional information can be found at `http://www.w3.org/TR/xpath`.

**XPointer (XML Pointer Language)** Non-XML syntax based on XPath that supports addressing the internal structures of XML documents. Additional information can be found at `http://www.w3.org/TR/xptr/`.

**XSL (eXtensible Stylesheet Language)** A language used to write XML output templates. XSL data can be transformed into XML, HTML, WML, and any other plain text format through these templates. The process of transforming an XML document via an XSL stylesheet is called XSLT (XSL Transformation).

**XSLT (eXtensible Stylesheet Language Transformation)** A language for transforming XML documents into other XML documents. Can be used as part of XSL or independently of XSL. Additional information can be found at `http://www.w3.org/TR/xslt`.

**XSLT Stylesheet** An XML document that contains templates or rules used by an XSLT processor to transform an XML document. XSLT stylesheets can be used to convert XML documents to other formats (for example, HTML or CSV) and into filtered XML documents.

# Index

## A



## B-C

## D

## E

## K-L

# M

## N



## O-P

## Q-R



## S

## T



## U-V

# Solutions from experts you know and trus

www.informit.co

OPERATING SYSTEMS

WEB DEVELOPMENT

PROGRAMMING

NETWORKING

CERTIFICATION

AND MORE...

**Expert Access. Free Content.**

**New Riders** has partnered with **InformIT.com** to bring technical information to your desktop. Drawing on New Riders authors and reviewers to provide additional information on topics you're interested in, **InformIT.com** has free, in-depth information you won't find anywhere else.

- **Master the skills you nee when you need them**
- **Call on resources from some of the best minds i the industry**
- **Get answers when you n them, using InformIT's comprehensive library or live experts online**
- **Go above and beyond wh you find in New Riders books, extending your knowledge**

As an **InformIT** partner, **New Rider** has shared the wisdom and knowledge of our authors with you online. Visit **InformIT.com** to see what you're missing.

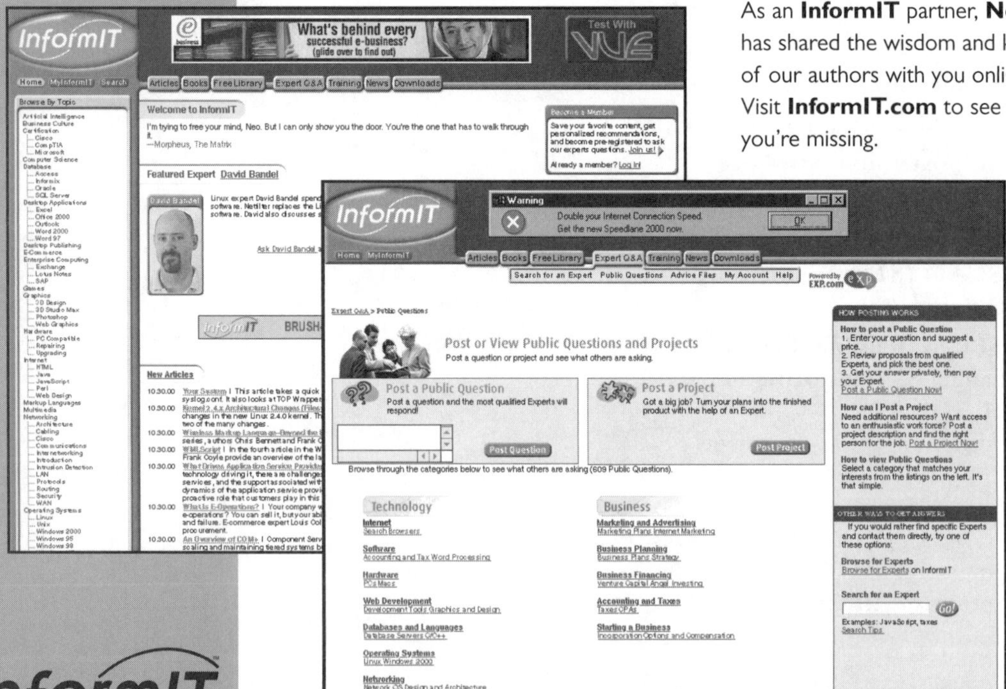


InformIT

www.informit.com ▪ www.newriders.com

Ne
Rid

VIEW CART

search

Registration already a member? Log in. Book Registration

OUR AUTHORS

PRESS ROOM

web development | design | photoshop | new media | 3-D | server technologies

EDUCATORS

ABOUT US

CONTACT US

You already know that New Riders brings you the **Voices that Matter**. But what does that mean? It means that New Riders brings you the Voices that challenge your assumptions, take your talents to the next level, or simply help you better understand the complex technical world we're all navigating.

## Visit **www.newriders.com** to find:

- 10% discount and free shipping on all purchases
- Never before published chapters
- Sample chapters and excerpts
- Author bios and interviews
- Contests and enter-to-wins
- Up-to-date industry event information
- Book reviews
- Special offers from our friends and partners
- Info on how to join our User Group program
- Ways to have your Voice heard

WWW.NEWRIDERS.COM

0735711143
Chris Radcliff
US$44.99

073571228X
Steve Oualline
US$49.99

0735712352
Matthew Langham and Carsten Ziegeler
US$39.99

0735712271
Vikram Vaswani
US$39.99

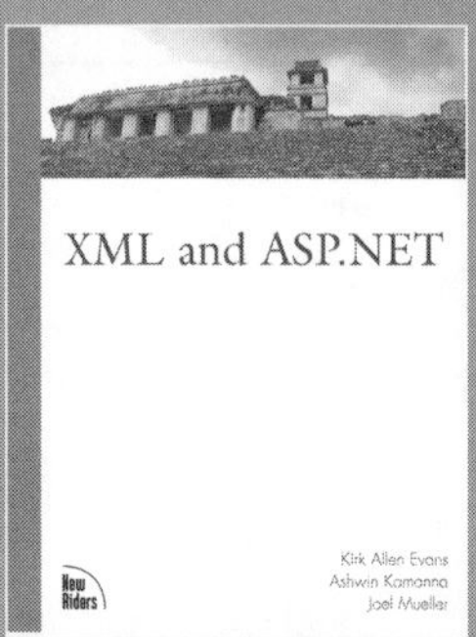


073571200X
Kirk Allen Evans, Ashwin Kam
and Joel Mueller
US$49.99

0735710201
Steven Holzner
US$49.99

VOICES
THAT MATTER™

WWW.NEWRIDERS.COM

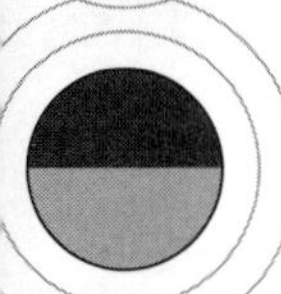

# HOW TO CONTACT US

## VISIT OUR WEB SITE

WWW.NEWRIDERS.COM

On our Web site you'll find information about our other books, authors, tables of contents, indexes, and book errata. You will also find information about book registration and how to purchase our books.

## EMAIL US

Contact us at this address: **nrfeedback@newriders.com**

- If you have comments or questions about this book
- To report errors that you have found in this book
- If you have a book proposal to submit or are interested in writing for New Riders
- If you would like to have an author kit sent to you
- If you are an expert in a computer topic or technology and are interested in being a technical editor who reviews manuscripts for technical accuracy
- To find a distributor in your area, please contact our international department at this address. **nrmedia@newriders.com**
- For instructors from educational institutions who want to preview New Riders books for classroom use. Email should include your name, title, school, department, address, phone number, office days/hours, text in use, and enrollment, along with your request for desk/examination copies and/or additional information.
- For members of the media who are interested in reviewing copies of New Riders books. Send your name, mailing address, and email address, along with the name of the publication or Web site you work for.

## BULK PURCHASES/CORPORATE SALES

The publisher offers discounts on this book when ordered in quantity for bulk purchases and special sales. For sales within the U.S., please contact: Corporate and Government Sales (800) 382-3419 or **corpsales@pearsontechgroup.com**. Outside of the U.S., please contact: International Sales (317) 581-3793 or **international@pearsontechgroup.com**.

## WRITE TO US

New Riders Publishing
201 W. 103rd St.
Indianapolis, IN 46290-1097

## CALL US

Toll-free (800) 571-5840 + 9 + 7477
If outside U.S. (317) 581-3500. Ask for New Riders.

## FAX US

(317) 581-4663

WWW.NEWRIDERS.COM

# Colophon

The image on this book's cover depicts Hadrian's Wall, which runs across northern Britain. The Wall was built by order of the Emperor Hadrian, probably around A.D. 122, and was likely intended to serve as the northern border of the Roman Empire. Many remains of the wall still exist, and it is listed as a World Heritage Site by UNESCO. Originally, the wall was approximately 73 miles long and 5 meters high. The photograph was captured by PhotoLink/PhotoDisc.

This book was written and edited in Microsoft Word, and laid out in QuarkXPress. The font used for the body text are Bembo and Mono. It was printed on 50# Husky Offset Smooth paper at R.R. Donnelley & Sons in Crawfordsville, Indiana. Prepress consisted of PostScript computer-to-plate technology (filmless process). The cover was printed at Moore Langen Printing in Terre Haute, Indiana, on Carolina, coated on one side.